D1453165

The Door of Purgatory

The Door of Purgatory
A Study of Multiple Symbolism in. Dante's
Purgatorio

Peter Armour

CLARENDON PRESS · OXFORD
1983

Oxford University Press, Walton Street, Oxford OX2 6DP

London Glasgow New York Toronto
Delhi Bombay Calcutta Madras Karachi
Kuala Lumpur Singapore Hong Kong Tokyo
Nairobi Dar es Salaam Cape Town
Melbourne Wellington

and associate companies in
Beirut Berlin Ibadan Mexico City

© *Peter Armour 1983*

*Published in the United States by
Oxford University Press, New York*

British Library Cataloguing in Publication Data

Armour, Peter
 The door of purgatory.
 1. Dante Alighieri. Divina commedia
 Purgatorio
 I. Title
 851'1   PQ447
 ISBN 0–19–815787–8

Library of Congress Cataloging in Publication Data

Armour, Peter.
 The door of purgatory.
 Bibliography: p.
 Includes index.
 1. Dante Alighieri, 1265–1321. Purgatorio.
2. Dante Alighieri, 1265–1321—Allegory and
symbolism.   3. Symbolism in literature.   4. Doors in
literature.   I. Title.
PQ4448.A7   1983   851'.1   83–4254
ISBN 0–19–815787–8 (Oxford University Press)

Printed and bound in Great Britain by
Biddles Ltd, Guildford and King's Lynn

CONTENTS

Foreword

The critical method adopted in this study of canto ix of Dante's *Purgatorio* is not one for which any great claims can be made. The investigations began with a mere intuition—that the traditional interpretation of the episode of the door simply did not fit Dante's narrative or normal technique. The next stage was to seek clues to an alternative explanation in sources indubitably known to Dante, sources, moreover, which he could legitimately have expected to be known also to his readers, directly in the case of the learned and the clergy, indirectly—through sermons, school-books, and the like—in the case of the ordinary layman. After some searching, these clues emerged from just such sources—the Bible, Virgil, Lucan, and Statius, major writings of St. Albert, St. Thomas, and St. Bonaventure, and Dante's own works, especially the poem itself. The task was then to view the episode as one of the early commentators might have done, explaining the symbols and citing the relevant authorities, and avoiding modern critical terminology as far as possible. Basically, therefore, the approach is the oldest one of all. At the same time, an attempt has been made to present the arguments, even the theological ones, in a way which is accessible to any modern reader interested in Dante.

The aim of this study is to explore half a canto of the *Divine Comedy* together with those aspects of its fourteenth-century background which cast light upon this single episode. Some of the conclusions, however, raise problems concerning the basic structure and the interpretation of the whole poem. These have been treated as fully as possible within the context of *Purgatorio* ix, although it will be clear that very much more could be said—and debated—on these points. This study led into unexpected areas, and it is hoped that the reader will not be too disappointed if the conclusions remain somewhat open-ended.

I am grateful to Professor G. H. McWilliam, who first suggested that I follow up the above-mentioned intuition, and to Professors P. M. J. McNair, T. G. Griffith, and C. Grayson for encouragement at various stages in this project. I am particularly grateful to Jonathan Sumption for providing me with references which proved invaluable in the formation of some of the concluding arguments. My thanks go also to Virginia Llewellyn Smith and her colleagues at the Oxford University Press for their help and advice.

This book is published with financial assistance from the British Academy and from Bedford College (University of London). I am deeply indebted to them, especially to Mr Peter Brown of the British Academy, for helping to bring this work, at last, on to the printed page.

PETER ARMOUR
Bedford College, London

Preliminary Note

Principal Works Cited and Abbreviations

(1) *Text*: *La Commedia secondo l'antica vulgata*, ed. G. Petrocchi, Milan, Mondadori, 4 vols., 1966–7.

(2) *Sources*:

a) *Biblical and liturgical*: all biblical quotations and references are taken from the Latin of the Vulgate, with literal translations. Liturgical references to the Mass can be found in the *Missale Romanum*, and to hymns, antiphons, and responsories in the *Liber Usualis*.

b) *Patristic*: *Patrologiae Cursus Completus*, ed. J.-P. Migne: *Series Latina* (abbrev. *P.L.*) and *Series Graeca* (abbrev. *P.G.*).

c) *Scholastic*:

St. Albert, *Commentarii in Quartum Librum Sententiarum*, in *Opera Omnia*, ed. S.-C.-A. Borgnet, vol. xxix, Paris, Vivès, 1894.

St. Bonaventure, *Breviloquium*, ed. J.-G. Bougerol, Paris, Éditions Franciscaines, 1966.

St. Thomas, *Summa theologica*, ed. Nicolai, Sylvius, Billuart, and C.-J. Drioux, 17th edn., Paris, Bloud and Barral. Most of the references are to the *Tertia Pars* (abbrev. *S.Th. III*), the *Tertiae Parti Supplementum* (abbrev. *S.Th. III Suppl.*), the *Appendix*, and the *Articuli duo de Purgatorio*.

St. Thomas, *S. Thomae Aquinatis in Evangelia S. Matthaei et S. Joannis Commentaria*, Turin, Marietti, 1925.

(3) *The Works of Dante*:

These are abbreviated as follows: *Vita nuova (V.N.)*, *Convivio (Conv.)*, *De vulgari eloquentia (D.V.E.)*, *Monarchia (Mon.)*, *Epistles (Ep.)*, *Inferno (Inf.)*, *Purgatorio (Purg.)*, *Paradiso (Par.)*.

NOTE: Throughout this study the word 'porta' in *Purg.* ix is translated as 'door' rather than 'gates'. The reasons for this choice will become obvious. However, the translation 'gates' would be equally correct (as in *Inf.* iii and viii-ix), provided that the reader imagines not some barred structure, but the solid, door-like gates of a medieval city.

(4) *Early commentaries on the episode of the door*:

The Anonimo, *Commento alla Divina Commedia d'Anonimo Fiorentino del secolo XIV*, ed. P. Fanfani, Bologna, Romagnoli, 1868, vol. ii, pp. 155–61.

Benvenuto, *Benvenuti de Rambaldis de Imola Comentum super Dantis Aldigherij Comoediam*, Florence, Barbèra, 1887, vol. iii, pp. 263-73.

Buti, *Commento di Francesco da Buti sopra la Divina Commedia di Dante Allighieri*, ed. C. Giannini, Pisa, Nistri, 1860, vol. ii, pp. 206–18.

Lana, *Comedia di Dante degli Allagherii col commento di Jacopo della Lana bolognese*, ed. L. Scarabelli, Bologna, Regia, 1866, vol. ii, pp. 98–9 (introduction), 106–10 (notes).

The Ottimo, *L'Ottimo Commento della Divina Commedia*, Pisa, Capurro, 1828, vol. ii, pp. 125–6 (introduction), 138–47 (notes).

Pietro di Dante, *Petri Allegherii super Dantis ipsius genitoris Comoediam Commentarium*, Florence, Piatti, 1845, pp. 359–65.

Text: The Door of Purgatory
(*Purg.* ix. 70–145)

Lettor, tu vedi ben com'io innalzo
la mia matera, e però con piú arte
non ti maravigliar s'io la rincalzo.

Reader, you can see clearly how I elevate my theme,
and so do not be surprised if I reinforce it with greater art.

Noi ci appressammo, ed eravamo in parte
che là dove pareami prima rotto
pur come un fesso che muro diparte,

We approached and found ourselves in a place where, at a point which previously had appeared to me as broken, just like a fissure which divides a wall,

vidi una porta, e tre gradi di sotto
per gire ad essa, di color diversi,
e un portier ch'ancor non facea motto.

I saw a door, and below it three steps of different colours leading to it, and a doorkeeper who as yet said nothing.

E come l'occhio piú e piú v'apersi,
vidil seder sovra 'l grado sovrano,
tal ne la faccia ch'io non lo soffersi;

And as I opened my eyes wider and wider to look, I saw he was sitting above the topmost step, and his face was such that I could not bear the sight;

e una spada nuda avëa in mano,
che reflettëa i raggi sí ver' noi,
ch'io dirizzava spesso il viso in vano.

and in his hand he held a naked sword, which reflected such bright rays upon us that several times I directed my gaze towards it in vain.

"Dite costinci: che volete voi?",
cominciò elli a dir, "ov'è la scorta?
Guardate che 'l venir sú non vi nòi."

'Speak from where you are; what do you want?', he began to say; 'where is your escort? Beware lest coming up here should harm you.'

"Donna del ciel, di queste cose accorta",
rispuose 'l mio maestro a lui, "pur dianzi
ne disse: 'Andate là: quivi è la porta'."

'A lady of heaven, wise in these things', my master answered him, 'said to us just now: "Go over there; there is the door".'

"Ed ella i passi vostri in bene avanzi",
ricominciò il cortese portinaio:
"Venite dunque a' nostri gradi innanzi."

'And may she further your journey towards good', the courteous door-keeper continued; 'Come forward therefore to our steps.'

Là ne venimmo; e lo scaglion primaio
bianco marmo era sí pulito e terso
ch'io mi specchiai in esso qual io paio.

We arrived there, and the first step was white marble, so polished and bright that I saw myself mirrored in it as I appear.

Era il secondo tinto piú che perso,
d'una petrina ruvida e arsiccia,
crepata per lo lungo e per traverso.

The second was darker than perse, of a coarse stone, rough and scorched, split lengthwise and across.

Lo terzo, che di sopra s'ammassiccia,
porfido mi parea, sí fiammeggiante
come sangue che fuor di vena spiccia.

The third, dominating with its mass, seemed to me to be porphyry, flaming like blood which spurts forth from the vein.

Sovra questo tenëa ambo le piante
l'angel di Dio sedendo in su la soglia
che mi sembiava pietra di diamante.

Upon this the angel of God rested both his feet, as he sat upon the threshold which seemed to me to be a rock of diamond.

Per li tre gradi sú di buona voglia
mi trasse il duca mio, dicendo: "Chiedi
umilemente che 'l serrame scioglia."

My master led me willingly up the three steps, saying: 'Humbly ask him to open the lock.'

Divoto mi gettai a' santi piedi;
misericordia chiesi e ch'el m'aprisse,
ma tre volte nel petto pria mi diedi.

Devoutly, I threw myself at the holy feet; I asked for mercy and that he should open the door to me; but first I struck my breast three times.

Sette P ne la fronte mi descrisse
col punton de la spada, e "Fa che lavi,
quando se' dentro, queste piaghe", disse.

Seven P's he inscribed upon my forehead with the point of the sword, and said: 'When you are inside, see that you wash away these wounds.'

Cenere, o terra che secca si cavi,
d'un color fora col suo vestimento;
e di sotto da quel trasse due chiavi.

Ash or earth which is dug up dry would be the same colour as his garment, and from beneath this he drew two keys.

L'una era d'oro e l'altra era d'argento;
pria con la bianca e poscia con la gialla
fece a la porta sí, ch'i' fu' contento.

"Quandunque l'una d'este chiavi falla,
che non si volga dritta per la toppa",
diss'elli a noi, "non s'apre questa calla.

Piú cara è l'una; ma l'altra vuol troppa
d'arte e d'ingegno avanti che diserri,
perch'ella è quella che 'l nodo digroppa.

Da Pier le tegno; e dissemi ch'i' erri
anzi ad aprir ch'a tenerla serrata,
pur che la gente a' piedi mi s'atterri."

Poi pinse l'uscio a la porta sacrata,
dicendo: "Intrate; ma facciovi accorti
che di fuor torna chi 'n dietro si guata."

E quando fuor ne' cardini distorti
li spigoli di quella regge sacra,
che di metallo son sonanti e forti,

non rugghiò sí né si mostrò sí acra
Tarpëa, come tolto le fu il buono
Metello, per che poi rimase macra.

Io mi rivolsi attento al primo tuono,
e '*Te Deum laudamus*' mi parea
udire in voce mista al dolce suono.

Tale imagine a punto mi rendea
ciò ch'io udiva, qual prender si suole
quando a cantar con organi si stea;
ch'or sí or no s'intendon le parole.

One was of gold, the other was of silver; first with the white one, and then with the yellow, he did to the door that which I desired.

'Whenever one of these keys fails so that it does not turn straight round in the lock', he said to us, 'this path is not opened.

One is more precious, but the other requires extreme skill and intellect before it will unlock, for it is the one which unties the knot.

From Peter I have received them, and he told me to err rather in opening than in keeping the door closed, provided that people prostrate themselves at my feet.'

Then he pushed the door of the sacred portal, saying: 'Enter, but I warn you clearly that he who looks back returns outside.'

And when the angles of that holy door, which are of metal, sonorous and strong, were turned in the hinges,

the Tarpeian did not roar so much nor seem so unwilling, when good Metellus was taken from it, so that then it was left empty.

I turned, intent upon the first thunder, and I seemed to hear *Te Deum laudamus* in a voice mingled with the sweet sound.

What I heard reminded me exactly of the impression which one often receives when one is present at singing with organs, when now one hears the words, now not.

Part I

Introduction

Before describing his entry through the door of Purgatory, Dante addresses his reader:

> Lettor, tu vedi ben com'io innalzo
> la mia matera, e però con piú arte
> non ti maravigliar s'io la rincalzo   (*Purg*. ix. 70–2)

(Reader, you can see clearly how I elevate my theme, and so do not be surprised if I reinforce it with greater art).

From the earliest times, from the commentary of Jacopo della Lana in fact, the episode which follows has been interpreted as an allegory of the Sacrament of Penance.[1] Some commentaries express doubts or introduce minor variations, as will be seen, whilst others occasionally hint at the wider themes which are the subject of this study, though always within the context of the sacramental interpretation.[2] The result has been that the second half of *Purg*. ix has come to seem a cold allegory,[3] a 'multiplication of symbols' which 'is apt to be tedious and irksome to us and needs Dante's apology'[4] and in general as schematic, emblematic, didactic, mechanical, and sketchy.[5] Yet despite these negative conclusions, and despite the obvious importance of the episode in the narrative of the *Purgatorio*, the interpretation of it as an allegory of confession has rarely been questioned, and, even where doubts have emerged, no comprehensive alternative theory has been offered in explanation of the details and general significance of the episode both in itself and as regards its place in the structure of the whole *cantica*.

There are good reasons, however, for doubting the traditional interpretation of the episode of the door of Purgatory. In the first place, there seems to be no other passage in the *Commedia* in which the allegorical elements are so clearly, not to say rigidly, expressed. The extended allegories of *Inf.* i–ii and *Purg.* xxix–xxx are considerably more complex in symbolism and rich in allusion than the compressed and schematic account of the steps and door of Purgatory, if this is interpreted as a straightforward allegory of the Sacrament of Penance; moreover, by introducing Beatrice, they also include that intensely personal element which seems totally lacking in the episode of the door. Besides the actual interpretation of the symbols—the dark wood, the hill, the three beasts, and so on—studies of such aspects as the imagery of the Exodus in *Inf.* i are indications of an underlying multiple symbolism closely connected with the analysis of the poem's technique as given in the Epistle to Can Grande,[6] whilst, as regards the allegory of the Church in the earthly Paradise, this study will open the way to identifying further possibilities of multiple symbolism there also.

The allegorical presentation of the 'noble castle' (*Inf.* iv. 106 ff.) and the ritual of the dew and the reed (*Purg.* i. 94 ff.) may seem superficially similar to the episode of the door, but neither has the same obvious structural importance in the poem, and in any case the context, the details, and the classical and other allusions make each considerably more complex on closer reading.[7]

The same can be said of the two occasions on which Dante actually tells the reader to look for the truth beneath the allegorical 'veil' (*Inf.* ix. 61–3; *Purg.* viii. 19–21). Both of these refer to dramatic representations of divine help given against temptations, but each shows levels of meaning apart from this clear moral lesson, and each contains details which are by no means easy to explain—for example, the psychological interaction between Dante and Virgil and the precise meaning of Medusa and the Furies in *Inf.* viii–ix, and in *Purg.* viii the reference to Mary, the details concerning the angels' robes and swords, and indeed the whole problem of the appearance of a tempter to souls who are already saved. The allegory of the snake in *Purg.* viii must certainly be considered in the context of the evening scene in the valley, among souls who sing the *Salve, regina,* with its themes of exile, the valley of tears, and Mary's protection, and the *Te lucis ante terminum,* another evening hymn, containing a prayer against the nocturnal attacks of the tempter (*Purg.* vii. 82; viii. 13); as regards the actual threat which the snake, the 'adversary' (*Purg.* viii. 95), poses to souls who are beyond temptation, one must also take into account the audience for whom this *sacra rappresentazione* is staged.[8] Taken with the sensual beauty of the setting and the presentation of the negligent rulers (*Purg.* vii. 73–81, 91–136), the episode of the snake recalls the temptations to worldliness which surround a monarch and so acquires another level of meaning, as an *exemplum* or message to rulers who neglect not only their true political responsibilities—though in this respect the souls in the valley are contrasted favourably with their decadent successors—but also their personal spiritual duties.[9] A closer definition of this aspect of their negligence will emerge later in this study.

In comparison with all these examples, the allegory of Penance in *Purg.* ix seems unusually cut and dried. The parallel with *Inf.* viii–ix is particularly important, for, as Sapegno has shown,[10] the overtly allegorical episode of Dante's entry through the gates of the city of Dis forms a dramatic and coherent whole which cannot be broken down into independent allegorical elements. Its rich and allusive complexity arises from, and expresses, the vital place which the episode occupies in the structure of the *Inferno*. As will be seen, the same or similar themes, the same complexity, and the same structural importance can be traced in the parallel, though contrasting, episode of Dante's entry through the door of Purgatory.

The traditional interpretation of *Purg.* ix. 73–145 requires one meaning for each detail and one meaning for the episode as a whole. It thus goes against the clear indications in the Epistle to Can Grande that the allegory of the poem is not simple but multiple and that the poem is an exploration of the technique of polysemy.[11] Moreover, the address to the reader which links the two halves of *Purg.* ix, stressing their 'greater art', can easily be referred back to the elevated symbolism and significance of the dream of the eagle but seems to contribute nothing towards identifying the elevated theme and artistry of the second half of the canto. It would seem quite untypical of the mature Dante almost immediately to break a clear promise of an elevation or 'reinforcement' both of his material ('matera') and of his poetic technique ('arte') at this crucial stage in his journey-poem.

The first arguments against the sacramental interpretation of the episode of the door are largely intuitive, but the fact is that, given Dante's normally free allegorical technique, and with his solemn address to us ringing in our ears, we do expect at this point a greater complexity of both doctrine ('matera') and symbol ('arte'); we expect evidence of multiple meaning and a wider choice of interpretations; and whilst it is clear that the episode has a strong ritual emphasis, we do not expect, in a narrative which illustrates the definitive anagogical exodus of the souls of the saved after death, a reference to such an ordinary and repeatable rite as the Sacrament of Penance, which is limited to the person of Dante in his moral journey and is wholly inappropriate to the state of the souls after death, who can neither sin nor even be left open to temptations to sin (cf. *Purg.* viii. 19–39, 97–108; xi. 19–24; xxvi. 132).

If one interprets the episode as a simple allegory of the Sacrament of Penance, it is uncharacteristic of Dante in another respect also, becoming as a result illogical within the structure of the poem as a whole. It is uncharacteristic because of the complete absence from the poem of any equivalent reference to the other Sacraments or to the most important of all the Christian rituals, the Mass. If an important episode in the *Purgatorio* is a re-enactment of one of the Sacraments, one would certainly expect some allusion somewhere to the most conspicuous and regular of all the Sacraments, the Eucharist, which links Christ to man and heaven to earth, which is the food of the Church Militant, and which expresses the unity of the Christian community, Christ's Mystical Body. Yet the Eucharist is nowhere mentioned nor used as a symbol, nor is the crucial mystery of Transubstantiation investigated. Indeed, for Dante the Eucharistic phrase, the 'bread of angels', has a different meaning; it is wisdom, the food of man's mind on earth, and the wisdom of God the Son which feeds the angels in heaven.[12] The symbol of wisdom as bread and the doctrine of Christ as Wisdom incarnate cause the brief sacramental reference to be absorbed into, and superseded by, a much more extended and elevated scheme of thought and imagery.

Elsewhere too Dante does occasionally use imagery with sacramental overtones, but wherever he does so it is always in a much wider and more allusive context. The most obvious example is the association of water with Baptism, but it is clear that the symbol of water can be used without specific reference to the Sacrament. Twice, at the beginning and at the end of the *Purgatorio*, Dante uses the image of cleansing with water, and each time the reference goes far beyond the merely sacramental and indeed is not really sacramental at all. The washing of his face with dew (*Purg.* i. 121–9) is clearly not a baptism: it is not a pouring of water on the head, and it lacks the words of Baptism; it is not a cleansing from original sin nor a bestowing of faith nor an admission of the soul into the Church Militant; and anyway Dante has already been baptized in his 'bel San Giovanni' in Florence (*Inf.* xix. 17; *Par.* xxv. 9). The introduction of the extra symbol of the reed has no obvious connection with the Sacrament at all. In fact, this ritual cleansing has a much wider and structurally more important reference. It is a washing-away of the dirt of hell and the tears Dante has shed when seeing the eternal results of actual, not original, sin; it also makes him worthy to enter the presence of the angel-doorkeeper:

> 'Va dunque, e fa che tu costui ricinghe
> d'un giunco schietto e che li lavi 'l viso,
> sí ch'ogne sucidume quindi stinghe;
> ché non si converria, l'occhio sorpriso
> d'alcuna nebbia, andar dinanzi al primo
> ministro, ch'è di quei di paradiso' (*Purg.* i. 94–9)[13]

(Go therefore and see that you gird him with a straight reed and wash his face, so that you remove all dirt from it; for it would not be fitting to enter, with eyes clouded by any mist, into the presence of the first minister, who is one of those of Paradise).

This rite may have an indirect association with Baptism, but it is certainly not a simple *allegory* of Baptism. In the structure of the narrative, it refers back to the darkness and grief of hell and forward towards Dante's meeting with a heavenly minister. It may also be noted that the ritual cleansing from the effects of sin is somewhat illogical if the primary function of this 'first minister' of Purgatory, the angel-doorkeeper, is going to be to preside over another ritual representing the forgiving of sin.

The cleansing of Dante in *Purg.* i also looks forward towards his immersion in the Lethe, but here too any baptismal connotations are indirect and subsidiary. The waters of the Lethe do not baptize but take away the memory of actual, not original, sin and in particular of Dante's infidelity to Beatrice. Moreover, like those of the Eunoè, they must be drunk to be effective, and this fact connects them with the theme of internal quenching, the waters of wisdom and grace, the disposition of the soul away from sin and towards good, as a prelude to Dante's ascent from the earthly to the heavenly Paradise.[14]

The only passages in which Dante refers directly to the Sacrament of Baptism as such underline the fact that it does not and cannot exist in the afterlife at all (*Inf.* i. 125–6, 131; iv. 33–9; *Purg.* iii. 40–5; vii. 7–8, 25–36; xxii. 59–60, 67–9, 89; *Par.* xix. 76–8). Baptism is essential for salvation, but it is needed in this life. To die unbaptized, as Virgil well knows, precludes the soul from entry into Purgatory and Paradise. Pagan Ulysses could not explore Purgatory; Virgil visits it but temporarily; Cato's presence there is absolutely exceptional. With the one other exception of Rhipeus, also an example of God's mysterious Providence, all the souls whom Dante meets in Purgatory and Paradise must have believed in Christ to come or in Christ after his coming and have formally acknowledged this fact by faith, by circumcision, or by Baptism (*Par.* xxxii. 76–84). All the souls who reach Purgatory must have been already baptized, and not only that but must also be repentant. Neither Baptism nor, as will be seen, repentance are possible in the afterlife.

As regards the other Sacraments, Matrimony is used by Dante as a theological image of the union of Christ and the Church, so that abuse of power by the Pope, especially by simony, becomes adultery or prostitution (*Inf.* xix. 2–3, 56–7, 106–11; *Par.* ix. 142; x. 140; xxxi. 3). He also uses marriage as an extended image of the union of St. Francis and Lady Poverty (*Par.* xi. 55–117). But the actual Sacrament is entirely absent from the afterlife, and indeed Dante quotes the chief text, *Neque nubent*, against its continuance after death (*Purg.* xix. 137; cf. Matt. 22: 30). Like all the Sacraments, marriage belongs exclusively to earthly life, where it is a sacred rite and institution involving obligations to virtue and fidelity; adultery is a sin which leads to hell (*Inf.* v; *Purg.* xxv. 133–5). Some of the souls in Purgatory look back upon their marriages, sadly, reproachfully, or lovingly, and love for dear ones certainly continues in Paradise (*Purg.* v. 135–6; viii. 73–81; xxiii. 85–93; *Par.* xiv. 64–6). But marriage as a Sacrament does not continue after death; what does last into eternity is ennobling and transcendent love, such as Dante's for Beatrice, which exists in both worlds, beyond the limited context of marriage and yet excluding the otherwise damning possibility of adultery.

The only other use of sacramental symbolism by Dante occurs in Virgil's 'crowning' and 'mitring' of him after he has completed the process of purification (*Purg.* xxvii. 142). This implies some sort of confirmation or ordination or, more specifically, episcopal consecration of Dante as of the high priest, Aaron (Ecclus.[= Sir.] 45:14). Nevertheless, the sacramental reference is vague, indirect, and polysemous, and the principal meaning of Virgil's words refers not to a Sacrament but to a crucial moral event—Dante's acquisition of perfect liberty of will in the temporal and the spiritual spheres as the link between his purification, now completed, and his entry into the garden of original innocence.

For Dante, therefore, the Sacraments belong to life on earth, and they play no direct part in his representation of the afterlife. If in *Purg.* ix he makes a single exception for the Sacrament of Penance, the uniqueness of this fact requires further investigation, and even those who believe that he is using sacramental symbolism must still decide if any further meanings or references are involved.

The reason for the absence of the Mass and the Sacraments in the *Comedy* is not necessarily that Dante was adhering to the Joachimite doctrine of the abolition of all these in the new age of the Spirit. The fundamental reason is the perfectly orthodox one that the Sacraments, traditionally defined as outward signs of inward grace, pertain solely to man's life on earth. They are impossible in hell, unnecessary in Paradise. As regards Purgatory, the question is more complex. There has long been a tendency to see the *Purgatorio* as basically a representation of man's moral journey in this life, and the sacramental interpretation of *Purg.* ix has either confirmed this or has had to be viewed as a somewhat mechanical and typically medieval allegorical inset in the otherwise realistic structure of the narrative. This moral approach to the *Purgatorio* and to this particular episode mars the unity and narrative realism of the whole poem, which describes a visit to the afterlife where human affairs are seen as projected into a world in which they have already been judged by an infallible Justice. Even though Purgatory has time and is not eternal, the figural realism of the whole poem applies to the central *cantica* just as much as to the other two. The fundamental subject of the *Purgatorio* is Dante's visit to the world where the souls are making their anagogical, that is, their definitive, exodus to liberty after death.[15] All the souls in Purgatory are inevitably destined to achieve their eternal fulfilment in Paradise, and indeed the episode of the door is a crucial stage in this journey, for the door of Purgatory is also the gate of Heaven. Thus the Sacraments have no more place in Purgatory than they do in hell or Paradise. St. Thomas says unequivocally: 'The Sacraments do not remain in the afterlife.'[16]

The Sacraments are outward signs which assure man, who in life is limited to knowledge through signs and the senses (*Par.* iv. 37–48), that grace is operative in him with regard to his future eternal fate; the *Comedy* is concerned with the afterlife itself, in which eternal Justice acts upon the souls according to their past merits or demerits in the use of their free will. The *Purgatorio* in its entirety is a complex investigation of the inward effects of divine justice and the refining of love after death, expressed by means of poetic outward signs of a visual, realistic nature. This may sound as though the Sacraments are some sort of earthly equivalent of Dante's symbolist technique, a form of poetry in action, but in fact they conflict with all the theoretical definitions which Dante gives of poetry. A Sacrament is not a 'truth hidden beneath a beautiful lie' but a real earthly ritual which represents, effects, and assures man of spiritual benefits; by no stretch of the imagination can a Sacrament be called a 'fiction fashioned with rhetoric and music'; nor does a Sacrament explore the realms of polysemy and multiple allusion on the model of theological interpretations of the story of the Exodus (*Conv.*

II. i; *D.V.E.* II. iv; Ep. to Can Grande, 7). The sacramental symbols belong exclusively to the world of sensed knowledge in this life; Dante's poetry elevates all symbols to a higher plane and presents them as the ultimate, eternal realities and the instruments of God's justice. Any terrestrial associations in Dante's symbols, whether sacramental or not, are but shadows or prefigurations of their supernatural significance.

In investigating Dante's unified and realistic presentation of the afterlife, the critic must first identify this elevation of earthly symbols on to a non-terrestrial plane of eternal and infallible judgement; only afterwards can the message be read back as an *exemplum* to men who still live among these earthly symbols. The landscapes, the symbols, the rites, the penances, and so on, of Purgatory as a whole must be seen first not as abstractions but as the ultimate realities. They are not allegorical representations of their earthly equivalents; rather, the earthly equivalents are but figures or adumbrations of them. The symbols used in the episode of the door belong primarily to the realm of the afterlife, but because they are based upon earthly symbols, they take with them into the afterlife all the multiple associations which they have on earth and become supraterrestrial realizations of those earthly symbols and part of the scheme of God's judgement of man after death and of Dante's discovery of that scheme. The earthly Sacraments have no place in Dante's figural world, which supersedes them. The *Comedy* portrays a world in which the seven Sacraments of the earthly Church are logically unnecessary, theologically impossible, and poetically confusing.

This does not exclude the possibility that Dante, a man conscious of the burden of evil in the world and of sin in himself, might have wished to make an exception in this one case and introduce, at this point in his narrative, an allegory of the Sacrament of forgiveness and cleansing. But it does indicate that the reader should transpose any such allegory to a higher plane and search within it for extraterrestrial and eternal significance and for a broader spectrum of meanings. In this respect, it is true that of all the Sacraments Penance has the most complex nature and the most direct moral reference to the themes of Purgatory. It has both remote matter (sin) and proximate matter (which consists of three *actus humani*—contrition, confession, and satisfaction); the form consists in the words, 'I absolve you', which are an invocation of the power of the keys.[17] Its uniqueness as a Sacrament derives from the fact that it depends absolutely upon a moral state, contrition, without which it is invalid; the word *poenitentia* applies both to the interior virtue and to the outward sign of the Sacrament. If Dante is using a sacramental allegory in *Purg.* ix, it must be for some exceptional reason,[18] and this reason can only be that the essential part of the Sacrament of Penance is sorrow for sin. But this raises a series of problems in addition to the more general ones already discussed.

In the first place, the supposition that Dante intended to base the episode upon an allegorical transformation of the rite of Penance is undoubtedly weakened by the fact that he has omitted essential aspects of the matter and form of the outward sign—oral confession and the words of absolution. Without these, the Sacrament lacks the very things which make it a Sacrament, the outward signs of interior sorrow and spiritual pardon. Nor, as will be seen, are the references to interior sorrow and pardon simple and univocal but complex and oblique. On investigation, the theory of a simple sacramental allegory begins to dissolve. The interior virtue of contrition may remain in general terms, but the outward, specifically sacramental element is absent. Dante does not confess his sins, nor does the angel absolve him. Indeed, on the surface the angel appears to do the opposite by imposing on Dante the marks of the Seven Deadly Sins. If the episode is an allegory of the Sacrament, then its method of proceeding by symbols can only be: some process involving contrition (the steps), the imposition of the duty of satisfaction (the seven P's), and absolution (the opening of the door). Even so, none of these symbols can be called clear and simple, and oral confession and the words of absolution continue to be conspicuous by their absence. The Sacrament begins to look curiously empty: Dante ascends three steps; instead of confessing his sins, he merely beats his breast; after he has been marked with seven wounds, a door is opened for him to enter the seven cornices of Purgatory proper. The scene resembles a formality, a ritual. Its exterior and stylized form seems unsuitable for the presentation of a Sacrament to which Dante here intends to give unique importance in an eternal setting, and which consequently might be expected to reveal his deep sense of interior sorrow, of God's pardon, of cleansing and renewal. The general atmosphere of repentance and forgiveness may be admitted, but the details are unclear, the essence of the Sacrament is lacking, and the event is stripped of personal involvement, of the sense of personal sin, sorrow, and forgiveness. We are left with a formality, not a Sacrament which pardons and redeems. The artificiality and the impersonal, ritualistic quality of the episode have, of course, been noted from the time of Buti. One could argue that these derive, not from the fact that the episode is an allegory of the Sacrament of Penance, but precisely from the fact that it is not such an allegory, that it bears no direct reference to the Sacrament of repentance but alludes to another theme, perhaps connected with this Sacrament but altogether wider and more general, more complex in its theological symbolism and more formal in its application.

If interpreted as a hollow enactment of a sacramental rite, this episode also anticipates, obscures, and even contradicts the memorable scene which forms the personal climax of the process of purification for Dante—the dialogue between him and Beatrice in the earthly Paradise (*Purg.* xxx. 76 to xxxi. 145). There we have, transposed on to an intensely personal level, nearly all the elements of the Sacrament of Penance: Dante sees himself as he is (xxx. 76–7), is ashamed (xxx. 78), is converted from hardness to contrition (xxx. 85–99), is accused of guilt, the pursuit of false pleasures, and risking damnation (xxx. 108, 130–8); he is required to repent (xxx. 144–5) and to confess (xxxi. 6); with shame, fear, and sorrow he confesses (xxxi. 13–21, 31–6), and his confession is required as a vital element in his forgiveness (xxxi. 40–2); his repentance is complete and overwhelming (xxxi. 85–90), and so he is cleansed (xxxi. 94–102), admitted to the company of the Virtues and Beatrice and to the mystery of the Griffin (xxxi. 103–26), and finally rewarded by complete reconciliation with Beatrice (xxxi. 136–45). Although this scene clearly goes beyond the Sacrament of Penance in its personal and dramatic elements and in its position as the climax of the *Purgatorio*, nevertheless the chief interior and spiritual elements of the

Sacrament are present, wonderfully transformed within a richly articulated narrative of a deeply felt and necessary rite of confession, absolution, and even oblivion of sin. The only element of the Sacrament of Penance which is lacking here is the one element which is indubitably present in *Purg.* ix—the imposition of the duty of penance, that is, of satisfaction. By the time that Dante meets Beatrice, he has performed, or at least travelled through, the required process of making satisfaction for sin in the afterlife. He is free of this duty now, and his final, complete contrition, his confession to Beatrice, and his immersion in the Lethe mark his definitive release from the world of sin, the punishment due to sin, and the very memory of sin. This is the moment of Dante's personal confession of sin and his final absolution. The episode of the door must therefore be something less than, or different from, this, and, even if one regards it as a vague anticipation of this important concluding scene, one can only be struck by the great differences in presentation and, once again, by the impersonal and hollow ritualism of the scene between Dante and the angel.

Other episodes and references in the *Comedy* also militate against the purely sacramental interpretation of *Purg.* ix. 73–145. According to theologians, contrition alone is necessary for the forgiving of sins. God, and only God, can forgive sin, and contrition by itself suffices for this. When grace is infused and accepted, and the sinner is contrite, then both the stain of sin and the obligation to eternal punishment in hell are removed directly by God. Oral confession and satisfaction are not essential for forgiveness of sin but have a different function deriving from this, as will be seen. The Sacrament, the outward sign of forgiveness, is normally needed in the earthly life of Christians, but it is not essential.[19] But as regards contrition it is absolutely essential that the sinner should repent of all mortal sins before he dies. Only thus will he be absolved from the stain of sin and from the obligation to eternal punishment in hell. Contrition is impossible after death: 'For contrition it is necessary that some sorrow be felt, and that this sorrow should be informed by love (*caritas*) and should be meritorious; but since none of these elements can be found in the souls after death, it is therefore impossible that they can have contrition.'[20] This statement applies primarily to the souls in hell but also, in part, to the souls in Purgatory. 'The souls in Purgatory have sorrow for sins, informed by grace, but it is not meritorious sorrow, for they are not in a position to earn merit (*non sunt in statu merendi*)'; the souls in Purgatory lack true, efficacious contrition.[21]

Dante constantly stresses this fundamental doctrine in the *Purgatorio*: contrition is sufficient for salvation, but it is essential that it should be achieved before death (*Purg*. iii. 118–23, 133–5; iv. 132; v. 53–7, 100–8; xi. 89–90, 127–8; xix. 106; xxii. 37–48; xxiii. 79–81; xxvi. 92–3). Thus the souls, both in Antepurgatory and on the cornices, have of necessity already repented of their sins and are now incapable of that meritorious contrition which is the one absolutely indispensable part of the Sacrament of Penance. The souls in Purgatory have no need of the ritual of the steps in a sacramental sense. They have already repented and been forgiven—some of them only in the nick of time—and the angel-boatman, in bringing them over the seas and making the sign of the Cross over them, confirms their final forgiveness, their release from the world of sin, and their entry on the path of final redemption and eternal salvation. Their psalm, *In exitu*, celebrates their definitive anagogical exodus to freedom and to a new and more real life.[22] Contrition, as Dante deliberately states by means of the episodes of Manfred, Belacqua, and Buonconte, is not a formal part of entry to the seven cornices above the door but an essential precondition for access to the whole mountain. The souls in Antepurgatory must all go before the angel-doorkeeper (*Purg*. iv. 128–9), but it cannot be to acquire contrition, which they already have, or absolution from the stain of sin, which contrition has already earned for them. Since the souls are also subject to the authority of the angel and the ritual of the seven P's,[23] the episode of the door cannot be a sacramental allegory which only Dante, in his moral exodus from sin to grace, must undergo. It is clear that Dante knows he too must die contrite in order to earn access to Purgatory and entry through the door for the second time; on his return to this life, he will have to strive for repentance lest he should forfeit what he has experienced once (*Inf*. xxvi. 19–24; *Purg*. viii. 59–60; xi. 118–19; xiii. 133–8; xxvi. 58, 75;

xxxi. 44–5; *Par.* xxii. 106–8; xxvii. 64–6; xxxi. 88–90; xxxiii. 34–7).

The exploration of the motives for contrition, for Dante and his readers, are in the whole poem and not just in one small part. The *Inferno* has taught Dante the negative reasons for contrition, namely, the nature and eternally horrible consequences of sin; his release from this world of sin is symbolized by his exit from hell and the washing of his face (*Purg.* i. 97–9, 127–9); Antepurgatory has then taught him the absolute necessity for the soul to have acquired contrition before death; and finally, with the entry through the door of Purgatory proper, the omnipresent theme of sin and sorrow takes a crucial turn towards the positive themes of purification and eternal reward. Thus even the element of contrition, in the realm of Purgatory in general and at this important stage in Dante's journey in particular, seems to need more precise investigation with the aim of defining the distinctive qualities of this episode of the door.

For these general reasons, the sacramental interpretation of the episode seems to be at best only partially true, if not downright dubious. Particular reasons against it will also emerge. At all events, there seems to be a case for re-examining the episode in its details and in its entirety. After all, by any reckoning, it is one of the most obvious examples of theological symbolism in the entire poem and, in its juxtaposition and agglomeration of such symbols, might prove to be a good basis for testing the term 'polysemy' as it works out in practice as the principal method by which Dante covers and communicates his vast range of material. It is unfortunate, therefore, that a recent critic should have remarked that to construct a 'fairly consistent philosophical-theological interpretation of this canto' would be 'to disregard the poem which Dante actually wrote' and equivalent to 'looking up the answers in the back of the book'.[24] Perhaps such statements derive from the fact that the traditional interpretation of *Purg.* ix makes it seem artificial and cold, a moralizing allegory unworthy of the mature Dante. If this is so, it is even more important to attempt to rehabilitate the episode in order to avoid perpetuating such notions that philosophy and theology are somehow extraneous to the actual poetry of the *Comedy*, and that Dante's sources are appendages rather than vital intellectual inspirations in the construction of such episodes.

In this re-examination, the weight of the traditional interpretation is an obstacle both because it is necessary to impugn, or rather adapt, the authority of the early commentators and because it stands in the way of a fresh and unprejudiced approach to the episode. However, as regards the first point, Dante did not write the *Comedy* primarily for commentators, but for readers, who all have equal rights. For Dante the job of the commentator would probably have appeared to be that of guiding the reader by conducting an ingenious investigation of the doctrine and symbols in his work. He might well have relished the subtleties of his earliest disciples, but he has also left sufficient obscurities and indications of multiple meanings as to make no single interpretation necessarily exhaustive. The early commentators, though they are unanimous in their overall interpretation here, knew and used their right to independence, especially in the interpretation of details. They would not have objected to further subtleties and ingenuities designed to uncover other possible levels of meaning which, for certain reasons to be seen later, they had not themselves perceived. The real problem is not so much one of deference to the fourteenth-century commentators as the ultimate obligation to be true to Dante and to the text. This requires that we put ourselves, as far as is possible, into the position of Lana or of Pietro di Dante and try to look at the text as if for the first time. Then, in the company of those early commentators, we may attempt to produce an analysis of which we hope Dante .would have approved.

With this in mind, let us examine independently the details of the episode, identifying some of the difficulties and uncertainties which have led to anomalies from the earliest times, and suggesting some new possibilities with regard to those details. By examining the various fragments of Dante's design in this way, it is in fact possible to trace the recurrence of certain constant patterns, and thus, like archaeologists, we may finally be able to rebuild these fragments into a single object, a beautiful artefact which is complex indeed but which has at the same time a fascinating clarity both of concept and expression, a perfect matching of the material to the art.

Part II

Investigations

1. *The Three Steps*

Of all the symbols employed in this episode, the three steps are the most difficult to explain with certainty, for they contain possible allusions to a vast number of themes. It could be that they, if not the whole episode, might conceal some personal allusion, present in Dante's mind but now lost to us.[1] What is certain is that as symbols of the three parts of the Sacrament of Penance they are remarkably unconvincing, and yet it is upon the steps that the whole sacramental interpretation is based. They have in fact posed difficulties from the earliest times, and the early commentators themselves disagree both in defining the order of the steps as symbols and in several details. The sacramental interpretation, which derives from them, rests upon a foundation already divided against itself. Yet at the same time, if we suspend belief in the sacramental theory, the early commentators themselves provide the means of resolving the anomalies and difficulties, and even if a definitive logical conclusion may be unattainable, it is possible to furnish a coherent reconstruction in terms of poetic symbol.

The earliest clear evidence of uncertainty is provided by Pietro di Dante. After discussing the three types of sin (of word, heart, and deed), the three elements in mortal sin (*impudicitia, delectatio, perpetratio*), and the three remedies for sin (shame, the bitterness of contrition, and satisfaction by works), he implies that the steps represent oral confession, contrition of the heart, and satisfaction by works, in that order. However, he then goes on to give an altogether more psychological explanation of the steps as the recognition of sin, compunction, and shame (*reminiscentia peccati, compunctio, erubescentia*). In other words, he presents both a 'sacramental' theory (the steps as elements in the Sacrament of Penance) and a 'moral' theory (the steps as stages in the interior process of repentance). Although continuing to associate the steps with the Sacrament, he moves away from the triple theological division of the Sacrament and treats the steps as three stages in the psychology of the true penitent, that is, as three stages in contrition alone.

This simultaneous presentation of two theories is evidence of Pietro's difficulty in matching the steps to the three parts of the Sacrament. The moral interpretation is certainly the more convincing. Since the image of steps naturally implies progress through stages each of which depends upon and is somehow contained in the preceding one, the clear indications in the text that the first step represents self-examination require that the other steps refer to interior stages in the process of self-knowledge. Pietro concentrates on the fact that the second stone is split, and thus, by associating it with the biblical rending of garments and with Joel 2:13 ('rend your hearts, not your garments'), he identifies the second step as compunction or contrition of the heart, and the etymology of the words 'compunction' and 'contrition' must have seemed appropriate to the image of a split, crushed, or worn stone.[2] With the third step Pietro, concentrating exclusively on its red colour, sees a reference to shame, which is primarily a part of contrition and only tenuously connected with making satisfaction for sin.[3] The two main problems with Pietro's interpretation are that he ignores the dark colour and dryness of the second step and that Dante's image of blood spurting from the vein in his description of the third step is extremely confusing, not to say ridiculous, if that step represents merely blushing. Nevertheless, Pietro indicates the necessity for a spiritual or moral, and not merely a sacramental, interpretation of the three steps.

The sacramental theory taken up so ambiguously by Pietro di Dante originates in the commentary of Jacopo della Lana, who had likewise interpreted the steps as oral confession, contrition, and satisfaction, in that order. Of the other early commentators only Buti follows this, the original order.[4] No doubt it rests mainly on the association of the split second step with the etymology of the word 'contrition'. Pietro's uncertainty presumably derives from the fact that, whilst finding Lana's sacramental theory quite persuasive in general terms, he was not so convinced of the validity of his interpretation of the steps. In fact, a hint of exactly the same ambiguity can be found in Lana himself. In his notes to the canto he states unequivocally that the steps represent 'confession by mouth', 'the weight and difficulty of contrition', and 'the arduousness of satisfaction by works'. However, in his introduction to the canto he too had already put forward an interior explanation, by which the steps signify the conditions required in the man who goes to confession: *recognescenza* (a 'mirroring' of the sins to be confessed), contrition (arduous, dark, and with fissures for emitting sighs and tears), and the sinner's firmness and constancy in loving the Creator (red for charity and bloody because of the arduous task of satisfying God's justice). Once again we find a simultaneous presentation of a moral and a sacramental theory. Moreover, Lana indirectly exalts the moral interpretation over the sacramental, for he refers his reader to his own notes to *Inf.* xxvii, where he stresses the absolute primacy of contrition in the process of forgiveness. The exterior elements of the Sacrament are not as important as interior contrition, which alone forgives sins. Indeed, without contrition no confession or absolution can be valid. Not even the Pope's power of the keys can absolve Guido da Montefeltro:

> ch'assolver non si può chi non si pente   (*Inf.* xxvii. 118)

(for no one can be absolved without repentance).

The tenor of Lana's reference to *Inf.* xxvii at this point undoubtedly exalts the interior process of contrition over the triple form of the Sacrament.

Buti's ingenious and pedantic investigation absorbs the tiniest detail into the general theme of the Sacrament of Penance. Oral confession, like the marble step, must be whole, firm, white, clean, polished. Contrition requires the five conditions symbolized by the second step and must be hard, harsh, burnt by the love of the virtues abandoned, black, and split. Satisfaction must be firm, solid, and multicoloured, although red, associated with the warmth of blood and of fire and thus representing the fervour of charity, must predominate. The interested reader may consult for himself the lengthy detail of Buti's analysis and his conclusion that the steps represent accurately the theological divisions of the Sacrament of Penance. Suffice it to note that, in summing up, Buti talks of 'compunction of the heart, confession of the mouth, and satisfaction by works', which is the correct theological order, but which, by inverting the order of the first two steps, vitiates Buti's own laboured exposition.[5]

Aware of the primacy of contrition, the other early commentators all apply the strict theological order and put contrition first in their interpretation of the steps. This immediately raises difficulties. The Ottimo Commento explains the steps as contrition, which washes away the stains of sin; as the dark, cold heart which is opened up by confession; and as satisfaction by works, which vivify the soul just as blood is the seat of the soul's life. Similarly, for Benvenuto da Imola the steps represent, respectively, the conscience cleansed by contrition and tears; the dark, ashamed, sinful heart as revealed by the act of oral confession; and penitence by living works. Apart from the neglect of certain details and the rather oblique ways of associating the fissures of the second step with oral confession, the main argument against the Ottimo and Benvenuto is that, if the first step represents the soul already cleansed from sin by contrition, then it is illogical for the second step to represent the heart still dark, cold, and sinful. In terms of landscape and symbols which describe moral states, Dante is not given to such examples of *hysteron proteron*. Had the order of the first two steps been the other way round, the penitential meaning would have been clear: the dark, broken, 'contrite' soul is cleansed by pardon and then restored to love. One could then have drawn further conclusions as regards the rite of Penance. It seems unjustifiable to draw those conclusions when the order of the steps as Dante has given it indicates that they are illogical, if not wrong. Moreover, if the first step represents Dante's recognition that he has repented and been forgiven and that his conscience mirrored in it is now white and clean ('io mi specchiai in esso qual io paio') (I saw myself mirrored in it as I appear), then this element anticipates and mars his whole presentation of the process of purgation. If any direct reference to complete forgiveness is admitted in *Purg.* ix, then one of the most fundamental images in the entire scheme of Purgatory is, if not contradicted, at least seriously blurred. This is Dante's consciousness of the weight of sin, which decreases as his soul is redirected by the refining of love towards liberty and Beatrice (*Purg.* iv. 88–95; xi. 37–9, 43–5; xii. 11–12, 116–26; xxii. 7–9; xxvii. 121–3; *Par.* i. 98–9). Also, as has been seen, a clear conscience in *Purg.* ix contradicts the intensely painful confession of guilt in *Purg.* xxx–xxxi. Thus, for reasons both of logic and of poetic symbol, the first step cannot represent repentance and cleansing pardon.

The interpretation of the Anonimo Fiorentino shows the same difficulties and anomalies in the adaptation of the three steps to the theological triad of contrition, confession, and satisfaction. It is also a good example of the dubious method of argument by which the sacramental theory was formed. The arguments put forward by the Anonimo move from moral premises to sacramental conclusions. The first step represents self-examination (the mirroring of the heart) and therefore contrition and the restoration of the sin-stained soul to whiteness. The second step, dark and broken, represents the shame of sin and therefore the duty to confess and, by confession, to reveal the stony hardness and broken, contrite state of the heart. The third step represents the ardour of love which impels the sinner to do penance for his sins. This, in simplified terms, is the substance of the argument which, largely because of Sapegno's authoritative commentary, may be regarded as the corner-stone of contemporary criticism of the episode.[6] It looks quite convincing and is bolstered by clever, though not always relevant, quotations from St. Augustine, St. Paul, and even Petrarch.

The method, however, is clear. The Anonimo first sees each step as a symbol of a moral state and then, impelled by the *a priori* conviction, already traditional, that the steps represent the three parts of the Sacrament of Penance, he proceeds, more imaginatively than logically, to draw the required conclusions. But there is no justification for making the first step describe a triple process—self-examination, contrition, and forgiveness. Indeed, as in the case of the

Ottimo and Benvenuto, the fact that the next step is made to represent an ashamed, broken, and hard heart implies that the sin has not yet been forgiven. The identification of the colour of the second step as a symbol of shame is also dubious, especially as Pietro di Dante had already seen as more natural the association of the redness of the third step with the moral state of shame for sin. The Anonimo also attributes a dual function to the fissures of the second step, which express the shame of contrition in two ways—internal, in the stony heart, and external, on the tongue in confession. This perhaps is evidence of his secret desire to identify this broken stone step with contrition rather than with confession. As regards the identification of the third step as satisfaction, the argument from the moral state of love to the third and final part of the Sacrament of Penance is not so forced logically, but it is still clearly conditioned by the desire to arrive at the expected symmetry.

The early commentators are thus divided into two camps by the question of the order of the steps, and they also show some confusion and experience some logical difficulties in arguing from the steps as moral states to the steps as the three parts of the Sacrament of Penance. Yet, despite these anomalies, their overall interpretation has rarely been questioned.

From time to time, however, doubts and uncertainty have been expressed. One such doubter was G. Rossetti, who found the allegory quite implausible and says that many interpretations of it are 'chimeras'.[7] He admits a fairly conventional explanation of the steps as self-examination, contrition, and penance and then proceeds to draw an ingenious political parallel according to which the three steps correspond to the three ages of the Papacy—the age of purity, the age of corruption, and the age of Guelphism and partisan bloodshed.[8] Curiously, as regards the episode as a whole, this theory, the least credible of all, relying as it does on Foscolo's presentation of the 'papal fury' and of Dante as 'the fugitive Ghibelline',[9] does contain a granule of truth which eluded the earlier 'sacramentalists'. One of Rossetti's daughters, however, returned to the safer sacramental theory, following the order of the steps as established by Lana, Pietro di Dante, and Buti: 'We need hardly be told that the Gate of St. Peter is the Tribunal of

Penance . . . The triple stair stands revealed as candid Confession mirroring the whole man, mournful Contrition breaking the hard heart of the gazer on the Cross, Love all aflame offering up in Satisfaction the life-blood of body, soul, and spirit.'[10] Ruskin seems to stress the interior and moral references: 'The white step is said to mean sincerity of conscience; the black contrition; the purple (I believe) pardon by the Atonement.'[11]

These quotations from Maria Francesca Rossetti and Ruskin serve to show how criticism of the episode continued to oscillate between the moral and the sacramental interpretations. More especially, they are good examples of the two main ambiguities in Dante's presentation of the steps—the exact nature of the fissures of the second step and the colours of both the second and the third steps.

As regards the fissures, Dante's phrase 'crepata per lo lungo e per traverso' (split lengthwise and across) could mean that the step is completely broken by criss-cross lines or, as Miss Rossetti says, that it is broken in the form of a single cross.[12] On this subject the early commentators are silent. Pietro di Dante's phrase, 'the rending of the heart', and Buti's reference to the 'length and breadth of sin' may indicate that these two saw the stone as broken in the form of one cross, but the others seem to have visualized it as completely broken (*con-tritus*), though for different reasons—to reveal the sins (the Ottimo, Benvenuto), to show that the hardness of the heart is broken (the Anonimo), or to provide outlets for sorrow (Lana). The visual ambiguity of this step has been ignored by commentators, but illustrators, who have no visual freedom in this respect, were uncertain. Domenico di Michelino shows the second step as brownish and scarred with many fissures,[13] whilst an early miniaturist presents this step quite clearly as black and with a single cross scored on each surface.[14] However, even those who may have visualized the step as marked with a single cross do not seem to have wanted to see in it any reference to the one Cross of Christ, even though such a reference would form a significant link with the image of blood in Dante's presentation of the next step.

As regards the colours of the second and third steps, the earliest commentators again diverge. The second is black

(Benvenuto, Buti), dark (Lana, the Ottimo), or 'tinted' with the colour of shame (the Anonimo). The third is flame-red (Lana, the Anonimo), blood-red (the Ottimo, Benvenuto), red for shame (Pietro di Dante), or multicoloured with red predominant (Buti). Although the general colour scheme of the steps is easily comprehended, the details of the visual imagery are ambiguous, and this surely indicates that the solution to the symbolism of the three steps lies in exploring their allusiveness and in restoring to the reader more freedom of interpretation than he has had hitherto. To destroy this allusiveness would be rash, for a definitive and univocal explanation is, in fact, impossible. The early commentators drew definitive conclusions which are open to doubt, but at least their investigation of the premises for these conclusions was justified by current methods of literary criticism. What is unjustifiable is to accept their conclusions whilst rejecting their premises.

Two modern critics have in effect done just this. Whilst accepting that the whole episode is an allegory of the Sacrament of Penance, they have found it impossible to believe that the steps represent contrition, confession, and satisfaction in any order or in any way. S. Aglianò says that the traditional interpretation 'is undoubtedly to be considered erroneous', and he explains the steps by means of concepts taken from the writings of St. Bonaventure; they represent three phases in the process of contrition: awareness of guilt, sorrow, and the ardent desire for purification.[15] G. Fallani also interprets the steps as moral events: examination of conscience, the *remotio obicis* (removing the darkness of sin by sorrow), and charity and the love of God.[16] Strangely, neither of these critics realizes that, by rejecting the traditional triad, they deprive the sacramental interpretation of its chief foundation. Without the steps as the three parts of the Sacrament, all that remains is an angel with a sword and two keys, a curious ritual of submission and wounding, and a door which resounds as it opens. If the steps are elements in contrition alone, the sacramental interpretation, at least in its traditional form, disappears. To preserve it, as has already been noted, the symbols must be reallocated in the following order: contrition (the steps), 'confession' (Dante's beating of his breast), satisfaction (the imposition of the seven P's), and absolution (the opening of the door). This is feasible, but again it raises a series of problems: the remarkable absence of any oral confession or the words of absolution, the strangely impersonal ritualism of the episode, and the unclear relationship between the seven wounds and the duty of satisfaction imposed for sins committed and supposedly confessed. Despite their divergences in detail, the early commentators knew that, to support their overall interpretation, they had to use the steps to argue from moral symbolism to the sacramental triad. Critics who limit the steps to the sphere of moral symbolism alone throw doubt upon the sacramental interpretation as a whole.

The crux of the matter is that, logically and theologically, in terms both of allegorical meaning and of poetic symbol, it is impossible to argue from the moral to the sacramental interpretation of the steps. All the anomalies examined so far arise from this. Yet all the commentators from Lana to Fallani, with the sole exception of the arch-sacramentalist Buti, agree that the steps are symbols of moral states. They differ in detail, but they unite in accepting this basic premiss. If, therefore, we can establish some moral reference in the symbolism of the steps without drawing the sacramental conclusions, then the way is open for a new interpretation of this whole section of the *Comedy*. It is not easy, nor should one hope for a definitive allegorical explanation to replace the cosy but fallacious symmetry of the sacramental theory. However, Dante's text provides us with ample material to furnish, if not an all-embracing definition, at least a convincing and allusive synthesis in terms of word and symbol.

*   *   *

With regard to the three steps in general, F. D'Ovidio has pointed out that they correspond to other triple symbols in Dante's works.[17] He also indicated the Virgilian reminiscences which underlie the whole episode: the steps correspond to the triple wall of Tartarus; the angel is a pacific transmutation of Tisiphone, guardian of the 'massive gate and columns of solid diamond'; and the opening of the door of Dante's Purgatory is contrasted with Virgil's gate of Tartarus, which opens 'screeching on the horrid-sounding hinge'.[18]

Besides the indirect Virgilian reference, Dante's symbol of the steps may also conceal an allusion to Ezekiel's description of the very high mountain of God, with the steps (seven, in fact) which lead up to the Temple gate which faces to the East; this gate, which must normally remain shut, is associated with the performance of seven days of expiation by sacrificing goats.[19] The whole of mount Purgatory, on the opposite side of the earth to Jerusalem, may allude to the description, in the Epistle to the Hebrews, of the heavenly mount Sion, which is immovable, and which is characterized by the justice of God, the mediation of Jesus, and the sprinkling of blood.[20] It is indeed tempting to try to find in the steps some reference to Dante's most frequent triple symbol, the Trinity, but any such reference would be, at most, very indirect. The first step, of self-examination or self-knowledge, could only obliquely evoke the justice and power of the Father. The dark, dry step can hardly be a symbol of the Son, although, as has been seen, there may be an allusion to the Cross. The third step, however, does summon to mind the main aspects of Dante's presentation of the power of the Holy Spirit. That the first two steps do not correspond to the Trinity but yet culminate in a reference to the fire and love of the Holy Spirit may be significant in a way, by defining the steps as a transition from a Godless state to Love.

The other main triple image in the *Commedia* is the triad of faith, hope, and charity. Here, the colours of the first and third steps correspond exactly to Dante's use of white for faith and red for charity in *Purg.* xxix. 121–9 (cf. also xxx. 31–3). The fact that the second step contradicts this neat scheme induced an anonymous commentator to gloss his definition of this step as contrition with the addition of a parenthesis, 'and here is hope'.[21] Dante's rejection of greenness, freshness, and the water of hope (cf. *Par.* xxv. 71, 76–8) in his description of this step might be a deliberate indication that it should be associated, in some respect at least, with hopelessness.

The three colours of white, dark, and the red of fire or of blood might also suggest three elements in the first cornice of Purgatory: the white marble sculptures which reveal mankind in acts of humility or pride; the definition of sin as the 'smoke of the world'; and the shame and vein tremors of Provenzan

Salvani's atonement for pride (*Purg*. x. 31 ff.; xi. 30, 135–8; xii. 10 ff.). Or, more generally, the steps could anticipate the three cornices in which Dante's personal involvement with the penance seems most strongly emphasized: white marble for the knowledge of his own pride; the 'darkness of hell' of the cornice of the wrathful; and the red flames of the cornice of lust (*Purg*. xiii. 136–8; xvi. 1; xxv. 112 ff.). The conclusion of Dante's *Epistle* xi describes a triple process of purity which is followed by the 'infamous scar' of corruption which, in turn, is to be purged by fire and fighting.

It can be seen that these varied possibilities are not mutually exclusive. Taken together, they indicate that the steps represent a process which moves from some aspect of candour, through a phase associated with sin, to a final purification by love.[22] If each step is now examined individually, a clearer picture will emerge.

The white step, as has been seen, cannot represent the purity of a clean conscience or of sin forgiven, for the second step immediately appears to contradict this, and in any case the whole episode, if not the whole process of purgation, is rendered meaningless if we eliminate all aspects of Dante's sense of guilt and sin at this early stage before his entry to the cornices. The early commentators diverge in interpreting this step as contrition or as oral confession, but in general they agree that, as an image of a moral state, it represents the act of self-examination. To draw any further conclusions is unwarranted. The text says no more than that this step is a mirror: 'I saw myself mirrored in it as I appear'. The fact that it is white, polished, and bright serves this purpose alone, just as the Heaven of the Moon, described in almost identical terms (as a pearl, 'bright, dense, solid, and clean'), is the reflector or mirror of the sun's light, and in fact these qualities lead Dante to mistake the Moon for a mirror (*Par*. ii. 31–4; iii. 17–22). As a mirror, the function of the first step is similar to that of the Lethe in the process of self-knowledge (*Purg*. xxix. 69; xxx. 76–8). The whiteness implies that the image reflected is true (cf. *Par*. viii. 112), and so this step applies the maxim, 'Know thyself', the necessary prelude to any process of repentance or purification: 'The just man is first of all his own accuser.'[23]

The second step is more complex, for Dante describes it as

dark, rough, dry, and split. As regards the colour, on which the early commentators and illustrators disagree, one need only turn to Dante's own definition of the colour of perse: it is 'mixed of purple and black, but black prevails, and from black it derives its name' (*Conv.* IV. xx. 2). The colour of this step, 'darker than perse', is thus very close indeed to black, if not identical with it. The association of this step with sin is obvious, since Dante uses the same words, 'tinto' and 'perso', to describe Hell.[24] Its darkness and hardness are also associated with ignorance, as Beatrice later tells Dante:

> 'Ma perch'io veggio te ne lo 'ntelletto
> fatto di pietra, e impetrato, tinto ...' (*Purg.* xxxiii. 73–4)

(But because I see that in your intellect you are made of stone and, being turned into stone, dark ...).

The image of a transition from whiteness to darkness also clearly implies a progress towards corruption (cf. *Par.* xxii. 93; xxvii. 136). The qualities of hardness and roughness in this 'petrina ruvida' recall the traditional concept of the hardness of the sinful heart and the stony ground which rejects the seed of the Gospel.[25] The dryness of the stone implies the lack of the dew of grace, the water of life, the green of hope: 'My heart has dried up'; 'My soul is to you as earth without water.'[26] It is as the waterless desert of the unclean spirit,[27] and the adjective 'arsiccia' (scorched) also refers back to the *Inferno* (*Inf.* xiv. 74). The fissures of the stone, together with its roughness, seem to have been associated by the early commentators with the etymology of the word *con-tritio*, and they have been interpreted as the rending of the heart in penitence,[28] as outlets for grief, and later as a symbol of Christ's Cross. But there is nothing against regarding them as yet another detail in the image of the sinful soul, as the scars of sin,[29] the divided kingdom of Satan,[30] the wounds of sin described in the hymn sung on the eve of Ash Wednesday:

> Mentis perustae vulnera
> Munda virore gratiae

(Cleanse with the dew of grace the wounds of the scorched mind).[31]

The whole imagery of steps implies a coherent process, and

so it is reasonable to assume that, since Dante looks into the
first step as into a mirror, the second step is the truth which he
sees, the truth about his sinful nature and the corrupted state
of his soul due to the effects of sin: 'I recognize my iniquity,
and my sin is always before me'; 'My sorrow is always in my
sight; for I shall announce my iniquity, and I shall take thought
for my sin'; 'I rejoice in the law of God according to the inner
man, but I see another law in my members . . . the law of sin.'[32]
Unless the second step is interpreted in this way, the first step
remains a simple reflection, and the reader is given no clue as
to the self-knowledge which Dante gains from this mirror. But
if the second step is taken as part of the same stairway, as the
next stage in the same process of self-examination, then it is a
reflection of an interior state and reveals the soul of the sinner
as dark, hardened, dry, and scarred. In this sense, it is one of
the most simple of all Dante's visual images. Indeed, it is
exactly the sort of picture which a child might form when
taught that sin is a dark stain on the soul, a stony resistance to
God, a loss of the cleansing and refreshing waters of grace,
and a disfiguring disease of the soul.

It is quite possible that Dante wished to allude here to the
etymology of the words 'attrition' and 'contrition', for in the
context the recognition of the soul's sinful state implies sorrow
for it at the same time. On the one hand, this stone, described
as 'tinto piú che perso' (darker than perse) and as 'arsiccia'
(scorched), makes one think of hell and therefore of attrition,
sorrow for sin due merely to fear of hell. On the other hand,
attrition was considered imperfect and only an initial motive
for true contrition, which, as the standard acts of contrition
show, arises from the acknowledgement that sin crucified
Christ and that it offends the infinite goodness of God. In this
respect, the obscure phrase, 'crepata per lo lungo e per
traverso' (split lengthwise and across), could be interpreted as
describing a single cross and so contain a brief reference to the
Cross by which Christ redeemed all sinners; the sinner moves
from attrition to contrition through awareness of Christ's
sacrifice and through trust in the Cross.

This identification of multiple allusion in the description of
the second step is confirmed by the aural and rhythmic qualities
of line 99. The harsh word 'crepata' is linked to 'ruvida' and

'arsiccia', implying that the stone is split by heat and dryness. But the phrase 'per lo lungo e per traverso' introduces a calmer sound and rhythm, and, taken in isolation, it does most naturally indicate a single cross. One cannot be sure, and the choice must be left to the reader. The true interpretation could, however, lie precisely in this allusive ambiguity: the soul is split and wounded by sin, but when this is recognized the sinner can move to true repentance and salvation through awareness of the Cross and the wounds of Christ. If there is a hidden reference to the Crucifixion here, then the second step is linked to the image of blood in the description of the third step, and the multiple imagery of wounds, the Cross, and the cleansing blood of Christ resembles the moral state of the Christian soul as described in the *Stabat Mater*:

> Sancta mater, istud agas,
> Crucifixi fige plagas,
> Cordi meo valide . . .
>
> Fac ut portem Christi mortem,
> Passionis fac consortem,
> Et plagas recolere.
>
> Fac me plagis vulnerari,
> Fac me Cruce inebriari,
> Et cruore Filii.

(Holy mother, grant me this: fix firmly on my heart the wounds of Christ crucified . . . Make me bear the death of Christ, make me a sharer in his Passion, make me meditate upon his wounds. Let me be wounded with his wounds, let me be inebriated by the Cross, and by the blood of your Son.)

The third step, which concludes this triple moral process, contains a wealth of possible moral and theological allusions. The colour, taken with the allusions to flames and to blood, indicates four main possibilities: shame, the fear of hell-fire, love, and the remembrance of the blood of Christ.[33]

Pietro di Dante, citing St. Augustine ('shame is part of forgiveness') and St. John Chrysostom ('he who blushes is worthy of pardon'), identified this step as *erubescentia* or shame for sin. As the *Dies irae* says, knowledge of sin brings the blush of shame: 'culpa rubet vultus meus' (my face is red with guilt). Dante often mentions shame, sometimes associating it with the colour red (*Inf.* xxx. 134; *Purg.* v. 20–1; xi. 135–8; xxx. 78; *Par.* xxix. 84). Shame is an important element in contrition and forgiveness (*Inf.* xxx. 142). St. Thomas also stresses its importance and says that it can even diminish the temporal punishment due to sin.[34] Dante too says that shame is a subsidiary element in the process of purgation from lust (*Purg.* xxvi. 81). So Pietro di Dante's theory is not entirely inappropriate here, though the image of blood is used in such a different way from a description of blushing that the theme of shame is at best a minor allusion in this context.

The remembrance of sin was also traditionally associated with the fear of judgement and the flames of hell: 'ne perenni cremer igne' (lest I be burnt by eternal fire) (*Dies irae*). This also was considered to be one of the main motives leading to contrition, but of itself it does not suffice, for it is a servile fear which produces merely attrition, and attrition by itself can never become contrition.[35] Fear of punishment only becomes meritorious when it is filial fear and inspires the penitent to love of good and to remembrance of the Passion of Christ.[36] Dante's reference to flames here may contain the idea of filial fear of God's eternal punishments, but, connected with the element of love in his use of the imagery of fire, it suggests rather the related concept of desire for the temporal fire of Purgatory (*Inf.* i. 119; *Purg.* xxvii. 127).[37] The transition from imperfect contrition, associated with the fear of hell, to the type of true contrition required before entry into Purgatory would be one of the simplest ways of defining the underlying significance of the second and third steps.

The association of the third step with *caritas* or love is to be found in Lana, the Anonimo, and most modern critics, and Dante's use of the word 'fiammeggiante' (flaming) suggests above all his constant application, in the *Purgatorio* and the *Paradiso*, of the symbol of fire to the theme of love. *Caritas* too is a principal part of contrition, being both a motive and a consequence of it; it can even remit venial sins. It is needed for oral confession and for satisfaction, but it is not part of the Sacrament nor exclusively associated with either of these two parts of the Sacrament.[38] The concept of *caritas* is fundamental to Dante's poetry, but it applies to all stages of repentance and perfectibility in the *Comedy* and not just to that element of

Purgatory known as satisfaction, though clearly it is a vital part of that too, as the central cantos on the doctrine of love will show. For Dante love does guarantee access to the kingdom of heaven (*Par.* xx. 94–5), but on a level much deeper and more extensive than any single reference to a Sacrament or part of a Sacrament.

Finally, in Dante's presentation of the third step, there is the simile evoking the shedding of blood, 'come sangue che fuor di vena spiccia' (like blood which spurts forth from the vein). Rather than referring to living works of charity (the Ottimo, Benvenuto, Buti), this surely alludes primarily to the theme of sacrifice, the biblical sacrifices of atonement and in particular the blood of Christ which was shed for mankind and which washes the soul of sin: 'The blood of Christ . . . will wash our consciences free from dead works . . . Without the shedding of blood there is no remission'; 'Blessed are those who wash their robes in the blood of the Lamb that they may have a right to the tree of life and may enter in by the gates of the city.'[39] The simile may include the idea of works of atonement and satisfaction performed by the individual Christian, but it is not limited to this, and the dramatic phrase, 'which spurts forth from the vein', evokes the shedding of real blood and thus first and foremost Christ's infinite act of sacrifice, atonement, and satisfaction for sin (cf. *Par.* vii. 19 ff.). Christ delivered man by the blood of his veins; he is the pelican who feeds man on his blood; by his blood he became the bridegroom of the Church (*Purg.* xxiii. 75; *Par.* xxv. 113; xxxi. 2–3; xxxii. 128–9). In this sense, the pattern of thought behind the transition from the second step to the third resembles St. Ambrose's prayer:

My heart and my body are stained with many crimes . . . To you, O Lord, I show my wounds, to you I reveal my shame. I know my sins to be many and great, and I fear for them; I put my hope in your mercies which have no bounds . . . Hail, saving victim, sacrificed for me and for all mankind on the gibbet of the Cross. Hail, noble and precious blood, flowing from the wounds of my crucified Lord Jesus Christ, and washing away the sins of the whole world.[40]

Moreover, the satisfaction for sin to be made in Purgatory is inspired by and modelled on Christ's shedding of his blood (*Purg.* xxiii. 73–5).[41]

The fact that Dante's description of the steps closes with this brief but reasonably clear reference to the merits of Christ's Passion in the context of Purgatory has implications which will become apparent later in this study. Meanwhile, it should be noted that these four related possibilities in the interpretation of the third step go well beyond the very limited theme of satisfaction and penances imposed in confession. They are all connected with the crucial theme of interior contrition, but even so they allude to wider and more positive concepts. Moreover, since as has been noted above, meritorious contrition is technically impossible for the souls in Purgatory, the episode of the three steps must also be viewed in its narrative context, as part of the prelude to entry into a completely new division of the afterlife, the cornices of Purgatory.

Without constricting Dante's allusions too severely, we can summarize the episode of the steps in the following general terms. They represent a threefold act of introspection and are a visual expression of a moral process associated primarily, but not exclusively, with repentance for sin. Self-examination leads to awareness of sin, and this in turn causes the soul to ascend to a more complex and elevated state dominated by the ardour of love and the sense of the magnificent effects and example of Christ's sacrifice on the Cross.

Dante's language reflects this process with absolute precision. The first step is described objectively, with almost scientific emphasis on the optical elements, the smooth and polished mirroring qualities of the marble. The second, in dramatic contrast, conveys a more emotive mass of sombre detail, with its reminiscences of hell and its insistence on the hardness, the sterility, and the mutilation of the stone. The third, again in contrast, rises above the others: 'di sopra s'ammassiccia' (dominating with its mass). It is of the more precious and exotic porphyry and acts as a resolution of the darker mood by means of the dynamic images of the flame and of the blood 'which spurts forth from the vein'. As the top step it is the moral and poetic climax of the triple process and represents the essential stage to be reached before entry into Purgatory. The infernal qualities of the second step are superseded by a complex spiritual state which is a mixture of the qualities required in the soul before he can enter into the realm of the seven cornices.

The terrestrial symbolism of the steps can thus be read as a visual-conceptual code which Dante wishes his reader to project into the afterlife and specifically to this crucial stage in his journey before he enters through the door 'where Purgatory really begins' (*Purg.* vii. 39). Dante, and presumably all the souls who aspire to purification (cf. *Purg.* iv. 128–9), must first approach the steps and pass through the moral states which they represent. As Dante himself looks upon them and describes them, they denote a crisis of spiritual awareness. Once this has been experienced and overcome, he is ready to proceed on his journey, up the steps, to the angel on the diamond threshold, and so into the new realm of Purgatory. This is indeed a form of moral allegory based upon the description of objects, or indeed upon what T. S. Eliot would call 'objective correlatives', but the moral allegory is firmly based, as will be seen, upon the anagogical realities of Dante's world. At all events, the sacramental division of the steps into contrition, confession—or confession, contrition—and satisfaction is not only unconvincing and unnecessary but positively hinders the full appreciation of Dante's complex and allusive technique at this point in his poem. The steps, together with the other elements in the episode, are not an allegory of the Sacrament of Penance but belong here and only here in Dante's journey, where he is describing the moral and theological significance of the whole of the sevenfold realm of Purgatory. The steps are part of a preliminary definition of the rest of the *cantica* and the entire process of purification.

Fallani adduces the analogy that confessions in Dante's time were heard in the apse of the church, but it seems impossible to regard this as in any way relevant to Dante's climbing of three steps leading to a locked door, and the parallel is best considered as a case of *petitio principii*.[42] Had medieval confessions been heard in the piazza or on the church steps, and had it been necessary in Dante's day to confess before one was allowed into the locked church, then the analogy would have been self-evident, but such was not the case. However, there were classes of persons who, in the Middle Ages, were compelled to remain, either metaphorically in the piazza or indeed literally on the church steps, and who were refused entry into the church, or indeed the Church, without prior absolution.[43] These, the various classes of public penitents, and not the ordinary penitents in confession, provide the relevant illustration to the true significance of the three steps and the door of Purgatory.

2. The Angel-Doorkeeper

Dante's presentation of the angel is in two parts. Firstly, he describes him as sitting above the three steps; his face is dazzling, as are the faces of other angels in the *Purgatorio* (*Purg.* ii. 39; xii. 89–90; xv. 10–33; xxiv. 137–42; xxvii. 59–60); he holds a naked sword which reflects the rays of the sun and likewise dazzles Dante's eyes; he breaks his previous silence (line 78) with a stern warning to Dante and Virgil to come no nearer without revealing the source of their authority to ascend the steps and enter Purgatory; when he is informed that the travellers have the authority of a heavenly lady, the angel becomes 'courteous' and, with words of encouragement and hope, invites them to approach the steps; he himself sits on the diamond threshold with his feet on the porphyry step. Afterwards, when Dante has ascended the steps, performed the ritual of admission, and been marked with the symbol of the seven P's, the description of the angel is resumed with the information that his garment is the colour of 'ash or of earth which is dug up dry' and that he holds two keys, one of gold and one of silver, consigned to him by St. Peter for the opening of the door; after his explanation of the keys, his final words, as he allows Dante to enter, are a warning to him not to look back.

Before investigating the meaning of the angel-doorkeeper, it is necessary to consider briefly all the angels in the *Purgatorio*, for such is the power of Dante's invention that one rarely questions the strange fact that ten of them are in temporary exile from Paradise in order to control Purgatory on God's behalf and, it may be added, to stress the positive theme that ascent through the cornices is ascent to the heavenly light which shines in their faces. Dionysius the Areopagite and his paraphraser, Pachymera, had expounded the triple function of angels (*expiatio* or *purgatio*, *illuminatio*, and *perfectio*), the episode of the seraph who purified Isaiah's mouth with a coal,[1] and the doctrine that angels can punish men.[2] St. Thomas, citing Dionysius, believed that angels could indeed punish men, but only living men, such as Jacob in Gen. 32:24–5; although Sylvius later held that the opposite theory was difficult to refute, St. Thomas maintains that the souls in Purgatory are not punished either by demons or by angels, 'but it is possible that they lead them to the places of the punishments (*ad loca poenarum*)'.[3] Dante takes up this idea: the angels do not punish the souls but act as guides or ushers *ad loca poenarum*. The angel-boatman and the angel-doorkeeper are the first such guides, and the position of the latter in *Purg.* ix confirms his benign and redemptive function in contrast to the hostile fallen angels of *Inf.* ix. The last angel is similarly a guide to salvation, welcoming Dante, Virgil, and Statius to the steps up to the earthly Paradise, and so ultimately to the heavenly Paradise, with the words of Christ promising to the blessed the kingdom prepared for them from the beginning of the world (*Purg.* xxvii. 58–60).[4] In between, the main function of the angels of the seven cornices is to act as welcoming guides between the *loca poenarum*. At the same time, according to the traditional triple duties of angels, they perform a rite of purification or expiation (erasing the seven P's imposed by the doorkeeper), they illuminate with their light, and they pronounce, or are associated with, words which promise perfection (the Beatitudes). The angel-doorkeeper plays a leading part in this scheme of guides and ministers. In the anagogical exodus of the souls, he confirms and continues the redemptive process begun by the angel-boatman; in imposing the seven P's, he initiates the ritual of purification completed by the seven angels of the cornices along the road to the final angel and the earthly Paradise.

The sacramental interpretation of the episode, however, is more or less compelled to ignore this scheme. It requires, and has received, virtual unanimity in explaining the angel's chief function, although there are slight divergences in detail. All the early commentators see the angel as a symbol of the priest-confessor, the 'spiritual judge' (the Ottimo), who sits in tribunal and must examine, know, and condemn (Pietro di Dante). The brightness of the angel represents the wisdom or authority of the confessor, and the sword is the priest's 'examining power of speech' (Pietro di Dante) or his tongue

(Benvenuto) or, in general, the justice with which the priest must dispense the Sacrament of Penance (Lana, Buti, etc.). The robe represents humility or virtuousness (*onestà*) or both. Lana apparently interprets lines 103–5 as meaning that the angel, not the threshold, is like a diamond, and he draws the moral that the confessor must be firm, adamantine, and himself spotless. Buti, of course, extracts from the smallest detail some allegorical reference and moral lesson in what he believes is Dante's picture of the ideal confessor.

The desire to detect the element of the ideal is common to all these commentators and is perhaps the factor which goes to the heart of the matter. As a symbol of the ideal priest, however, this angel is curiously isolated from his fellows and from the scheme described above. No one, to my knowledge, has tried to interpret the other angels of the *Purgatorio* as symbols of the priest on earth. The angel-boatman has a clearly non-terrestrial function in transporting the souls of the dead across the seas to Purgatory. The angels of the cornices are agents of the doorkeeper in erasing the seven P's, and thus, if the doorkeeper is a priest who absolves, then they too must be linked to the priestly function, and the reader must infer that Dante undergoes some sort of sevenfold absolution. But in this case, the opening of the door ceases to be a symbol of forgiveness and complete absolution, as the sacramental interpretation requires it to be, and the process of absolution has to be seen as continuing through most of the rest of the *cantica*, which neither fits the doctrine of the Sacrament nor is in any way tenable in the context of Dante's presentation of the process of purification. The cornices are not part of a process of absolution from guilt but a ritual expiation of the effects of guilt and, at the same time, a redirecting of the soul to love and liberty, and it is to these elements that the angels are related in their dual function, both negative (erasing the seven P's) and positive (guiding the souls and pronouncing the Beatitudes).

Since the angel-doorkeeper initiates the whole process of Purgatory, one would expect him also to be related to this scheme and not to sit isolated from the general plan by being the only angel to symbolize the everyday ministry of the priest on earth. Moreover, Pietro di Dante's argument that 'the priest is the angel of the Lord', deduced from a doubtful interpretation of 1 Cor. 6:3, does not reflect his father's usual judgement on the clergy nor his sad knowledge that many Popes, Cardinals, bishops, priests, monks, and friars of his day were far from angelic.[5] If, therefore, one accepts that this angel represents the priest, then he can only represent a transformed and idealized priest, a projection of the earthly priesthood into the afterlife and on to the figure of an angel. Thus the symbol has an indirectly polemical value: Dante is describing the priest as he should be, not the priesthood as it is. The thorny theological problems of the wicked, ignorant, excommunicate, or heretical priest and the validity of his ministration of the Sacraments would in this way be seen to be resolved by Dante in the symbol of the perfectly just spiritual judge, who receives illumination and grace directly from God, like an angel.[6] The early commentators saw Dante's implicit polemic. 'Let the spiritual judge beware . . .', says Pietro di Dante, launching into an exhortation concerning the duties of the confessor, and the others also moralize along the same lines, especially with reference to the ignorant priest, when they come to discuss the silver key as a symbol of the learning (*scientia*) required in the ideal confessor.

That the angel is an ideal expression of some element found in the earthly Church seems reasonably clear, but whether that element is the ordinary priest requires further investigation in view of the special function and importance of this angel in the whole scheme of the *Purgatorio*. In fact, an examination of Dante's imagery will show that his imagination is working on a higher and more complex level and that the angel has a significance which teems with allusions to important themes in the *Comedy*, which matches his general presentation of Purgatory as a real figural or anagogical world, and which is in fact fundamental at this particular stage in the poem. In giving a new dimension to the episode, it is also possible to restore to it the one thing which commentators and editors have found largely lacking, namely, the personal element, some glimmer of a state of mind and a moral attitude in an episode usually considered cold and exterior. If the metaphor may be permitted, the angel may also provide a key to a fuller understanding of Dante's personal journey, in his moral and religious life and in his poem, and maybe also to a real journey which he once made.

*   *   *

The angel's primary function is, of course, that of doorkeeper, and it has long been noticed that the door of Purgatory is also St. Peter's Gate, the traditional entrance to heaven, which Dante has already said he hopes to reach in the company of Virgil (*Inf.* i. 134).[7] The 'porta di san Pietro' mentioned in *Inf.* i by an as yet ignorant Dante turns out to be the door of Purgatory as well as of Paradise. The angel says that he has received the keys of the door from St. Peter (line 127), and he is in fact later called 'the vicar of Peter' (*Purg.* xxi. 54). These basic facts immediately suggest that the symbolism of the angel rests upon the concept of the '*successor Petri*', St. Peter's vicar on earth, the Pope (cf. *Inf.* ii. 24; *Purg.* xix. 99; *Par.* xxvii. 47). Buti and Lana both talk of the angel as the 'vicar of Christ', and this phrase too refers primarily to the Pope (*Purg.* xx. 87; *Par.* xxv. 14–15).[8] Perhaps because of the remoteness of the Avignonese Papacy or because of their obsession with the sacramental interpretation, they do not draw the most obvious conclusion from their own words: that the angel, the vicar of St. Peter, the doorkeeper and holder of the keys, is above all a projection into the afterlife of an idealized Papacy, and thus an indirect polemical reference to the ideal of a reformed Church, of which the Pope is the chief representative and holder of the supreme powers. By derivation, one could also see this as containing the concept of the lower ministers of the Church, but the primary reference remains to the Pope.

The angel guards a door which has a dual function: it is the door 'where Purgatory really begins' (*Purg.* vii. 39), and it is St. Peter's Gate to heaven, here anticipated by Dante because he wants to present his and the souls' journey beyond the door as a single, continuous, and inevitable road to salvation, to Paradise, and to God. Just as St. Peter holds the keys of Paradise (*Par.* xxiii. 139), so does his angel-deputy hold the keys to Purgatory, and since the doors are the same, the keys are in a sense the same keys. The keys were also left by St. Peter to his vicar on earth (cf. *Par.* xxvii. 49–51; xxxii. 124–6).

In fact, all the keys, of St. Peter, of the angel, and of the Pope, are three aspects of the same keys given by Christ to his Church to open the door of the kingdom of heaven. This is the basic reason why Dante anticipates the door to heaven. He wishes to present the three keyholders and their keys in their relationship to the three parts of the Mystical Body of Christ, the three communities of the Church—on earth, in Purgatory, and in Paradise. This fact, moreover, confirms the theory of the figural realism of the *Comedy*,[9] for the earthly Church prefigures and, ideally, is fulfilled in the afterlife in Paradise. The papal symbolism of this angel 'vicar of St. Peter' is the first element in Dante's definition of Purgatory too as a Church, the Church Suffering, the link, both theologically and in the structure of the poem, between the Church Militant and the Church Triumphant. This is also vital in his presentation of Purgatory as a positive place, a Church of transition between the earthly Church and Paradise, for the eternal fulfilment of the Church Suffering will, after the end of time, be the same as that of Paradise.[10]

If in *Purg.* ix the traditional two terms of comparison (the angel and the priest) are replaced by a triad (St. Peter, the angel, and the Pope), clear parallels can be seen. With reference to St. Peter, the angel is his vicar or deputy, keeper of the door to heaven. The merging of the two doors into one in the scheme of the *Comedy* emphasizes the fact that for Dante the door of Purgatory denotes a frontier between a more earthbound community outside and a more spiritual community inside, now definitively and inevitably travelling on the path to Paradise. The souls in Antepurgatory are still subject to laws of time linked to their earthly lives and perhaps also to natural earthquakes, but the mountain above the door is not subject to normal earthly conditions of time and weather (*Purg.* xvi. 26–7; xxi. 43–57). For Dante, the door is a link between earthly and heavenly, between temporal and spiritual, just as indeed, on earth, the Church is the bridge between the two worlds, and the Pope is the *Pontifex*. In his relationship to the Pope, who controls membership of the earthly Church, the angel-doorkeeper controls entry into Purgatory. He would refuse entry to Belacqua (*Purg.* iv. 128–9) and, by implication, to all the other souls obliged to remain in Antepurgatory, 'on the outside of this shore', namely, the excommunicates who died 'in contumacy of Holy Church', those who died repentant but *in extremis*, before formal reconciliation with God through the mediation of the earthly Church, and finally the group of rulers negligent in the temporal sphere and also, obviously, in their personal spiritual duties (*Purg.* iii. 136–8; iv. 130–2; v. 52 to vi. 24; vii. 91–136; viii. 46–139). Each of the souls in Antepurgatory adopted some sort of negative attitude to the duties of the Christian in the earthly Church, and for this, after death, they must undergo a negative punishment of waiting for a fixed period of time outside the door where Purgatory, the Church Suffering, really begins.

The angel, with the authority of St. Peter and by the power of the keys of heaven, excludes these more earthbound souls in Antepurgatory from entering the spiritual community of the saved who are performing the positive process of purification. In this respect, his function is analogous to that of the Pope, supreme arbiter and holder of the keys on earth, and in fact the angel's first stern admonition to Dante and Virgil not to proceed without declaring their authority for entry is better adapted to a figure of supreme authority with the absolute right to refuse entry, rather than to the ordinary priest preparing a penitent for the Sacrament of forgiveness.

> 'Dite costinci: che volete voi?'
> cominciò elli a dir; 'ov'è la scorta?
> guardate che 'l venir sú non vi nòi' (*Purg.* ix. 85–7)

('Speak from where you are; what do you want?', he began to say; 'where is your escort? Beware lest coming up here should harm you').

These words contain reminiscences of the Sibyl's 'procul, o procul este, profani' ('stay well away, well away, unhallowed ones'), of the episodes in which hell tries to resist Dante's entry, of Nessus' similar words with their bloodthirsty significance, and of the similar words and function of Cato, who also guards Purgatory and whose face also shines with light.[11] All these elements stress the severity of the words and heighten the authority invested in the figure of the angel.

Two further, though less evident, points may help to support this theory that in the figure of the angel Dante was thinking primarily of St. Peter and of his vicar on earth, the Pope.

Firstly, there are in the *Comedy* several examples, apparently deliberate, of a system of cross-references by which Dante links two episodes by means of the rhyme-words.[12] It may be a coincidence, but it is also a fact, that Dante introduces the angel with the same rhyme-words (*rotto-sotto-motto*), used in the same order, as in the description of his meeting with Pope Nicholas III in the *bolgia* of the simoniacs (*Inf.* xix. 44–8). No one can know if this fact was deliberate, unconscious, or purely accidental, but it does raise an interesting series of possibilities relating to known symmetries and themes in Dante's presentation of the Papacy in the *Comedy*. The clear symmetry between *Inf.* xix and *Purg.* xix, two episodes which are also linked by several shared details, shows that Dante intended the latter to be in part a recantation and in part a development of the former.[13] Between the harshly sarcastic and reformist condemnation of the avaricious Papacy in *Inf.* xix and the presentation of a more humble Papacy being purified from avarice in *Purg.* xix, Dante's view of the office of Pope has been adjusted and developed and its corrupt earthly reality elevated in the direction of its ideal spiritual nature. A comparison between, for instance, *Inf.* xix. 90–6 and *Purg.* xix. 103–20, confirms that in the *Purgatorio* Dante is dealing with the ideal of the Papacy, poor like St. Peter, a heavy religious burden, with the Pope, though supreme, as a servant of God like any other Christian, indeed as the *servus servorum Dei* (*Purg.* xix. 134–5; cf. *Inf.* xv. 112). He has come to present the papal office, even in the hands of such a man as Boniface VIII, as the office of vicar of Christ, even of an *alter Christus* (*Purg.* xx. 86–91). This reappraisal of the office coincides perfectly with one of the arguments adduced in the *Monarchia*, where Dante accepts the Pope's title of 'Vicar of God', but not in the political sense in which Boniface used it in his struggle with Philip the Fair; Dante analyses the phrase in a deeper theological sense, limiting the meaning of the word 'vicar' to exclude the extravagant claims to temporal power made by Boniface VIII (*Mon.* III. vi–vii).[14] The process of redefining the Papacy continues in the *Paradiso*, so that towards the end of his journey Dante, through the mouth of St. Peter, finally condemns the man, Boniface VIII, in terms which imply that the office is vacant (*Par.* ix. 127–36; xi. 118–20; xii. 88–96; xxvii. 22–4). If, in the rhyme-words of *Purg.* ix, Dante intends to refer back to *Inf.* xix, then the angel-doorkeeper looks forward to the repentant and humble Pope of *Purg.* xix, and maybe also to another episode, otherwise rather puzzling, namely, the condemnation of the Pope and Cardinals for avarice, neglect of the Holy Land, and 'adultery' of the Church, in the superficially unlikely context of the Heaven of Venus, in the corresponding canto of the *Paradiso* (*Par.* ix. 126–42).

In this way, the angel, guardian of the principal frontier between earth and heaven, could mark an allusion to Dante's personal attempt, in his life and in his poem, to reconcile the earthly Papacy to its spiritual ideal, the unworthy men to the exalted office. Even if the angel is seen merely as a symbol of the perfect priest, exactly the same process of idealization and reappraisal is involved, but if the primary reference is taken as being to the Pope, then the angel ceases to be an isolated example of the allegorized priest and becomes linked to one of the most fundamental and personal themes of the whole *Comedy*. As G. Rossetti concluded from different premisses, Dante's humble submission to the angel becomes a dramatization of his journey from disillusionment with the Popes as men to recognition of the supreme authority of the office.[15] Dante recognizes that for salvation it is necessary to be associated with the Church and with the Pope, as St. Jerome says in his letter to Pope Damasus: 'I, following none but Christ, associate myself in communion with your Holiness, that is, with the Chair of Peter.'[16]

The second corroborative detail concerns the angel's final admonition to Dante:

> 'Intrate; ma facciovi accorti
> che di fuor torna chi 'ndietro si guata' (*Purg.* ix. 131–2)

(Enter, but I warn you clearly that he who looks back returns outside).

These solemn words contain reminiscences of the myth of Orpheus and Eurydice (especially in Boethius's version) and of the fate of Lot's wife.[17] Pietro di Dante, followed today by Sapegno, cites also the warning given by Christ: 'No one who puts his hand to the plough and looks back is worthy of the kingdom of God.'[18] But Pietro also adduces another, even more appropriate, scriptural reference which, after contrasting the damnation of the fallen angels with the salvation of Lot and after condemning the false liberty, in reality slavery, promised by false teachers and sensualists, concludes:

If, fleeing from the corruptions of the world by acknowledging our Lord and Saviour Jesus Christ, they then become entangled and overcome by them again, their latter state is worse than their former. For it would have been better for them not to have known the way of justice than, after knowing it, to turn back from the holy law which was given to them. For they have fulfilled the truth of the proverb, 'The dog has returned to his vomit, and the washed sow to the quagmire.'

This powerful and unforgettable statement on recidivism comes from St. Peter himself.[19]

*   *   *

Although there are various possible reasons for their oversight, it is still remarkable that the early commentators were not immediately struck by the clear parallels between the angel and St. Peter. Apart from the stated connection (line 127), the two traditional symbols of St. Peter are the keys and a sword.[20] Leaving aside for the moment the conclusive evidence of the keys, let us examine the first symbol or attribute which the angel is described as possessing.

The sword contains many possible allusions beyond the traditional one, that it represents the justice required in the perfect confessor. St. Thomas distinguishes three swords: the material sword, which brings punishment upon those who wield it; the sword of God's justice, which is that of the angel of the garden of Eden; and the sword of the word of God.[21] None of these, he says, is to be abused by man.

The material sword is a function of the secular, not the ecclesiastical, authorities, and its use by the Church is perilous.[22] Dante emphasizes exactly this point in *Mon.* III. ix and in *Purg.* xvi. 109–12:

'ed è giunta la spada
col pasturale, e l'un con l'altro insieme
per viva forza mal convien che vada;
però che, giunti, l'un l'altro non teme'

(and the sword is joined to the crozier, and, put together by living force, they cannot go well together, for, so joined, one does not fear the other).

The sword of divine justice is clearly the aspect of the angel's sword which appealed most to the early commentators. The obvious parallel with the sword of the angel who guards the garden of Eden makes this interpretation very appropriate here, because the dazzling sword of the angel-doorkeeper is also in its way the flaming sword which expelled fallen man from the earthly Paradise and prevents him returning there before his time. The theme of God's sword of retribution is frequent in the Old Testament and is used by Dante in *Epistles* v. 2 and vi. 1. The absolute justice of God's sword is described by Beatrice with reference to the punishment of the Church invoked by Pier Damiani and the souls in the Heaven of Saturn (*Par.* xxii. 16–18), and this aspect of the sword as the instrument of just punishment underlies the metaphor of *Purg.* xxx. 57 and xxxi. 2–3.

The third sword, the sword of God's word, is a sword which pierces the soul and discerns the inner man.[23] It is particularly associated with St. Paul, champion of the light of the faith (cf. *Purg.* xxix. 139–41) and Dante's predecessor in the journey through the afterlife and through the door of heaven (*Inf.* ii. 28–32; *Par.* i. 73–5; xv. 29–30).

The sword of the angel-doorkeeper, as the early commentators saw, clearly requires interpretation in one or both of the last two senses, as the sword of God's justice and his discerning word. The angel's sword reflects the light of the sun, and so Dante's angel, like the angel who protects the garden of Eden, is presented as the minister of the direct light of God's justice, the same light which, as we are told in *Par.* ix, is reflected from the Thrones:

'Sú sono specchi, voi dicete Troni,
onde refulge a noi Dio giudicante' (*Par.* ix. 61–2; cf. xxviii. 103–8)

(Above there are mirrors – you call them Thrones – from which God in judgment is reflected to us).

As a sword of just retribution, the angel's sword is used to mark upon the souls the seven P's, the signs of the duty to do penance for past sins. But at its first appearance, when it dazzles Dante, it is presented rather as the sword of God's discerning word, the sword of faith which reflects heavenly light upon the eyes of man, but whose light is distorted by the false swords of heretics (*Par.* xiii. 128–9). To a medieval reader, the sword might at this stage evoke the figure of St. Paul, and this would not contradict the later explicit associations of the angel with St. Peter, for the two saints are traditionally closely linked as the joint founders of the Church, St. Peter as the source of its hierarchical power, St. Paul of its dogmatic supremacy.[24] Both saints were martyred and buried in Rome. Their bodies, according to a sixteenth-century account at least, were divided by Pope Sylvester on a porphyry stone and were shared between St. Peter's and St. Paul's and, in some versions, also the Lateran.[25] According to St. John Chrysostom, they are the shining eyes, the lanterns of Rome, and their bodies, especially that of St. Paul, protect the city of Rome.[26] Thus, upon St. Peter and St. Paul together were based the primacy and authority of the See of Rome.

The angel's sword is thus connected with the Papacy, the Petrine and Pauline authority of Rome and the Church in general, and the light of the true Faith and divinely inspired spiritual justice. But it will be noticed that the angel has only one sword, lit from heaven, and thus a purely spiritual sword. If we now recall the doctrine of the material sword, described above, another possibility presents itself. If the early commentators saw in the episode a hidden polemic against bad confessors, it is now possible to trace in the symbol of the sword another level of polemic, and one very typical of Dante. The angelic vicar of St. Peter, bearing one sword alone and that a spiritual one, could well suggest Dante's known rejection of the notorious doctrine of the two papal swords, a doctrine which in Dante's own time was asserted by Boniface VIII in the most absolute terms in the Bull, *Unam sanctam*:

The Gospels teach us that in the power of the Pope there are two swords, namely, the spiritual and the temporal. For when the Apostles say, 'Behold, here are two swords' (and, since the Apostles were speaking, this means the Church), the Lord does not reply that it is too many, but that it is enough. Certainly anyone who denies that the temporal sword belongs to the power of Peter misinterprets the words of the Lord which say, 'Put back your sword into its scabbard.' Both swords, the spiritual and the material, are in the power of the Church, but the latter is to be wielded on behalf of the Church, the former by the Church. The one belongs to the priest, the other to kings and soldiers but at the will and with the permission of the priest. But it is necessary that one sword should be beneath the other and that the temporal authority be subject to the spiritual power.[27]

The Bull, which ends with a solemn definition of the Pope's supremacy over all creatures, also accuses those who believe in the independence of the two powers of being dualists, like the Manichaean heretics, but this is in fact the whole thesis of Book III of Dante's *Monarchia*, and especially of chapter ix, in which Dante argues against Boniface's chief text, 'Behold, here are two swords.'[28]

In this way, the symbol of the angel, vicar of St. Peter, bearing the spiritual sword alone, appears as an indirectly polemical element, oblique for reasons both of poetic technique and of prudence, in Dante's presentation of a Church and a Papacy restored to the ideal state, custodians of the true Faith against heresy and supreme ministers of God's justice in the spiritual sphere alone. The obliquity of the reference and the heterodoxy of the theory may explain why the early commentators, motivated perhaps by caution or by the desire to avoid the imputation of Manichaean heresy to their author, seem either not to see it or deliberately to set it aside. Nevertheless, the theme is one close to Dante's heart, as is amply proved by the *Monarchia* and by the constant recurrence, throughout the *Comedy*, of references to Dante's political and religious conception of the relationship between Church and Empire, between the spiritual and the temporal, in God's plan for man and for human society.[29] Far from being an intrusion in *Purg.* ix, such a reference to Dante's ideal of a purely spiritual Church is entirely appropriate, in that Dante is here passing from a more temporal world into the spiritual community of the Church Suffering and so to the kingdom of heaven. Moreover, in this interpretation, the symbol of the angel with the sword acts as a prelude, not only to the discourse of Marco Lombardo on the two swords (*Purg.* xvi. 106–12) and to the episode of the reformed Pope (*Purg.* xix. 88–145), but also to the climax of the whole of the *Purgatorio*: the triumphal procession of Beatrice in the chariot of the Church, in the garden of man's active life on earth and of ideal temporal and spiritual innocence, and the final visionary re-enactment of the corruption of the earthly Church and the prophecy of the coming of the reforming DXV, the heir of the imperial eagle (*Purg.* xxix ff.). The presentation of the earthly Paradise is the culmination of the political and religious thread which runs through *Purgatorio* and of Dante's view of a Church founded through the Bible, surrounded by the Virtues, and guided by Beatrice, as contrasted with the earthly reality of a corrupt Church which awaits imminent reform by a mysterious 'emissary of God' (*Purg.* xxxiii. 43–5). To transpose the angel-doorkeeper to this plane not only provides a striking example of the overall unity of the *Purgatorio* but also reveals the existence in the episode of those two levels upon which Dante's poetry regularly operates—the universal and the personal.

*   *   *

The angel, acting with hieratic authority, first halts Dante and Virgil, but when he is told of their heavenly guide he becomes 'courteous' and benevolently invites them to approach the steps, which in papal fashion he calls 'our steps', thus also stressing from the beginning the idea of Purgatory as a community or Church (lines 91–3). These lines are the start of a process by which the angel, at first so dazzling and severe, becomes more natural and even 'humanized'. After Dante has ascended the steps and been marked with the seven P's, he tells us of the colour of the angel's robe:

> Cenere, o terra che secca si cavi,
> d'un color fora col suo vestimento   (*Purg.* ix. 115–6)

(Ash or earth which is dug up dry would be the same colour as his garment).

The fact that Dante gives us this detail only at this later stage implies a contrast with his earlier inability to look at the angel. The ascent of the steps and the ritual have given Dante the power to come close to him and look upon his robe. This element continues the process of 'humanizing' the angel, as if Dante, at first overcome by his severe and blinding authority, now begins to appreciate his essential benignity and affectionate interest. Indeed, whilst retaining some of his elevated, otherworldly character, the angel becomes comparatively intimate as he confides to Dante the secrets of his office. His last words, however, re-establish the full severity and authority of his first.

The description of the robe is not only a stage in the narrative presentation of a more 'human' angel; it is also an essential element in this process. All the early commentators saw this when they interpreted the robe as a symbol of humility. Pietro di Dante quotes Ps. 131:9: 'Let thy priests be clothed in justice'; but this is not the same virtue as humility and anyway makes the colour of the robe irrelevant and the connection of it with justice improbable. The other commentators may well have associated the robe with the habits of religious orders, especially of the Franciscan friars, in the same way that Dante later uses the metaphor of 'grey cloths' for the religious life (*Purg.* xx. 54). This factor should not be excluded, but it is a secondary reference, deriving from the fact that the early commentators were conditioned by their belief that the angel represents the perfect confessor. Suspend belief in this theory, and one can return to a far more obvious and appropriate interpretation of the symbol, indeed to its primary meaning, supported by innumerable biblical and liturgical texts.

Dante's choice of words points directly to this primary interpretation. The colour of the angel's robe is described ambiguously: it is the same as the colour of ash or of dry earth which has been dug up. It is unclear whether this means grey or brown or some indeterminate mixture or colour in between. The comparatively direct colour symbolism of the steps, by which we see them, at least in general terms, as white, dark, and blood-red, here gives way to something more vague and allusive. The reason can only be that Dante does not particularly wish his readers to have a clear picture of a distinct colour, but he very much wants us to associate the two concepts of ash and dry earth.

Ash, throughout the Bible, symbolizes penitence. Repentance, in the Old Testament, consists in the use of sackcloth and ashes,[30] and so the angel's ash-coloured robe recalls both these outward signs of inward repentance. Since the angel is the 'first minister' of Purgatory (*Purg.* i. 98–9), and since, as has been seen, he is associated with the Pope and the Church, the robe recalls the words of the responsory for Holy Saturday, which presents the pastors and priests of the Church repenting in sackcloth and ashes: 'Howl, pastors, in sackcloth and ashes, for the day of the Lord is coming, great and exceedingly bitter. Priests, gird yourselves and weep; ministers of the altar, sprinkle yourselves with ash.'[31] Ash is also the principal liturgical symbol for repentance and is marked on the foreheads of the faithful on Ash Wednesday, the first day of Lent, the season of penance. The liturgy for Ash Wednesday shows that the ash symbolizes repentance, humility, and the hope of pardon, as for the Ninevites at the time of Jonah.[32] It also implies a change of life: 'Let us be changed in habit, in ash and sackcloth.'[33]

Dante's reference to dry earth complements the symbolism of ash: 'He has remembered that we are dust; man's day is as grass; he shall flourish as the flower of the field, for the spirit will pass in him and will not endure.'[34] The Ottimo Commento does in fact connect Dante's phrase, 'terra che secca si cavi' (earth which is dug up dry), with the definition of man as 'earth to earth', and Dante himself takes rhetorical pleasure in the concept with the words of St. John to him: 'in terra terra è 'l mio corpo' (my body is earth in earth) (*Par.* xxv. 124). The reference to dry earth, therefore, concerns man's mortality, his lowly and transient state on this earth, from which he comes and to which he returns as dust. Thus, in the earthy colour of the robe are further motives for repentance, poverty, and reform.[35] The penitential liturgy of Ash Wednesday associates both ash and dust as symbols of mortality: 'We recognize that we are ash and that, for the punishment of our wickedness, to dust we shall return.'[36] The words addressed to each person as his forehead is marked with ash in the form of a cross are: 'Remember, man, that thou art dust, and unto dust thou shalt return.'

The colour of the angel's robe thus signifies primarily repentance and a change of life, accompanied by awareness of mortality, with strong associations with Lent and penance. In this respect, it is part of the introduction to the whole purgatorial process of doing penance for sins, as well as anticipating the theme of man's transience in the episode of the cornice of the proud (*Purg.* x. 121–6; xi. 91–120). Only secondarily does it refer to the specific virtues of humility and poverty and to the idea of admission to the ascetic life, with its allusion to the indeterminate colour of the Franciscan habit. This secondary reference, however, is also appropriate in the context of the whole episode, for it adds to the figure of the angel, St. Peter's vicar, those elements of humility, poverty, and simplicity which Dante, with the Franciscan Spirituals, saw as the basis of the ideal of the reformed Church. The simple garb of the angel who guards the spiritual Church of Purgatory contrasts strongly with the extravagant dress of the prelates of the earthly Church, castigated by Pier Damiani in Paradise (*Par.* xxi. 130–4). To the greedy, wolfish pastor of the earthly Church (*Par.* ix. 132) Dante contrasts this *Pastor angelicus*, who controls entry to a true, reformed Church, the community of the penitents and the saved.[37]

In conclusion, the angel is a projection, into the context of Purgatory, of the Pope and the Church, idealized and reformed, administering perfect spiritual justice and the direct light of faith, free from claims to the sword of temporal power, restored through repentance to poverty and humility, and with the authority, derived from Christ through St. Peter, to allow or to refuse entry into the kingdom of heaven. On earth the Pope is the chief doorkeeper and pastor of the flock, and these offices he has inherited from St. Peter, who received them from Christ.[38] The doctrine of the Communion of Saints identifies three parts of the Mystical Body of Christ: the Church Militant on earth, the Church Suffering in Purgatory, and the Church Triumphant in Paradise.[39] Traditionally, the Pope, with the keys to the Church Militant, corresponds to St. Peter, who holds the keys to the Church Triumphant. Dante completes the triad by presenting the angel as St. Peter's other vicar, holding the keys to the community of the Church Suffering, which, beyond the door, leads inevitably to the Church Triumphant. In this way, Dante alludes to the fundamental theology of Purgatory besides establishing a relationship of prefiguration and ideal fulfilment between the earthly Church and the Church of Purgatory, a relationship which is also an *exemplum* and call for the reform of the former on the model of the latter. The angel's office is not to absolve Dante but to impose upon his forehead the marks of membership of this community, the signs of the duty to do penance for sins. Then, to the sound as of organ music and the singing of a hymn, the angel admits him to this new spiritual Church.

3. The Diamond Threshold

The angel-doorkeeper sits upon the threshold which appears to Dante to be a diamond rock, 'pietra di diamante' (line 105). The Petrine associations of the angel now give to this symbol new and fascinating implications. Again the early commentators provide half the truth. Leaving aside the comments of Jacopo della Lana, who applies the symbol of the diamond to the figure of the angel,[1] the others all associate the diamond rock with firmness and constancy: the priest must be firm in examining and judging (the Anonimo), in his own life of virtue (Buti), in maintaining the seal of confession (Benvenuto). The Ottimo adds a more sentimental touch: the diamond is the stone of reconciliation and love and here denotes that when a man is reconciled with God he ascends to the 'threshold of love'. Since the theme of reconciliation is identifiable in Dante's submission to the angel-vicar of St. Peter, this theory is possible, but it is not necessary to rely on such an additional subtlety, for the symbol of the rock of diamond has a much more obvious meaning. The two elements, rock and diamond, stress the absolute firmness of this threshold, above which the mountain is subject to no normal earthquakes (*Purg.* xxi. 52–7). For the image, Sapegno refers us to Ezek. 3:9 and, very significantly, to Matt. 16:18. To these texts may be added the presentation of the Apostles as the precious foundation-stones of the New Jerusalem.[2]

With these facts in mind, the adamantine and immovable rock upon which the angel sits recalls first and foremost the Rock of Christ and of St. Peter, upon which the Church is built. The Rock is primarily Christ himself, the rock which the builders rejected but which has become the corner-stone, the precious stone which is the foundation of mount Sion, the model for the Rock of the Church, founded on the priceless merits of the Redemption.[3]

According to the Fathers and Doctors of the Church, Christ first promised to transfer this quality to St. Peter, the Rock upon which the Church was to be built on earth, and he did so after the Crucifixion and Resurrection, in his words to St. Peter: 'Feed my sheep.'[4] St. Peter also is the corner-stone and the precious foundation-stone of Sion, and so are his successors, and to the Church founded on this Rock is committed the power of the keys.[5] Thus the association of the 'vicar of Peter', seated on an immovable and precious stone, and invested with the power of the keys, has an unmistakable reference to the words of Christ in Matt. 16:17–19, a text which in any case has always been seen as Dante's chief inspiration for the whole episode: 'And I say to you that you are Peter, and upon this rock I shall build my Church, and the gates of hell shall not prevail against it. And I will give to you the keys of the kingdom of heaven. And whatsoever you shall bind on earth shall be bound also in heaven; and whatsoever you shall loose on earth shall be loosed also in heaven.'

If the theme of the Sacrament of Penance is set aside and this fundamental text is applied to the more elevated symbolism of the Pope and the Church, rather than to the very limited allegory of the perfect confessor, a most significant symmetry is revealed between *Purg.* ix and the parallel episode of Dante's entry into the city of Dis in *Inf.* ix. The general symmetry has long been noticed. Apart from their position in each of the two *cantiche*, both deal with images of doors and locks, both contain admonitions to Dante not to enter, in both Dante addresses the reader, and both are dramatic descriptions of important stages in Dante's journey and of moral and psychological crises resolved (*Inf.* viii. 84–5, 94–6; ix. 52–4, 61–3; *Purg.* viii. 19–21; ix. 70–2, 85–7).

The gates of hell and the gates of heaven were traditionally contrasted in an ecclesiastical as well as a moral sense. The wide entrance to hell was associated with infidels, Jews, and heretics, as well as with sin in general, whilst in contrast the true Church is the door to the kingdom of heaven, and indeed the Apostles and their successors are the actual gates.[6] Dante's entry into the city of Dis is an entry into a Godless world, the infidel anti-Church, with its mosques, of Lucifer, its triune 'god' (*Inf.* viii. 70; xxxiv. 37–45). The first souls whom Dante meets inside the city-walls are those of the heretics (*Inf.* ix. 124–9), which is why, as a clear theological reference, this circle is not included in the moral scheme of hell in *Inf.* xi.[7]

In *Inf.* ix Dante is to enter a city forbidden to the soul who is saved. The Furies, Medusa, and the devils oppose his entrance, and the gates are barred. But God sends a 'heavenly messenger' to show that Dante's journey is willed by God and that the 'gates of hell shall not prevail' against him (*Inf.* ix. 64–105). To those acquainted with the frequent symmetries in the *Comedy*, the appearance of another angel at exactly the same point in Dante's journey through Purgatory cannot but suggest the other, more positive, half of the same quotation: 'and upon this rock I shall build my Church'. To the anti-Church of the city of Dis, with its heretics and other sinners, is contrasted the true Church of Purgatory, guarded by an angel with a bright, true sword of faith and justice.

The three doors of hell and Purgatory are thematically linked. The first gate of hell did not prevail against Christ when he entered to deliver the souls of the biblical patriarchs from Limbo; despite hell's resistance, it was broken by Christ and now remains open (*Inf.* iii. 1–11; iv. 52–63; viii. 124–6; xiv. 86–7).[8] The second, inner gate of the city of Dis, the gate of heresy and deliberately chosen *malizia*, does not prevail against the Christian Dante but is opened by an angel. In contrast to these, the door of Purgatory, which is also the door of heaven (the gates of St. Peter), is built upon a firm, bright rock, and Dante enters through it into a purely spiritual community or Church of purgation, redirection of love, and ascent to Beatrice and God. The first gate of hell is, because of Christ, 'without a lock (*sanza serrame*)', but yet its 'threshold is denied to none'; the second gates are firmly closed but then easily opened by God's emissary so that Dante and Virgil can pass over the 'horrible threshold' and into the fortress of torment; the lock ('serrame') of the door of Purgatory is opened after Dante has performed a rite and made a humble request for entry, and so Dante and Virgil cross the 'threshold of the door which weans the souls from bad love and makes the crooked way seem straight' (*Inf.* viii. 126; ix. 92, 107–11; xiv. 87; *Purg.* ix. 107–11; x. 1–3). After crossing two thresholds into negative worlds of sin, Dante now crosses the final threshold into a positive, spiritual realm of penance and purification, the straight path to God.

The translation just given of Purg. x. 1–3 confirms the vital importance of the threshold also in the definition of the purgatorial process to come. However, the common interpretation of these lines is that they refer to the small number of souls who achieve salvation (cf. *Purg.* xii. 94) and are to be construed as follows: 'the bad love of the souls [i.e. of living men], in making the crooked way [sin] seem straight [good], makes the door little used'.[9] A slight variation of this reading, which arrives at the same general meaning by a different route, takes 'disusare' with 'di' on the model of *Inf.* xxx. 144; 'bad love makes the door little used by the souls'.[10]

This reading seems improbable on philological and interpretative grounds. In the first place, the verb 'disusare', when transitive, has two basic meanings: 'to cease to use' and 'to disaccustom, to wean'. In the first sense, examples can be found in Odo delle Colonne and in Guittone d'Arezzo; in the second sense, the verb becomes equivalent to 'disavvezzare, divezzare, svezzare', and medieval examples of this usage include Bartolomeo da S. Concordio ('in due modi si disusa l'ira di possedere l'anima') (in two ways can one wean anger away from taking possession of the soul), Ugurgieri ('il cuore disusato d'amare') (the heart which has lost the habit of loving), and B. Giovanni Dominici, with 'disusanza' used by Brunetto Latini to mean 'not being accustomed', and 'disusato' by Bono Giamboni to mean 'not accustomed'.[11] Battaglia provides only *Purg.* x. 2 and Landino's commentary on it as an example of 'disusare' meaning 'to cause to be little used'.

Given this evidence, therefore, it seems legitimate and most natural to take the word 'che' as referring to 'porta' or maybe, without any material change of sense, to 'soglio' and as the subject, to take 'disusare' in its regular sense of 'disaccustom', and to consider 'il mal amor de l'anime' as the object. It is possible, again without material change of sense, that, on the model of the above examples from Bartolomeo da S. Concordio and Ugurgieri, 'de l'anime' stands for 'da l'anime': the door 'takes away from the souls the habit of bad love'. In either case, the sense is that, at the passing of its threshold, the door breaks the souls' habit of bad love, although, as Dante immediately goes on to say in relation to himself, this is provided that the angel's warning is heeded and no one looks back. In other words, the phrase refers to the process begun at entry into Purgatory and continued up the mountain, which is described in a strikingly similar expression as 'lo monte che salendo altrui dismala' (the mountain which weans from evil those who climb it) (*Purg.* xiii. 3).

This reading accords perfectly with the total context of the episode as Dante passes through a crucial stage into a new realm of weaning from bad love; he must not look back; the door and its threshold represent the start of a new process which Virgil will in fact define as the purification and re-direction of the souls' love, away from the 'mal diletto' (bad pleasure) which results from love of a 'malo obietto' (bad object), from the defective love of God, and from intemperate love of secondary goods (*Purg.* xvii. 94–102). Indeed, it is surprising that a concept so fundamental to Dante's presentation of Purgatory, expressed in such a clear phrase as 'disusare il mal amor de l'anime', has ever been interpreted otherwise. After all, the reference to the bad love of the 'anime', and the use of the definite article in this phrase, is a strong indication that we are dealing with the afterlife, with those souls who do actually reach and use the door and pass through it to purification. The alternative explanation requires that 'il mal amor de l'anime' (the bad love of the souls) be equivalent to 'il mal amor degli uomini' (the bad love of men), the sinful nature of living men on the other side of the world, men who, because of their sins, will never get to Purgatory or the door at all. The use of the word 'anime' to refer to men who are still both body and soul would at the very least be extraordinarily ambiguous in the context of the afterlife.

As a result of this reinterpretation of *Purg.* x. 2, it can be seen that line 3 then continues the idea of the door and its threshold as marking entry into a new realm of weaning and redirection. The door is again the subject of the verb, 'fa parer'. Not only does it begin the process of breaking the souls' habit of bad love, but it achieves this because it makes the narrow, tortuous path up to and through the cornices seem straight to them, for it is in fact the sole and necessary direct path to God. The broad gate and wide road which lead to perdition are replaced, in Dante's striking poetic and moral scheme, by a door opening on to a narrow, crooked path which, from now onwards, the souls see as straight.[12] Indeed,

Dante immediately goes on to stress the crookedness of the
path:

> che si moveva e d'una e d'altra parte,
> sí come l'onda che fugge e s'appressa (*Purg.*
> x. 8–9)

(which moved from side to side, like a wave which approaches and
recedes).

This zig-zag path is also difficult, slow, and narrow as a
needle's eye (*Purg.* x. 10–16). Dante's insistence on these
details shows that this must be the 'via torta' of line 3, the
crooked path which is now accepted by the souls as straight.

Purg. x. 1–3, therefore, is not a gloomy aside on human
nature, inserted between the references to the door in lines 1
and 4, but a positive and forward-looking definition of the
door itself in relation to the souls who cross its threshold and
to the purgatorial process which it initiates. The diamond
threshold is the foundation-stone of this new mount Sion and
the rock upon which the Church of Purgatory is built. Christ,
the first foundation-stone and rock, has by the infinitely
precious merits of his Passion made it possible for the door of
Purgatory to be opened to the souls of the saved, but first a
state of mind and spirit is required in the individual. This state
is represented by the porphyry step, on which the angel's feet
rest. From this, Dante, making his submission at the angel's
feet, can ascend to the threshold and so pass into the spiritual
Church founded on this unshakeable rock and leading directly
to God. The earthly Church, built on the rock of the Papacy,
is the door to heaven, and the city of Rome, burial-place of St.
Peter and seat of his successors, is known as the 'limen Petri',
the threshold of Peter.[13] When he kneels in submission to St.
Peter's vicar, who sits on the precious diamond stone, Dante
has reached a new 'limen Petri', the threshold of both Purgatory
and Paradise.

4. *The Rite of Submission*

> Divoto mi gettai a' santi piedi;
> misericordia chiesi e ch'el m'aprisse,
> ma tre volte nel petto pria mi diedi   (*Purg.* ix.
> 109–11)

(Devoutly I threw myself at the holy feet; I asked for mercy and that he should open the door to me; but first I struck my breast three times).

In this *terzina* Dante describes the ritual which, following the instructions of Virgil (lines 107–8), he has to perform before the door of Purgatory will be opened to him. It is equivalent to knocking on the door and is necessary (cf. line 129), since, as Pietro di Dante notes, the door of heaven 'is not opened unless it is knocked'.[1]

According to the sacramental interpretation of the episode, this is the moment when Dante confesses his sins (the exterior matter of the Sacrament). But, as has been seen, this does not in fact occur, and as a result the scene has a curiously stylized, ritualistic flavour. This can be largely explained if we consider the rite to be primarily an act, not of repentance, but of submission.

Dante's text in fact suggests this, for he inverts the chronological order of his actions in lines 110–11. This means that the element most associated with penitence, his beating of his breast, comes last, almost as an afterthought. The order in which the significance of the ritual is developed is therefore: humility (line 108), devout submission (line 109), request for mercy and for entry (line 110), and penitence (line 111). Moreover, the angel's own definition of the rite indicates that it is an act of submission and an acknowledgement of his authority (line 129). Thus, after a triple process of self-examination, culminating in the spiritual state required for Purgatory and represented by the porphyry step, Dante kneels humbly before St. Peter's vicar who is seated on the diamond rock. In this way, the whole tone of Dante's submission recalls that of St. Jerome to Pope Damasus, in which the saint, rejecting three heresies which have split the seamless tunic of Christ, and acknowledging the three hypostases of the Trinity, submits to the authority of Rome: 'I, following none but Christ, associate myself in communion with your Holiness, that is, with the Chair of Peter. I know the Church to be built upon that Rock.'[2] Dante makes a similar profession of loyalty to the Church when he states that his discussion of the powers of the Papacy is inspired 'by that reverence which a loyal son (*pius filius*) owes to a father, a loyal son to a mother, loyal to Christ, to the Church, to the pastor, to all who profess the Christian religion' (*Mon.* III. iii. 18).

Dante's first action, throwing himself at the angel's feet, expresses humility and devout submission. In terms of the narrative, Dante submits to the authority of the angel and to his sacred office as doorkeeper to the Church of Purgatory. But in terms of the earthly and papal symbolism on which Dante's narrative is based, it is hard to believe that the phrase, 'I threw myself at the holy feet', would not have evoked a very special association in the mind of anyone who had made a pilgrimage to Rome in the time of Boniface VIII. This association would not, however, have occurred so readily to the earliest commentators, who would have had to travel to Avignon to perform or witness this particular ceremony.

Dante's request for mercy and for admission to Purgatory forms the essence of the whole ritual: this is what Virgil has instructed Dante to do (lines 107–8), and this is what Dante really wants (line 120). The word 'misericordia' is somewhat indeterminate. On the one hand, it is linked to the act of humble submission and is a request for mercy and the favour of admission (cf. lines 127–9); on the other, it may imply an element of repentance required as a preliminary to admission and so be linked to Dante's beating of his breast. In this latter sense, the word is associated with the penitential psalms,[3] and since chronologically the request for 'misericordia' follows Dante's beating of his breast, there may be a reference to the prayer 'Misereatur', which followed the 'Confiteor' in the Mass, or to the 'miserere nobis' of the 'Agnus Dei'.

Line 111 is universally interpreted as meaning that Dante

struck his breast three times. The manuscript tradition is, however, confused, and Petrocchi's reading is a timely 'reminder that in fact the line is none too clear.[4] It could be read as a description of a moral state, a triple act of interior dedication required as a prelude to the receiving of a special grace, as in Dante's ardent self-immolation in the Heaven of Mars (*Par.* xiv. 88–93). Such a reading would be quite appropriate here and would further attenuate the theme of repentance. However, even in the normal interpretation, the reference to repentance does not exclude other possibilities. The rite of beating one's breast used to occur three times in the Mass: in the 'Confiteor' (at the words, 'through my fault, through my fault, through my most grievous fault'), in the 'Agnus Dei' ('Lamb of God, who takes away the sins of the world, have mercy on us . . . have mercy on us . . . give us peace'), and at the 'Domine, non sum dignus' ('Lord, I am not worthy that you should enter under my roof; but say only the word, and my soul shall be healed'). The early commentators all implicitly relate Dante's act to the first of these examples and connect it with the three ways of sinning (by thought, word, and deed) and, according to the Ottimo, sins against the Father, the Son, and the Spirit. However, the other two occasions are also in their way appropriate. The 'Agnus Dei' associates the themes of sin, Christ's sacrifice, mercy, and peace, whilst the 'Domine, non sum dignus' expresses unworthiness, and the phrase, 'my soul shall be healed', fits in with the angel's command to Dante to wash away the seven wounds (lines 113–14). Even with regard to the theme of repentance, the beating of the breast is by no means exclusive to the Sacrament of Penance. Its generic and daily use is explained by St. Albert who, after discussing repentance for pre-baptismal sin and repentance for mortal sins, adds a third type: 'The repentance of the good and humble faithful is also a daily punishment by which we beat our breasts and say, "Forgive us our trespasses." '[5] This is the habit of repentance which Dante learns from his whole journey and which causes him to beat his breast frequently lest, in the remainder of his life, he should forfeit his chance of returning to Paradise (*Par.* xxii. 106–8).

The whole ritual is thus predominantly one of submission, a submission mixed perhaps with an element of penitence and essential before the door will be opened. In the context of the journey, at a point when Dante is about to cross a threshold of tremendous spiritual importance, it assumes a greater prominence at a unique moment in the poem, and this implies that Dante wishes it to be interpreted on a higher level than that of a mere allegory of the regular and repeatable Sacrament of Penance. It marks the point at which Dante turns his back on a negative and defective world of exclusion and submits to the authority of the 'first minister' of a spiritual Church and to the duties which entry into this Church imposes upon its members (cf. *Purg.* i. 98–9; xxi. 22–4). Despite the additional elements of humility and repentance, however, the actions seem on the surface to add up to a purely ritual gesture required *pro forma* before admission to the path of salvation. There is no precise reference to the Sacrament of Penance, nor is there a dramatized sense of personal guilt. It reminds one rather of the quaint custom of the penitentiaries of St. Peter's in Rome: the visitor, tourist or pilgrim, can kneel before the priest and, without further formalities, he will receive a tap from the priest's rod and so many days of indulgence.[6] This analogy is useful for defining the tone of the episode rather than for arguing a direct reference, but it does illustrate how the balance of the intonation tips away from the theme of interior forgiveness and towards a purely exterior act of Roman ritualism. However, to Dante perhaps such rituals were not so empty as they may appear today. Perhaps for him there was no real conflict between the interior state and the exterior formality. Perhaps he saw in such a ritual some complex spiritual truth or some valid historical process or some personal event. Besides its universal and general theological and moral importance at this point in the journey, Dante's act of repentant submission may even be the poetic expression of a subjective experience, an acknowledgement of some personal sin or habit or error which in life kept him outside a certain door. Or maybe, since the elements of personal guilt and repentance are so attenuated and formalized, the rite represents, not so much his sense of personal sin, but rather the recognition of an external obstacle, some defect or source of scandal, which at some stage in his life prevented him from submitting to a legitimate authority and so from entering through a door which leads to heaven.

5. *The Seven P's*

> Sette P ne la fronte mi descrisse
> col punton de la spada, e "Fa che lavi,
> quando se' dentro, queste piaghe" disse   (*Purg.*
> ix. 112–14)

(Seven P's he inscribed upon my forehead with the point of the sword, and said: 'When you are inside, see that you wash away these wounds').

The imposition of the seven P's is, above all else, the basis of the whole process of purgation and fundamental to Dante's presentation of the theology and structure of Purgatory. Yet normally the seven P's are identified merely as the marks of the Seven Deadly Sins, and this raises anomalies in the flow of the narrative. If Dante is contrite, then pardon and absolution are the next natural stages, but in fact there is as yet no hint of absolution. On the contrary, instead of pronouncing the words 'I absolve you' (the form of the Sacrament), the angel immediately marks Dante with the signs of those very sins of which he is supposed to have been cleansed by his 'confession'. Instead of the expected innocence and freedom, he at once receives marks and obligations which are also a burden (*Purg.* xii. 115–26; xxii. 1–9; xxvii. 121–3). Moreover, as will be seen, the seven P's represent a universal purgatorial rite and not the marks of personal sin. The Ottimo Commento seems to sense these anomalies for it points out that since Dante sinned in all the Seven Deadly Sins he has a duty to make satisfaction for all of them. In this way Dante's personal confession is followed by a universal rite. But there is no justification for presuming that Dante sinned so extensively, nor in Purgatory does he actually undergo the process of purgation as applied to his personal sins. It is clear from the example of Statius, punished at length for accidie and prodigality (*Purg.* xxi. 67–8; xxii. 34–6, 92–3) but not for gluttony or lust, that all the souls pass through the seven cornices but are fully punished only in those which pertain to their actual, and particularly their besetting, sins. The rite is universal, the application personal. The washing-away of the seven P's is required from all the souls; the punishment which does this varies, with absolute justice, according to the past sins of each individual. Dante undergoes the universal process, but only after death will he return to certain cornices to wash away some of the P's at greater length, notably that of pride but not so much that of envy (*Purg.* xiii. 133–8).

That the imposition of the seven P's is a universal rite is confirmed much later on by Virgil's words to Statius about the P's which Dante still bears (*Purg.* xxi. 22–4). The most natural meaning of this passage is that all the souls are marked with the P's, which are therefore the signs that they are travelling to salvation.[1] Virgil has just alluded to his own eternal exile, and Statius has mistakenly assumed that both of them are souls banned by God from ascending to heaven. Virgil's reply points to Dante, who, though still alive, is marked with the signs of the saved inscribed by the angel, as opposed to Virgil himself, who is not so marked. The implication, as most critics see, is that Statius must be aware of the function of the angel and of the P's as the signs of salvation. To assume that only Dante is so marked involves some distortion of the natural sense of *Purg.* xxi. 22–4 (with its use of the present tense 'profila') and of *Purg.* xxv. 138–9. It also makes the angel-doorkeeper and the angels of the cornices redundant as regards the souls and the process of purgation: they operate only once, on the occasion of Dante's visit. This contradicts the whole universal and ritual scheme which Dante carefully builds up throughout the *cantica*. The reason why Dante does not usually mention the P's marked on the souls is because his own experience shows that each angel erases one. Thus, the proud have seven, the envious six, and so on. By a curious miscalculation, C. S. Singleton argues that in any case Statius would have no P's left, whereas it is clear that, even though he is not to spend any time being punished among the gluttons and the lustful, he, like Dante, must still bear the two P's associated with those cornices, and this is the whole point of Virgil's words to him about the marks. Presumably, Singleton supports the alternative theory because, if one interprets the letter P as referring only to *Peccatum*, then the souls cannot bear the signs of sin, nor can these signs be the marks of salvation, so that the symbol must therefore be applied solely to the personal allegory of the living Dante, uniquely travelling through Purgatory on his moral exodus to salvation. If it can be shown that the seven P's can be both the signs of sin and the signs of salvation, then this will dispose of the problem.

The sacramental interpretation of the episode of the door contradicts itself in its explanation of the seven P's. If Dante and the souls are repentant and have been absolved, then they cannot be the marks of the actual Seven Deadly Sins, nor, since they represent a universal duty, can they denote the personal duty of satisfaction imposed for personal sins in confession. Yet they are connected in some way with personal sin, and especially with a besetting sin—for Dante pride, for Statius accidie and prodigality. Except for pride (*Purg.* x. 136–7), Dante does not seem to distinguish between different degrees of severity in the punishment of individual souls, but he does use the idea of duration.[2] The stronger has been the attachment to the sin, the longer will the sinner remain on the cornice (*Purg.* xiii. 133–8), and the soul's liberation from a cornice is an interior process, dependent on his sense that his will has been released from the remains of that particular sin (*Purg.* xxi. 58–72). Indeed, Dante's emphasis on duration and on the purifying and liberation of the will is an important element in his presentation of the punishments of the cornices as positive rather than negative. In this respect too, the seven P's not only operate on the universal and the personal levels but are also simultaneously negative (aspects of the burden of sin) and positive (part of a process of washing or healing). So they point the way to the dual function of Dante's Purgatory—to punish and to purify.

The method by which the angel imposes the seven P's suggests the possibility of multiple meanings in the symbol. Remotely, it recalls the stigmatization of the saints and the ceremony of Ash Wednesday already cited with reference to the colour of the angel's robe. More directly, it rests upon two of Dante's chief visionary sources, the prophecy of Ezekiel and the Apocalypse (cf. *Purg.* xxix. 100–5). The seven P's recall the marking of the Hebrew letter Tau on the brows of the good who are to be saved, and the marking of the foreheads of the elect in opposition to the marks of blasphemy on the seven heads of the Beast and on its followers, before the punishment of the world by the seven plagues of the seven angels.[3] Dante follows these sources in presenting the seven P's also as the signs of the elect (*Purg.* xxi. 22–4). G. R. Sarolli has described St. Jerome's interpretation of the Tau of Ezekiel and has indicated several readings of this symbol.[4] The seventh man who makes the marks wears pontifical robes, and Tau, the twenty-second and last letter of the Hebrew alphabet, stands for the twenty-two books of the Jewish Bible and, in general, for the Torah (the Law); at the same time it prefigures the Cross of Christ. With the examples of Ezekiel and the Apocalypse before him, Dante too may have wished to convey a wider series of allusions in his symbol of the seven P's. Other suggestions have, in fact, been made, connecting them with the seven penitential psalms, the seven scrutinies of Lent, or with the custom of making malefactors bear cards indicating their crimes (for example, F for FUR, 'thief').[5]

That the letter P in some way represents *Peccatum* cannot be denied. The arrangement of the cornices relates the seven P's directly to the Seven Deadly Sins. But the Seven Deadly Sins were themselves traditionally linked with numerous sevenfold images in the Scriptures: the seven plagues and the seven sword blows for sins; the sevenfold washing of Naaman; the seven days of sacrifices of expiation; the seven penitential psalms; the seven heads of the Beast and the seven plagues of the seven angels; the seventy-times-sevenfold forgiveness of sins in the Christian era.[6] St. Bonaventure links the seven Cardinal and Theological Virtues and the seven Gifts of the Holy Ghost with seven of the Beatitudes, thus presenting these last, as Dante does, as sevenfold remedies for the Seven Deadly Sins.[7]

This long tradition of sevenfold sin, sevenfold punishment, and sevenfold forgiveness underlies Dante's presentation of the cornices. The possibilities for the letter P begin to multiply if these three elements of *peccato-pena-perdono* are further considered in relation to the overall themes of Purgation and Purification, to the Virgilian concept of *Piacula*, which Dante has already adapted to his presentation of the repentant *in extremis*,[8] and to the biblical concept of Expiation, which in itself involves the two main aspects of Dante's Purgatory— punishment and cleansing. G. Rossetti made the quaint, but not impossible, suggestion that in the symbol of the seven P's Dante was using a *figura etymologica* based upon the word *ex-PI-atio*.[9] Even if purely coincidental, this would express a real truth about Dante's Purgatory, which is the place both for the expiation of the effects of past guilt and for the removal of those impediments in love which stand in the way of full atonement and of being 'at one' with God, Supreme Good.

Of all these possibilities, the most fundamental is the con- nection between *Peccatum* and *Poena*. By analysing this, we can relate the seven P's to the overall presentation of Purgatory by Dante and to the concept, both negative and positive, contained in the word which the angel himself uses to describe them—*Piaghe* (wounds).[10]

If the letter P refers to *Peccatum*, then it certainly does not mean the stain of actual mortal sin. The souls in Purgatory have of necessity already been absolved from this by repent- ance before death. Without this repentance the souls of Manfred and Buonconte would be in hell like those of their fathers (cf. *Inf*. x. 119; xxvii. 1 ff., esp. 112–23). There is no stain of mortal sin in Purgatory,[11] nor, of course, can the souls sin there (*Purg*. xxvi. 131–2).[12] Nor are the P's the memory of actual sins, for this is only erased by immersion in the Lethe (*Purg*. xxviii. 127–30). Yet the removal of the seven P's has something to do with release from a burden and with some sort of remission or 'covering up' of sins, for Matelda, who later administers the Lethe, first sings: '*Beati quorum tecta sunt peccata!*' ('Blessed are those whose sins are covered up!') (*Purg*. xii. 115–26; xxix. 3).[13] Obviously, some other concept must link the sin, represented by the letter P, with the process of sevenfold purgation.

The answer is provided by St. Thomas: 'In sin there are but three elements: the stain, the obligation to punishment, and the remains of sin (*macula, reatus poenae, et reliquiae peccati*).'[14] The stain (*macula* or *culpa*) of sin is remitted by contrition alone, although on earth there should normally be also the intention to confess and to make satisfaction.[15] But the souls in Purgatory are incapable of contrition, confession, and satisfaction in the sacramental sense: the Sacraments do not apply in the afterlife; the souls in Purgatory are informed by *caritas* and can experience sorrow, but their contrition lacks efficacy, for they are not *in statu merendi*; and, since their contrition is not meritorious, they cannot strictly speaking make satisfaction for their sins. Only 'in a broad sense˜(*largo modo*)' can the paying of the debt of punishment in Purgatory be called satisfaction.[16] There is thus a theological distinction between the meritorious satisfaction enjoined in confession and the type of satisfaction required by divine justice in Purgatory.

On earth, the Sacrament of Penance is the outward sign that the penitent is liberated from the stain of sin, and the act of oral confession also liberates him from some of the temporal punishment, thus opening to him the door of heaven. The Sacrament also imposes on him the duty to remit more of the temporal punishment by performing works of satisfaction proportional to the stain and consisting of penances such as fasting, almsgiving, and prayer.[17] For the souls in Purgatory the stain of all mortal sins must have been erased by contrition before death (*Purg.* iii. 121–3; iv. 132; v. 52–7, 100–7; xxvi. 92–3), but the debt of temporal punishment remains after the removal of the stain, and the principal function of Purgatory is the remission of this temporal punishment which has not yet been paid off by works of satisfaction in life. By contrition, man is absolved from the stain and from the obligation to eternal punishment in hell, but there remains, in life and after death, the obligation to temporal punishment—to penances in life and to the 'temporal fire' of Purgatory after death (*Purg.* xxvii. 127).[18]

Dante, of course, presents this doctrine primarily as regards mortal sins, which carry the obligation to eternal punishment if the sinner dies unrepentant. The case for venial sins is slightly different, since they do not carry this sentence of eternal punishment. In life, the stain of venial sin can be removed by attrition or even by confessing to a layman; after death, the punishments of Purgatory remove the stain of venial sins which have not been formally forgiven in life. However, all sins—mortal sins already forgiven and venial sins whether forgiven in life or not—carry the obligation to temporal punishment, and, if the *poena* of venial sins is not remitted by works of satisfaction in life, it too must be paid in Purgatory before the soul can have full *caritas* and enjoy the vision of God. Only very exceptionally, as in the cases of the good thief and of Trajan after his resuscitation from the grave, are the *culpa* and the *poena* of all sins remitted simultaneously, and the soul travels directly to Paradise.[19]

Purgatory completes the process of the remission of the *poena* due to sin, a process which was begun, or should have been begun, by the soul performing works of satisfaction in life. Indeed, satisfaction not performed or not completed in life must be fully made to God in Purgatory (*Purg.* xi. 71–2). Moreover, the pains of Purgatory, being broadly analogous to works of satisfaction and, in fact, their completion, have like them a dual function. As acts of justice they pay off a debt to God, and as acts of virtue they uproot the causes of sin. In this second, positive sense, the *poenae* are the medicines of sins and so help to cure the *reliquiae peccati*, the tendency to, and habits of, sin.[20] Dante's conception of Purgatory embraces the elements both of justice and of curing (the erasing of the seven wounds), and these elements are linked by a method of *contrapasso* or relationship between the sin and the penance. This *contrapasso* expresses the penance both as a debt and as a purifying ascetic act. The proud are burdened down towards the earth in order to ascend eventually to the stars; those guilty of *invidia* cannot see (*invidio-invideo*);[21] a blinding smoke is the punishment for wrath, haste for the slothful, starvation for the gluttonous, and purification by fire for the lustful. The punishment of the avaricious may seem less obvious, but, if one examines the terms in which Dante or Virgil addresses the souls of the cornices, one finds a constant use of expressions and metaphors appropriate to the particular form of the punishment on each cornice (*Purg.* xi. 37–9; xiii. 85–90; xvi. 31–3; xviii. 106–8; xxiii. 58; xxiv. 42: xxvi. 61–3). Since only the fifth cornice seems to be missing from this scheme, it is very probable that we should give to the verb 'maturare', applied twice to the penance being performed by the avaricious Pope Hadrian V, an economic rather than a horticultural sense (*Purg.* xix. 91, 141). All the souls are paying their debt to God (*Purg.* x. 108; xi. 88, 125–6); in the case of the avaricious, this has a particularly appropriate application as they lie, bound and motionless, face downwards; in this inert posture, Hadrian is waiting for his spiritual money to mature in order that he may pay off his debt and redeem his soul.

In discussing the seven P's, it is therefore most important to distinguish between the stain of sin (*culpa*) and the punishment due to sin (*poena*). Dante himself applies this distinction when discussing the Crucifixion as an infinite act of satisfaction and expiation, and the terms in which he does so are remarkably close to the theme of the seven P's and Purgatory as the place for the redirection of love. Sin can only be expiated, and true human dignity reacquired, by a man who 'fills in where guilt (*colpa*) has made a void', and this is done by 'just punishments (*pene*) against bad love' (*Par*. vii. 83–4). All expiation in Purgatory is based upon that performed by Christ (*Purg*. xxiii. 73–5).

The erasing of the seven P's is thus not a remission of the stain of sin, for the souls have already earned this by repentance in life, and Dante knows that he too must die repentant, absolved, and healed of sin (*Par*. xxii. 106–8; xxxi. 88–90; xxxiii. 34–7). The P's are first and foremost the marks of the *Poena*, the temporal punishment which remains due after the sin has been forgiven.

The fact that this temporal punishment consists of two parts—satisfaction in life and Purgatory after death—suggests a solution to one of the most puzzling aspects of the *Purgatorio*, the unity of theme between Antepurgatory and Purgatory proper. It has long been noticed that the division into groups of the souls in Antepurgatory is apparently freer than anywhere else in the *Comedy*. The lower groups are as small bands of wandering sheep, excluded for a variety of reasons from the 'holy flock' of the cornices; the souls of the last group are set apart, but they too could wander downwards on the slopes at night (*Purg*. iii. 79–87; vii. 58–9; xxiv. 73). The different reasons why these various groups are excluded from the cornices seem unconnected. However, if the imposition of the seven P's is regarded as the sign of admission to the sevenfold process of remitting the *Poena* due to sin after death, then there is one factor which unites all the groups of souls in Antepurgatory: they are temporarily excluded from making final satisfaction on the cornices because they did not start the process of making satisfaction while they were still alive. Those who died excommunicate were juridically excluded from the Sacraments, the *suffragia*, and the prayers of the Church, which controls the methods of satisfaction.[22] Those who were lazy or were repentant *in extremis* had no desire or time to perform works of satisfaction before death. The souls in the Valley of the Princes are presented in a place which recalls sensual worldly pleasures and temptations (*Purg.* vii. 73–81; viii. 94–108), and as rulers they were preoccupied by temporal affairs at the expense of their spiritual duties. Of the four groups, the excommunicates and those who died violently experienced contrition *in extremis* but lacked confession and satisfaction, whilst the lazy and the princes may have died shriven but are presented as not having performed works of satisfaction and penance in life. St. Thomas says that those who repent at the last moment are punished more in Purgatory, whilst of those who die shriven he says: 'It is necessary that he who dies after contrition and absolution, but before making satisfaction, be punished in the afterlife.'[23]

What is common to all these groups is that they died without having made satisfaction for sin, so that each soul in Antepurgatory exemplifies the reference, in one of Dante's main sources for the whole episode, to the man who:

> distulit in seram commissa piacula mortem[24]

(postponed to the last moment of death the required acts of expiation).

Provenzan Salvani is, in fact, exempted from Antepurgatory precisely because he performed a great act of satisfaction for his pride during his life, Sapía and Forese because their defect has been supplied by the living on their behalf (*Purg.* xi. 127–42; xiii. 124–9; xxiii. 83–90). So, because for various reasons they delayed until death the required duty of satisfaction, they are all subject to corresponding statutory periods of delay before they can enter the realm of final satisfaction and purification. The excommunicates must wait for thirty times the length of their period of exclusion from the Church

Militant; the others must 'relive' their whole lifetime of sloth and negligence in their spiritual duties. Antepurgatory is a little like Limbo, a place 'sanza martíri' (without torments), where the souls must remain excluded from the Church Suffering, for, as Belacqua says, the angel-doorkeeper would refuse them access to the 'martíri', the positive punishments which make satisfaction after death (*Inf.* iv. 28; *Purg.* iv. 128). Their form of expiation resembles that of certain classes of public sinners who, in the Middle Ages, were excluded from the churches or obliged as a penance to stand on the church steps for statutory periods, especially during Lent, until the penance was completed, and they were admitted through the doors.[25]

The direct lesson of Antepurgatory to Dante is, therefore, the absolute necessity of contrition before death. Indirectly, he is taught that confession is also normally required and, more importantly, that satisfaction must be made for sins in this life through positive penances modelled on those of the cornices. Purgatory beyond the door is an *exemplum* of the only way of making or completing satisfaction through penances. Unless a man embarks upon this path during his earthly life, he too will be temporarily excluded from these penances after death. This is also the reason for Oderisi's obscure prophecy that, as for Provenzan Salvani, so too for Dante the shame, humiliation, and mendicancy which he will experience in exile will provide him with a positive opportunity to escape Antepurgatory by making satisfaction for his pride during his life, although Dante fears that much may still remain for him to expiate on the first cornice after his death (*Purg.* xi. 139–41; xiii. 136–8).

As the signs of the elements which remain after the *culpa* of the sin has been forgiven, the P's represent primarily the *poenae* or punishments, the reaping of the harvest of sin (cf. *Purg.* xiv. 85). But within this negative context Dante has included the positive idea of the purging-away of those other *reliquiae peccati*, the tendencies to, and habits of, sin. Chiefly by means of the device of the 'whips' inciting to virtue and the 'bridles' for curbing vice, Dante presents his Purgatory as a medicinal curing of the soul, a school of moral training, in the soul's redirection towards virtue and true *caritas*. These examples are nourishments which actually assist in purging away the sin by healing the wound (*Purg.* xxv. 138–9). Their constant presence in the ritual of each cornice helps to decrease the sense of punishment and torment in Dante's Purgatory and gives it a positive dimension of re-education to virtue, making it in this respect too a model for the study of virtue and the avoidance of vice in this life as well as in the next, indeed as preparation for the next. Purgatory is both negative and positive. It is the place for 'paying the debt' with the 'money to make satisfaction' and for sloughing off sinful habits, but it is also above all the place where virtue is taught and the source of all moral action, rational or elective love, is purified and redirected (*Purg.* ii. 122–3; xi. 88, 125–6; xvii. 91–139; xviii. 13–75). In so far as the P's weigh Dante down, they are the debt; in so far as they are erased in a process of education and moral healing, they are the signs of cleansing, release, and joy and contribute towards finally making his will 'free, upright, and healthy' (*Purg.* xi. 34–6; xii. 121–6; xiii. 106–8; xvi. 31–2; xxvii. 140). The seven P's, which are progressively erased through Purgatory (*Purg.* xii. 121–36), are the signs of the saved, as Virgil, who lacks them, says to Statius:

> 'Se tu riguardi a' segni
> che questi porta e che l'angel profila,
> ben vedrai che coi buon convien ch'e' regni'
> (*Purg.* xxi. 22–4)

(If you look at the signs which he bears and which the angel carves, you will see clearly that he must reign with the good).

So the *poenae* are ultimately a source of joy, as Forese says:

> 'io dico pena, e dovría dir sollazzo' (*Purg.* xxiii. 72, cf. xxiii. 12, 86)

(I say 'punishment' but should say 'joy').

Throughout Purgatory, Dante concentrates perhaps more on the positive than on the negative aspects of the process. Purgatory is a place not of sorrow but of contentment, hope, and expectation. The souls there are:

> 'color che son contenti
> nel fuoco, perché speran di venire
> quando che sia a le beate genti'   (*Inf*. i. 118–20)

(those who are content in the fire, for they hope some time to join
the blessed people).

Purgatory is:

> quel secondo regno
> dove l'umano spirito si purga
> e di salire al ciel diventa degno   (*Purg*. i. 4–6)

(that second realm, in which the human spirit is purged and becomes
worthy to ascend to heaven).

In this process of paying a debt, of casting off the remnants of
sin, of straightening the crooked (*Purg*. x. 3; xxiii. 126), of
purifying love, the place where the soul passes from one
cornice to another and where each of the P's is erased is in a
full and final sense the 'passage of pardon' (*Purg*. xiii. 42).
This significant phrase, with its positive connotations, occurs
precisely at the point where Virgil is explaining to Dante the
educative and remedial process of Purgatory's 'whips' and
'bridles'.

All these aspects are combined in the word which Dante
uses most frequently to describe the seven P's—*Piaga*
(wound). This is what the angel calls them (*Purg*. ix. 114), and
thus from their first appearance they represent the wounds
which remain after sin and which require healing in a process
of *ruptio vulneris* and *sanatio mentis*.[26] Dante uses the same
word to describe the wound of original sin, healed by Christ
becoming man in the Virgin's womb (*Par*. xxxii. 4–6). As
wounds of sin the P's recall the fissures of the second step, and
as debts of punishment applied by God's absolute justice in
proportion to the past sins of the individual, they fulfil the
biblical *lex talionis*, especially the verse which St. Thomas
cites on the subject of satisfaction both in life and in Purgatory:
'In proportion to the sin shall be the measure of the wounds
(*pro mensura peccati erit et plagarum modus*).'[27]

Dante retains this symbol of the wound to describe the
essence of the process of purgation. The wounds are 'closed

up by suffering', and God's justice is as a wound or scourge in imposing the penances (*Purg.* xv. 80–1; xxiv. 38–9). The final wound, remaining from the sin of lust, is closed up and healed both by the torment of fire and by the moral nourishment of the 'whips' and 'bridles':

> con tal cura conviene e con tai pasti
> che la piaga da sezzo si ricuscia   (*Purg.* xxv. 138–
> 9)

(by this task and by these foods, the wound must finally be closed up).

And this final healing is a true cauterization of the wound by purification in the 'refining fire' (*Purg.* xxvi. 148).

Thus, in three principal senses are the seven P's fundamental to the whole of Purgatory: schematically, as *Peccata*, by their connection with the Seven Deadly Sins; theologically, as *Poenae*, by their importance in the process of progressive remission of the temporal punishment due to sin after death; and morally, as *Piaghe*, because their removal denotes the gradual healing of the sinner's soul, so that, purified and remade in love, Dante's will becomes free, upright, and healthy and so is ready for the final acts of purification by water which make him:

> puro e disposto a salire a le stelle   (*Purg.* xxxiii.
> 145)

(pure and prepared to ascend to the stars).

6. The Keys

The symbol of the keys draws together Dante's presentation of the angel as the 'first minister' of the Church of Purgatory (*Purg.* i. 98–9) and the ritual of the seven P's as the basis of the process of remitting the temporal punishment due to sin after death. The angel's description of his keys also confirms the polemic implicit in the whole episode and points the way towards a definition of the concluding symbol of the door.

From beneath his robe the angel draws two keys:

> L'una era d'oro e l'altra era d'argento;
> pria con la bianca e poscia con la gialla
> fece a la porta sí, ch'i' fu' contento.
> "Quandunque l'una d'este chiavi falla,
> che non si volga dritta per la toppa"
> diss'elli a noi, "non s'apre questa calla.
> Piú cara è l'una; ma l'altra vuol troppa
> d'arte e d'ingegno avanti che diserri,
> perch'ella è quella che 'l nodo digroppa.
> Da Pier le tegno; e dissemi ch'i' erri
> anzi ad aprir ch'a tenerla serrata,
> pur che la gente a' piedi mi s'atterri"   (*Purg.* ix.
> 118–29)

(One was of gold, the other was of silver; first with the white one, and then with the yellow, he did to the door that which I desired. 'Whenever one of these keys fails so that it does not turn straight round in the lock', he said to us, 'this path is not opened. One is more precious, but the other requires extreme skill and intellect before it will unlock, for it is the one which unties the knot. From Peter I have received them, and he told me to err rather in opening than in keeping the door closed, provided that people prostrate themselves at my feet').

In the sacramental interpretation of the episode, the keys represent the double power of the confessor: the 'key of discerning between sin and sin (*scientia discernendi inter lepram et lepram, inter peccatum et peccatum*)' and the 'power of absolving and of binding (*auctoritas sacerdotalis consistens in absolvendo et ligando*)' (Pietro di Dante). All the early commentators use the same or similar terms and point out the moral message that, whilst the golden key operates automatically by the power of sacerdotal orders alone, the silver key of discernment or *scientia* requires that the priest himself be holy and learned. This interpretation allows discussion of the problems of the heretical, excommunicated, or ignorant priest, and in general terms it permits the commentators to exhort the ideal confessor to a life of sanctity and careful study of moral theology. The Anonimo adds a humanistic touch, stressing that the silver key is a key of wisdom and learning, and adding: 'Just as silver is bright and sonorous, so learning makes the mind bright and makes the man renowned and famous and makes his fame resound.'

The image of the keys and the whole theology of the power of the keys depend upon the words of Christ to St. Peter: 'And I will give to you the keys of the kingdom of heaven. And whatsoever you shall bind on earth shall be bound also in heaven; and whatsoever you shall loose on earth shall be loosed also in heaven.'[1] These keys, according to St. Thomas, were forged by Christ in his Passion and consigned to St. Peter after his triple confession of love, when Christ gave him the commission to feed his sheep. The keys were commonly explained as a metaphor for the Church's ministry of all the Sacraments, and in a special way of the Sacrament of Penance.[2]

The doctrine that the confessor uses the power of binding and loosing in administering the Sacrament of Penance goes back at least to St. Jerome, who warns bishops and priests in confession to decide correctly 'who is to be bound and who is to be loosed', lest, like the Pharisees, they should condemn the innocent and absolve the wicked.[3] From this derives the dual concept: within the single power of binding and loosing is both the actual power to do so and the related authority to discern between those who are to be bound and those who are to be loosed. Hence the metaphor of the two keys. It is important to note from the beginning the exact traditional interpretation of the 'key of discernment'. As will be shown, Pietro di Dante's phrase, 'discerning between sin and sin', is a secondary derivation.

In the thirteenth century, St. Bonaventure and St. Thomas use the symbol of the keys to explain the powers of the confessor.[4] They say that, although the door of the kingdom is open,[5] there is an impediment *ex parte nostra* (from man's side), namely, sin. In order to remove (or refuse to remove) this impediment in the individual, so opening (or closing) the door to him, the confessor holds the keys prophesied by Isaiah and consigned by Christ to St. Peter and so to the Church built upon the Rock of Peter.[6] The keys consist in the spiritual power to absolve or to refuse absolution, and in the authority to discern in individual cases. The traditional interpretation of the angel's keys rests almost entirely on *S. Th. III. Suppl.*, Q. 17, a. 3, and it is essential to note the exact terms in which St. Thomas defines the two keys of the priest-confessor. One key is for assessing the suitability of the man to be absolved and so for discerning who is to be brought out of sin and through the door of salvation; the other key is the power of absolution which actually opens the door. The confessor or 'ecclesiastical judge' must have both keys. It is sinful to accept the key of the power to absolve unless the priest already has the key of discernment, but not vice versa. However, the key of the science of discernment (*scientia discernendi*) is not a key of *scientia* alone, for secular judges, scholars, and other laymen can have wisdom and discernment. Strictly speaking, this key is not the key of wisdom but the key of the authority to exercise wisdom.[7] St. Albert is even clearer on this subject. After discussing three theories, he concludes: 'A third group, to which I belong, says that the key is not *scientia*, but rather the authority to discern and judge; every priest receives this at ordination, although he does not receive *scientia*.'[8]

On this basis we can discount the opinion of Pietro di Dante and others that the silver key represents primarily the science of moral theology, the wisdom to discern and judge the gravity of different sins. This opinion rests upon a secondary and comparatively trivial aspect of the key of discernment. No doubt it came into vogue because it was extremely rare for a priest to refuse absolution to an ordinary penitent, and so it seemed as though the confessor used only one key. Thus the silver key lost its principal function, to open or close the door of heaven, and became a metaphor for the ability to unlock the secrets of moral theology. Pietro di Dante's phrase, the 'science of discerning *inter lepram et lepram, inter peccatum et peccatum*' (between disease and disease, between sin and sin), demonstrates this devalued, if more practical, use of the symbol. The original phrase, used by St. Albert, is significantly different. For him the key is the 'science of discerning *inter lepram et non lepram*' (between what is a disease and what is not), i.e. between the sin which cannot be absolved and the sin which can, between the sin which makes a man a leper, an outcast from the community, and the sin which is not so contagious and so does not prevent a man from being re-admitted to the community of the kingdom of heaven.[9] In Pietro di Dante's theory, the two keys in a sense open different doors. In the correct theology of the power of the keys, they complement each other in administering the power of binding and loosing, and each represents a related aspect of the powers vested in the earthly Church to open or close the door of the kingdom of heaven.

Before defining the interrelated powers of the two keys, it is necessary to examine briefly their application in the context of the Sacrament of Penance, for this too is important with regard to the doctrines of Dante's Purgatory and to the present attempt to view any sacramental imagery in the episode as part of a higher, wider, and more complex scheme of polysemy and multiple allusion.

The rather complicated doctrine of the power of the keys in confession can be summarized as follows. Included in the power of the keys of heaven is the key of hell, the key which opens or closes man´to sin and which, in the power of the Church, remits temporal punishment due to sin.[10] The key of hell, forged in Christ's Passion, opened hell at the same time as it opened heaven. The key of hell leads the individual out of hell and closes the door behind him. By closing hell it opens heaven, and thus its function is subsumed into the power of the keys of heaven; the key of hell, the key to eternal and, in a sense, also to temporal punishment, is an aspect of the power of the keys of heaven, '*sed denominatur a digniori*' (but it takes its name from the more valuable one).[11] Heaven is open,[12] but man is impeded by sin, original and actual, from entering. The priest uses the power of the keys to admit the worthy or to exclude the unworthy from the kingdom of heaven. He does not exclude by placing an obstacle, but by refusing to remove the obstacle of sin until God has done so, upon the sinner's repentance. In this sense, the power of 'binding and loosing' has two aspects: *scientia* to discern the worthy from the unworthy, and the actual power to remit sin. But the use of the keys does not remit the stain (*culpa*) of sin. Only God can do this. The priest has no direct power over the kingdom, only over the Sacraments by which man arrives at the kingdom. Since only God can forgive sins, the priest uses the power of the keys as God's minister (*ministerialiter*), not causing forgiveness but in a way (*aliquo modo*) disposing a man to it, and so remitting the *culpa* of sin not directly but *dispositive*.[13] Contrition alone remits the *culpa* of sin and the obligation to eternal punishment in hell, but it cannot normally remit all the *reatus poenae*, the temporal punishment due to sin after forgiveness. This last is the primary function of the confessor's power of the keys.[14] As St. Albert also says: 'Through the keys the penitent's sorrow becomes capable of making satisfaction.'[15]

Even in confession, therefore, the power of the keys directly governs, not the remission of sin as such, but the duty of satisfaction. Only thus can the priest be said to have the two powers of binding and loosing. He cannot bind the *culpa* of sin, for this depends on contrition, although he may be said to bind it in a metaphorical and indirect sense, if he should ever refuse to grant absolution to an impenitent. But as regards the duty of remitting the *poena*, the temporal punishment, the priest can use the keys directly both for binding and loosing. He can bind either by imposing some penance or by refusing to lift one, and he can loose by remitting some temporal punishment and, in general, by administering the various methods of making satisfaction for sin. These powers require great discernment and discretion on the part of the priest. He cannot use the keys at will, but only in accordance with the will of God, prescribing medicinal penances proportional to the sin.[16] In this way, the two keys of the confessor represent the necessary blend of power, authority, and the science of discernment.

However, as has been seen, the key of discernment is not

merely wisdom; it is the authority to discern.[17] Both the keys are related aspects of the Church's authority to bind and loose. In one article only of the *Summa theologica* does St. Thomas, in the context of confession, define the keys respectively as the power to absolve and the science of discernment, and even so the latter is strictly speaking an aspect of authority. The full doctrine of the power of the keys is defined next, in two whole *quaestiones*, nine articles in all, and is then applied over a further four *quaestiones*.[18] In these, the narrow definition of the priest's dual authority in the tribunal of Penance is subsumed into the main doctrine, that the keys are respectively the key of orders or ordination (*clavis ordinis*) and the key of jurisdiction (*clavis jurisdictionis*).

The key of orders is a key of purely spiritual power. It belongs to all priests of whatever rank and consists in the ministry of all the Sacraments, especially Penance, to open the door of heaven to man. It belongs equally to all priests, even bad ones, but its use is impeded in heretics and excommunicates.[19]

The key of jurisdiction governs the disposition of men towards the use of the other key, and this it does first and foremost by controlling the individual's membership of the Church, i.e. by admitting him as a member of the community or by excluding him through excommunication. All priests must have the key of jurisdiction before they can receive the key of orders, although the key of jurisdiction can also belong to non-priests, for example, chapters, abbesses, and certain laymen. The key of jurisdiction is a necessary prerequisite before the priest can administer the Sacraments; in the case of Penance, he can absolve only those over whom he has received jurisdiction from his superiors, and specifically from his bishop. The key of jurisdiction is not equal in all priests but is distributed in different degrees hierarchically. The chief powers of the key of jurisdiction are reserved to bishops and higher prelates. This applies especially to excommunication. Excommunication and absolution from it regard a man's membership of the Church and only partially relate to entry into heaven. They are entirely acts of the key of jurisdiction, reserved to the higher prelates of the Church.[20]

The two keys are related to the two *fora*. All priests, having the key of orders, can act in the 'forum of conscience', i.e. in cases between man and God. Only bishops and higher prelates have the jurisdiction to act in the 'forum of public judgement', i.e. in cases between man and man. It is for his work in codifying the laws of both *fora* that Dante praises Gratian in the Heaven of the Sun (*Par.* x. 104–5). Only prelates who have jurisdiction in the 'public forum' have the power of binding and loosing by excommunication and recommunication, and six cases are in fact reserved to the Pope as the *juris conditor*, the source of all jurisdiction.[21]

If one examines the various definitions of the confessor's power of the keys, as described above, one can see that they all refer to this more fundamental doctrine of the key of orders and the key of jurisdiction. The confessor has a key to discern those who may enter from those to be excluded (St. Jerome), to distinguish non-contagious sins from offences which are contagious (St. Albert), to define the community, or the part of it, over which the priest or prelate has the authority of jurisdiction (St. Thomas). In other words, the use of the keys in the forum of penance is to be explained by reference to their clearly defined powers as used in the public forum, and so, in its public aspect, the angel's silver key recalls first and foremost the earthly Church's power to exclude, to expel those who might contaminate the Church, in short, to excommunicate.

The relevance of the key with the power to excommunicate is obvious in the context of *Purg.* ix. The angel's chief function is to exclude the unworthy—those excommunicated on earth, the late penitents, and the negligent rulers—from the community of the Church Suffering. In this sense, all the souls in Antepurgatory are 'excommunicates', juridically or spiritually, from this Church. In the case of Manfred and those who died under sentence of excommunication, the effect of the key of jurisdiction, however unworthily administered, is seen as continuing into the afterlife: 'whatsoever you shall bind on earth shall be bound also in heaven'. Dante extends the same sentence to the other groups of souls in Antepurgatory. Excluded by their own sloth, delay, or negligence from true membership of the earthly Church, and so not having actively made formal satisfaction for their sins in life, they too are temporarily 'excommunicated' from the positive process of making satisfaction in the Church Suffering after death. The angel's function is not to discern sin from sin, but to decide, on these bases, who is to remain excluded and who is to be admitted to the Church of Purgatory (*Purg.* iv. 127–32). Like the priest's power of the keys, the angel's keys admit the soul to the realm in which the temporal punishment due to sin is remitted; like the bishop's power of the keys, they control the absolution from exterior impediments, such as the sentence of excommunication, and from the comparable spiritual impediments of sloth, delay, and negligence, and admit the soul to the community. The angel's keys of spiritual and juridical authority work in perfect accordance with God's justice. When they both turn cleanly in the lock, the soul may enter (lines 121–3).

The angel's description of his keys fits the theme of excommunication perfectly. The golden key of spiritual ministry is 'more precious', for, as St. Thomas says, the 'forum of penitence is more worthy', but the silver key of the public forum 'requires greater solemnity'.[22] The silver key is a necessary prerequisite for the use of the golden key, and an excommunicate cannot be absolved from sin until he has been absolved from the sentence of excommunication.[23] So the angel opens the door 'first with the white key, then with the yellow' (line 119). The key of orders works despite the unworthiness of the priest, but the key of jurisdiction can be abused in the hands of unworthy prelates, and so it requires 'extreme skill and intellect' in its use (lines 124–5). In particular, on earth the power of binding by excommunication can be wielded arbitrarily and not in accordance with the will of God.[24] For these reasons the angel, perfect minister of God's justice, describes the powers of the silver key in greater detail than those of the gold. In the angel's description of his perfect keys, there is a hidden polemic against the earthly Church's misuse of them, and especially of the silver key of jurisdiction.

Perceiving the polemic in the episode, the early commentators use the angel's description of the silver key as the starting-point for exhortations to the perfect confessor to acquire perfect knowledge of moral theology, to discern between sins, to deal with problems of conscience, to cut the knot of sin by absolution, and to use sparingly the power to refuse absolution. But, as has been shown, this is not the function of either of the keys in confession. In the forum of conscience, the silver key is the juridical authority to discern in controlling the duty of satisfaction, and its chief use in the public forum is the power of excommunication. Dante's hidden admonition to the earthly Church is to impose penances carefully, justly, and only in proportion to the sin, and in particular to use with extreme skill and wisdom the power to impose the punishment of excommunication. This last point has already been the main lesson of the episode of Manfred, with the condemnation of the sentence passed on his remains by the bishop of Cosenza:

> 'Per lor maladizion sí non si perde,
> che non possa tornar, l'etterno amore' (*Purg.* iii. 133–4)

(By their curses eternal love is not so lost that it cannot return).

The meaning of this passage is, of course, that the prelates of the earthly Church are fallible in their decrees, which often do not reflect the justice and mercy of God (*Purg.* iii. 124–6). But the word 'malediction' probably conceals also a deeper polemical reference against the sinful abuse of the power of excommunication, for St. Thomas says that excommunication is legitimate only when it is a medicine for the good of the soul; otherwise, it is a 'malediction' uttered for its own sake and as such is absolutely forbidden by St. Paul.[25] Later, Dante castigates John XXII for his arbitrary and unstable decrees of exclusion, which likewise do not conform to the mercy of God (*Par.* xviii. 128–9).

In order to wield the complex and dangerous power of excommunication, earthly prelates need great skill and wisdom, and when in doubt they should use mercy, not severity. This is the message contained in the angel's words that St. Peter has told him 'to err rather in opening than in keeping the door closed' (lines 127–8). Obviously the angel cannot err; therefore the sense is that he should use his powers with mercy, just as the earthly Church too should be sparing in the use of its binding powers. Both St. Peter's vicars, the angel and the Pope, should open the door of heaven to all who humbly acknowledge their authority (line 129). The keys of the earthly Church should be modelled on the angel's keys which administer God's perfect justice tempered with mercy.

The angel defines the silver key as 'quella che 'l nodo digroppa' (the one which unties the knot), and this phrase covers both aspects of the power of this key—to bind and loose with regard to temporal punishment in general and to excommunication in particular. Pietro di Dante's reference to discerning between sin and sin does not fit this phrase at all, and so it has led to the rather romantic interpretation that the silver key untangles ('digroppa') the twisted knot ('nodo') of the conscience.[26] But the word 'nodo' is never used in the *Comedy* to mean a tangle; it refers always to something tied. As a symbol (i.e. excluding its use in *Inf.* xvii. 15 and xxx. 28), the word is employed twice to describe things linked together, where the idea of a tangle is quite impossible (*Purg.* xxix. 133; *Par.* xxxiii. 91), and elsewhere 'nodo' refers exclusively to a bond which has to be untied before someone can see a truth (*Inf.* x. 95–6; *Purg.* xxiv. 55–7; *Par.* vii. 52–4; xxviii. 58).[27] The mixed metaphor of a key which discerns or which unravels a tangle is ludicrous. If the word 'nodo' is seen to mean simply a bond or impediment, then the metaphor, though still mixed, has at least the support of the original words in the Gospel and of the theology based upon those words, and the silver key retains its original sense as an aspect of the power of 'binding' and of 'loosing' and so of opening the door of heaven.

The word 'nodo' is in fact used twice by Dante in the *Purgatorio* to denote the bond of temporal punishment due to sin, which is at the same time an impediment to the weaning of the soul from sin and its redirection towards true love. The souls on the cornice of the wrathful:

> 'd'iracundia van solvendo il nodo'   (*Purg.* xvi. 24)

(are untying the knot of wrath).

Similarly, those on the cornice of the gluttonous are:

> 'ombre che vanno
> forse di lor dover solvendo il nodo'   (*Purg.* xxiii.
> 14–15)

(shades who are perhaps untying the knot of their debt).

Thus the silver key 'which unties the knot' is closely linked to the theme of the seven P's, the remission of the debt of temporal punishment and the casting off of earthly attachments and the remains of sin. These are the impediments to the vision of God which are removed by the just punishments of Purgatory (*Purg.* ii. 122–3; xiii. 85–90), and in this sense the angel's silver key, which starts the process of untying the knot, is analogous to the confessor's power to discern correctly the methods of making satisfaction. It also unties the public juridical impediment of excommunication from the Church Suffering and frees the soul so that he can participate in the spiritual effects of the golden key, namely, entry into the realm of remission, the community of salvation, and ultimately the kingdom of heaven.

In the earthly Church, the untying of any juridical bond of excommunication is an essential prerequisite for access to the spiritual benefits available to members; it is also an essential prerequisite for entry into Paradise, for the power of the keys 'extends not just to the living, but also to the dead', since the Church's power to bind binds also in heaven.[28] This is why Manfred and the other excommunicates who died repentant but 'in contumacy of Holy Church' must loose this bond after death by waiting thirty times the length of their contumacy before they can enter the Church of Purgatory through the door which is also the door of heaven (*Purg.* iii. 136–40). Otherwise, the key which 'unties the knot' after death will not work for them. For Dante, not so bound, both keys turn perfectly in the lock. A key of discernment or of unravelling sin would apply to him and to everyone, but the key which unties a juridical bond applies directly only to the excommunicates and to the other souls temporarily excluded from the Church Suffering. The silver key refers back to the negative world of waiting for statutory periods of time outside the door. The golden key looks forward to the positive spiritual world of Purgatory, where time itself is different (*Purg.* xvi. 25–7).

The perfect keys of the angel are thus based on the theology of the two keys, of orders and of jurisdiction, vested in the priests and, more especially, in the bishops of the earthly Church, and in the afterlife they can, in fact, loose bonds imposed by earthly prelates. But since the angel is the vicar of St. Peter, the main reference is to the man who holds the plenitude of the power of St. Peter's keys on earth, the Pope. The keys are primarily those which Christ gave to St. Peter and which St. Peter has left, in Purgatory, to the angel and, on earth, to the Pope (cf. *Par.* xxxii. 124–6). In the Pope are vested the supreme spiritual powers and the supreme jurisdiction over the earthly Church, and he alone possesses the full power of the keys: 'The Pope, who is in the place of St. Peter, has plenary power, the others derive theirs from him.'[29] St. Bernard addresses the Pope with these words: 'You are he to whom the keys are consigned, to whom the sheep are entrusted. There are indeed other doorkeepers of heaven and pastors of the flocks; but you have inherited both titles more gloriously and to a different degree above all the others.'[30] From St. Peter the Apostles derived their powers; from the Pope the powers of binding and loosing descend to the bishops, successors of the Apostles, and thence to the priests.[31] Dante himself reveres the 'supreme keys' of the papal office (*Inf.* xix. 101). In hell this is ironical for he is simultaneously attacking the corrupt holder of that office, but in Purgatory, when Dante attempts to show reverence for the office, he is rebuked by a Pope conscious of the shared nature of papal power as a ministry and of its purely spiritual duties (*Purg.* xix. 127–38). Together with the symbols of the threshold, the angel's sword, and his robe, so also are the keys of Purgatory an element in Dante's implicit polemic against the earthly Papacy, and in his poetic transference of its powers to a purely spiritual plane.

For Dante the papal keys are to the kingdom of heaven, and their function is exclusively spiritual. This is one of the main concluding arguments of the *Monarchia* (cf. III. i, iii). In his discussion of the relationship between the spiritual and the temporal orders, Dante accepts that the Pope, successor of St. Peter, holds the supreme power of the keys, but he insists that this power does not extend to everything. It cannot, for instance, apply to divorce, nor can even the Pope absolve an unrepentant sinner (cf. *Inf.* xxvii. 118). Nor does the Pope's power of the keys extend to the Empire any more than does the Pope hold the sword of temporal power (*Mon.* III. viii–ix). When Christ said to St. Peter, 'I will give to you the keys of the kingdom of heaven', he meant merely, 'I shall make you the doorkeeper of the kingdom of heaven' (*Mon.* III. viii. 9). The power of the papal keys applies solely to the spiritual sphere and to man's journey to salvation.

In the *Comedy* Dante insists on the purely spiritual nature of St. Peter's keys. They were not bought with gold and silver but are keys to the spiritual treasures of Paradise (*Inf.* xix. 90–3; *Par.* xxiii. 130–9; xxiv. 34–6). The Popes abuse the power of the keys by mixing their spiritual powers with temporal ambitions, by simony, the selling of these powers for gold and silver, or by making excessive and fraudulent claims for their powers (*Inf.* xix. 1–6, 91–117; xxvii. 85 ff.). On this last point is based the irony of the way in which Boniface VIII, the 'prince of the new Pharisees', totally obsessed by political and military intrigues against fellow-Christians in the heart of the Church, outwits the astute but theologically naïve Guido da Montefeltro by exaggerating the power of the keys as wielded by his hands, more appreciative of that power than were those of poor Celestine V:

> 'Lo ciel poss'io serrare e diserrare,
> come tu sai; però son due le chiavi
> che 'l mio antecessor non ebbe care'   (*Inf.* xxvii. 103–5)

(I can close and open heaven, as you know; for there are two keys which my predecessor did not consider precious).

But Boniface's claim to absolve an unrepentant sinner by the power of the keys is logically impossible and therefore fraudulent (cf. *Mon.* III. viii. 7), and his 'absolution' is ineffective:

> 'ch'assolver non si può chi non si pente,
> né penter e voler insieme puossi
> per la contradizion che nol consente'   (*Inf.* xxvii. 118–20)

(for he who does not repent cannot be absolved; nor can one repent and wish to sin at the same time, because of the contradiction which prevents this).

In the *Inferno*, therefore, Dante accuses Nicholas III, Boniface VIII, and Clement V of simony (*Inf.* xix) and Boniface VIII also of laying claim, for reasons of personal advantage, to a power which not even God possesses (*Inf.* xxvii). His invective against these abuses of the purely spiritual power of the keys reaches its climax in the words of St. Peter:

> 'Non fu nostra intenzion ch'a destra mano
> d'i nostri successor parte sedesse,
> parte da l'altra del popol cristiano;
>   né che le chiavi che mi fuor concesse,
> divenisser signaculo in vessillo
> che contra battezzati combattesse;
>   né ch'io fossi figura di sigillo
> a privilegi venduti e mendaci,
> ond'io sovente arrosso e disfavillo'   (*Par.* xxvii. 46–54)

(It was not our intention that part of the Christian people should sit at the right hand of our successors, and part at the left; nor that the keys which were given to me should become a symbol on a banner which wages war against baptized people; nor that I should be a figure on a seal for false privileges bought and sold, for which reason I often glow red and spark with fire).

To the corrupt use of the papal keys to divide the Church, to wage war on fellow-Christians, to deceive, and to practise simony in the earthly Church are opposed the angel's perfect keys of gold and silver. Thus, the sword, the robe, and the keys combine in the presentation of the angel as a projection of an ideal Papacy, just, repentant, and poor, bearing the spiritual sword alone, and using with skill and wisdom both its keys of authority to administer the purely spiritual treasures of the kingdom of heaven.

*   *   *

This, in general terms, may suffice to define the symbol of the angel's keys, but so far we have examined the keys in a predominantly negative sense, as keys which control the duty of untying the knot of temporal punishment and, in particular, of loosing the bonds of excommunication. But the essential function of keys is to open doors, and within the symbol of the angel's keys we can in fact trace a further level of allusion which links the whole episode of the steps, the threshold, and the angel to the opening of the door and so to the positive spiritual benefits of Purgatory in Dante's poem.

Dante himself indicates elsewhere another use of the power of the keys, and the similarity to the description of the keys of Purgatory is very striking. In the Heaven of the Moon, Beatrice explains to Dante the doctrine of dispensations and commutations of vows and warns that these must not be done privately and arbitrarily by the individual, but only after recourse to the spiritual and juridical authority of the Church:

> 'Ma non trasmuti carco a la sua spalla
> per suo arbitrio alcun, sanza la volta
> e de la chiave bianca e de la gialla'   (*Par*. v. 55–7)

(But let no one change the burden on his shoulders of his own accord, without the turning both of the white key and of the yellow).

The whole tenor of this admonition is that men should act as men and not as 'mad sheep', making and changing silly vows; they should rely on the two sole guides to salvation—the Scriptures and the authority of the Pope, 'the pastor of the Church who guides you' (*Par*. v. 76–81). The text requires that the reference be applied not to the ordinary confessor but to the supreme powers vested in the Church as a whole, in its prelates, and above all in the Pope. Sapegno's notes to *Par*. v. 56 refer back to his notes on the keys of the angel-doorkeeper, but his interpretation of *Purg*. ix does not make sense in the context of *Par*. v, for two main reasons: firstly, because the key of prudence and wisdom for examining guilt does not by any means define the function of this key in the context of the commutation of vows; and secondly, because in Sapegno's interpretation the minister of the keys is different in each case, being the ordinary priest in *Purg*. ix and specifically a prelate in *Par*. v. On this second point, Sapegno himself quotes St.Thomas: 'For commuting or dispensing from vows, the authority of a prelate is required.'[32]

If, therefore, a vow has to be changed, recourse must be made to the juridical and spiritual authority of the Church, and the law of satisfaction must be followed in making the second vow equal to or greater than the first (*Par*. v. 43–63). Obviously, the use of the silver key mentioned here has nothing to do with the imputation or discernment of personal sin but with the authority of the Church in the 'forum of public judgement'. For the annulment of sacerdotal, monastic, or matrimonial vows, a public judgement would literally be required, as the context of the vows of Piccarda and Constance also implies. In lesser cases, it is a function of the Church's key of jurisdiction to assess the proportions of any commutation in accordance with the law of satisfaction. In this respect also, as Beatrice emphasizes, the juridical key is essential for the achievement of the spiritual effects of the other key. Here too the dual power of binding and loosing is necessary for man's salvation.

Thus Dante refers to another aspect of the power of the keys. Not only does this prompt us to search for more, but it raises the question of the whole basis of the power of the keys. What element unites these various uses of the keys which were forged in Christ's Passion? What does the Church 'dispense' when it uses the keys to unlock a spiritual store for administering the Sacraments, for binding and loosing in the two *fora*, for annulling or commuting vows? The answer is that, through the keys, the Church has access to the merits of Christ.

Immediately after his discussion of excommunication, St. Thomas investigates another *actus clavium* (use of the keys)— the granting of indulgences. This power belongs to the same jurisdiction as excommunication. The difference between them is that, whereas excommunication depends on a formal pronouncement (*sententia*), indulgences are the dispensing of the treasures of the Church.[33] The doctrine of indulgences is a notoriously difficult one. It was not properly understood by some of Dante's contemporaries, the main mistake being the belief that indulgences removed the *culpa* of sin, whereas only contrition can remove the *culpa*, and indulgences relate solely to the *poena*. That a layman such as Giovanni Villani should make this mistake is understandable, but it seems that even papal notaries could slip, for there is one contemporary example of the granting of an indulgence *a culpa et poena*.[34] The doctrine was, of course, later rejected by Luther, together with the whole concept of Purgatory. This may seem a strange parallel, but in fact the doctrines of satisfaction, of commutation, of indulgences, and of Purgatory are all intimately connected.

The theology of indulgences depends upon the concept of the infinite merits of Christ, together with the superabundant merits of all those whose works of penance and satisfaction exceed their debts to divine justice, namely, the saints, all those who make atonement on behalf of the whole Church, and all those who bear unjust sufferings and do works beyond what is required of them for their sins. These merits constitute an infinite treasury which, because of the unity of the Mystical Body of Christ and the Communion of Saints, belongs to the Church: 'The aforesaid merits are the common property of the whole Church.'[35]

An indulgence is a way of commuting the satisfaction required for sin. Instead of doing acts of penance, a man draws on the treasury of merit to remit some of the temporal punishment due to sin: 'An indulgence or *relaxatio* is a remission of the imposed punishment and proceeds from the power of the keys and from the treasury of superabundance of the perfect.'[36] Indulgences do not cancel the duty of satisfaction but offer another means of paying off the debt, although not even the Pope could arbitrarily remit all the temporal punishment by means of indulgences.[37] What an indulgence does, therefore, is to assist the duty of satisfaction by helping to pay some of it off 'from the common wealth of the Church', and not only does an indulgence take the place of works of satisfaction in remitting the *poena* on earth, but it also thereby remits some of the *poena* or temporal punishment due after death in Purgatory. Normally, indulgences are valid only to those who have repented of mortal sin and confessed (*contritis et confessis*), but of itself an indulgence only means: 'I make you a participant in the merits of the whole Church.'[38] Indulgences, therefore, pertain to the opening function of the power of the keys, and since they are not a dispensation of the Sacraments but of the treasure of the Church, they are controlled primarily by the key of jurisdiction. Commutation by indulgences 'is a function of him who governs the Church'; whilst God alone remits the stain (*culpa*) of sin and the debt of eternal punishment, God and man together remit the temporal punishment (*poena*).[39] The jurisdiction over indulgences belongs primarily to the Pope but can be delegated to bishops and others. Ordinary priests can normally neither excommunicate nor grant indulgences. Plenary indulgences belong to the Pope alone, 'because of the plenitude of pontifical power'.[40]

St. Bonaventure's description of the powers of prelates—and therefore, in the highest degree, of the Pope—offers an even clearer parallel with Dante's presentation of the sword-bearing angel-vicar of St. Peter, who administers the sentence of 'excommunication' to the souls in Antepurgatory and at the same time controls the realm of remission of the *poenae* due to sin. He says that in the earthly Church the prelate has both the sword of excommunication and the 'power to distribute from the treasures of the merits of the Church', and this last power 'is for indulgences (*et hoc in relaxatione*)'.[41]

The angel's silver key to the Church Suffering is, therefore, also an allusion to the doctrine of the earthly Church's jurisdiction over indulgences. Indeed, the angel's words, that this key needs 'extreme skill and intellect before it opens', stress this opening function rather than the ideas of discerning the worthy or of binding the unworthy by excommunication. In its control of indulgences the key of jurisdiction 'unties the knot' of temporal punishment in life in the earthly Church and after death in Purgatory. In this context also does it require 'extreme skill and intellect' in its use. The main sinful abuses of the power of granting indulgences were: firstly, the excessive and disproportionate use of them, 'in such a way that men are absolved from acts of penance almost for nothing';[42] and secondly, the danger of simony. In this last respect, St. Thomas makes a distinction which Julius II was to employ, to the scandal of Luther and others, namely, that indulgences can be granted for temporal aids only when spiritual matters are at stake (e.g. for fighting the enemies of the Church, for building churches and bridges, and for almsgiving). Indulgences can never be given for temporal aids *simpliciter*, since the remission of punishment is spiritual, and 'to give the spiritual for the temporal is simony'.[43] Besides his general attack on simony (*Inf.* xix; *Par.* xxvii. 52–3), Dante also attacks the particular evil of the granting of false but lucrative indulgences (*Par.* xxix. 118–26).[44] Dante's kneeling before the angel, and his hostility to the abuse of indulgences in the earthly Church, can be illustrated also by the words of Chaucer's pardoner, accustomed to exploit a credulous populace by means of his relics and indulgences:

'But sirs, o word forgat I in my tale,
I have relikes and pardon in my male,
As faire as any man in Engelond,
Whiche were me yeven by the popes hond.
If any of yow wol, of devocioun,
Offren, and han myn absolucioun,
Cometh forth anon, and kneleth heer adoun,
And mekely receyveth my pardoun.'[45]

The word which Dante, like Chaucer, uses for indulgence is
'pardon' (*Purg.* xiii. 62; *Par.* xxix. 120), and this suggests a
new possibility for interpreting the 'pass of pardon' mentioned
in one of the same cantos (*Purg.* xiii. 42). In a real sense, the
place where a P of temporal punishment is erased is the place
where the soul receives final indulgence from the *poena* due to
that sin.

*   *   *

Dante's conception of Purgatory is based on the theological
principle that the punishment which has not been remitted by
works of satisfaction or by indulgences in life must be paid off
by the penances of Purgatory after death (*Purg.* xi. 70–2). All
satisfaction, in life and in Purgatory, is based upon the infinite
act of satisfaction for sin, the death of Christ, who:

'forato da la lancia,
e poscia e prima tanto sodisfece,
che d'ogne colpa vince la bilancia'   (*Par.* xiii. 40–
2)

(pierced by the lance, both before and after performed such satisfaction that it outweighs the balance of all guilt).

By Christ's infinite act, Purgatory, previously forbidden, was
opened to man (cf. *Inf.* xxvi. 133–42; *Purg.* i. 130–2; vii.
4–6). Christ died in order to open Purgatory, to make its
shore accessible on the way to purified love, so that man might
live and be 'pulled out of the sea of crooked love' and 'placed
on the shore of straight love' (*Par.* xxvi. 59–63). Just as the
earthly Church, with its keys to the door of heaven, is founded
on the firm Rock of Christ and his vicar, so too for Dante both
Purgatory and Paradise are based on the infinite and priceless

merits of the Redemption, and Purgatory above the precious, immovable threshold is the place where man uses these merits to 'pay off his debt' with the 'money to make satisfaction' (*Purg.* xi. 88,125–6). Since the door of heaven is the Church Militant on earth as a *figura* of the Church Triumphant after the end of time, and since Dante, in *Purg.* ix, is defining the intermediate stage, the Church Suffering, these concepts are closely linked to another vital and conspicuous element in the *Purgatorio.*

As has been seen, the earthly Church's power of the keys is related in two ways to the duty of satisfaction: by imposing penances in confession and by commuting the debt by means of indulgences. Both these methods thereby remit some of the punishment due in Purgatory after death. But the powers of commutation and of granting indulgences may affect Purgatory in two ways: directly, when a man gains an indulgence for himself, and indirectly, by means of the *suffragia mortuorum*, the prayers, penances, and indulgences performed by a living person and commuted on behalf of a soul in Purgatory. Since the souls in Purgatory cannot, strictly speaking, perform meritorious satisfaction, the living can supply this duty on their behalf, by works of satisfaction applied to the souls of dead relatives or, in general, to all the souls in Purgatory. The *suffragia* of the living applied to the souls in Purgatory help to remit the temporal punishment due to their sins; they allow a 'speedier remission of the *poena*' and so remove the final impediment to the 'attainment of glory'.[46] There are three types of *suffragia*: the Eucharist (cf. *Purg.*v.71–2), almsgiving, and prayers; the Church can also allow the living to apply indulgences on behalf of the dead.[47] Thus these *suffragia*, together with the superabundant merits of the saints and the other holy people on earth, join the infinite merits of Christ in the treasury which pays off temporal punishment after death, the treasury of indulgence or pardon to which the earthly Church has access by the power of the keys.

Dante's use of the doctrine of the *suffragia mortuorum* is one of the most conspicuous features of the theology of his *Purgatorio.* As for St. Thomas and St. Bonaventure, so also for Dante, the main link between the Church Militant and the Church Suffering consists in the Masses, prayers, and penances performed by the living who are good on behalf of the dead, and they are not a lifting but a commutation of divine justice.[48] This is also conclusive proof that Dante intends us to read the *Purgatorio* with the *Inferno* and the *Paradiso* as a projection into the real afterlife and not as a mere moral allegory of this life, for the *suffragia* apply only to the dead. Dante's enthusiasm for this doctrine is the more remarkable in that it contradicts Virgil's line: 'Cease hoping that the will of the gods can be changed by prayers.'[49] Dante resolves the anomaly in *Purg.* vi. 28–42, where he states the two main aspects of the *suffragia* of the Christian era: they do not diminish the debt of satisfaction but help to pay it off, and they must be inspired by the 'fire of love' and so 'joined to God' (*Purg.* vi. 37–9, 42). So he reconciles the doctrine with Virgil's words: God's justice is not in fact changed but, as in the case of indulgences and vows, the debt is commuted, and in any case in the pagan era, to which Virgil's words refer, prayers were not based on love of the true God.

Many souls in Purgatory ask Dante for prayers to help them pay off their debt, so speeding their remission and helping them to attain glory more quickly. Moreover, these prayers must come from good and innocent people, for others are invalid (*Purg.* iv. 133–5; viii. 71–2). Since the souls in Ante-purgatory failed to make satisfaction in life, they are particularly anxious for *suffragia* which will supply this defect and reduce their sentence of having to wait outside the door before they can be admitted to the positive process of remission (*Purg.* iii. 136–45; iv. 130–5; v. 70–2; vi. 1–27; viii. 71–2; xi. 127–30). Three souls have already been liberated from Ante-purgatory and admitted before their time to Purgatory proper: Provenzan Salvani because of his own great act of satisfaction performed in life, Sapía by the 'holy prayers' of Pier Pettinaio, and Forese Donati by the 'devout prayers and sighs' of his widow (*Purg.* xi. 133–42; xiii. 125–9; xxiii. 85–90). The *suffragia* apply also to the cornices (*Purg.* xxiii. 90), but here the requests are less direct, or else Dante offers the favour without being asked (*Purg.* xiii. 148–50; xix. 95–6, 142–5; xx. 37–9). Several of the souls, conscious of Dante's special importance, ask him to pray for them, especially when he reaches the sight of God (*Purg.* xiii. 147; xvi. 50–1; xxvi.

127–32, 145–7). Dante exhorts his readers to perform this pious practice on behalf of the souls in Purgatory, and later Cacciaguida instructs him to perform penances on behalf of his great-grandfather, Alighiero, who is still on the cornice of the proud (*Purg.* xi. 31–6; *Par.* xv. 91–6). These last two passages, linked also by the rhyme-words *cornice–dice–radice*, add an extra personal dimension to the themes of *Purg.* xi: Dante learns the results of family pride from Omberto Aldobrandeschi, and not from his own ancestor who shares the same punishment; he is then taught about the emptiness of artistic fame, and this deflates the swelling of his own other pride; and finally, the episode of Provenzan Salvani shows him how to use his exile to make satisfaction in life for this twofold pride (cf. also *Par.* xvi. 1–9).

Thus Dante's use of the doctrine of the *suffragia mortuorum* is another vital element in his presentation of Purgatory as the Church Suffering and as the place for the remission of the *Poena* still due to sin after death. It imposes a duty on good Christians in the Church Militant to help their comrades in the Church Suffering; it highlights the special position of Dante as a living visitor to the Church Suffering who will return to the Church Militant with messages, both general and particular, for the living; and it is an important part of the structure of the dialogues in the *Purgatorio*, for by the *suffragia* Dante can offer the souls real help on their way to salvation, as opposed to the mere promises of limited, and ultimately empty, earthly fame which he makes to the souls in hell. The *suffragia* are also related to the theme of the earthly Church's power of the keys, especially the key of jurisdiction, which opens the treasury of merit and commutes the prayers, penances, and indulgences of the living in favour of the dead. Through the earthly keys the Church of the living can help the souls of the dead, who are subject, either by exclusion for a while in Antepurgatory or by being granted admission to the Church Suffering, to the power of the keys of the angel-doorkeeper.

*   *   *

The silver key of the angel-doorkeeper is, therefore, the juridical key of Purgatory. It looses from juridical bonds and statutory penances of exclusion, Purgatory's equivalent of excommunication, involving the obligation to remain outside the door, as if doing public penance on the steps of a church. It confers on its holder the authority to discern those worthy to enter from those who are unworthy, and so it is an essential part of the angel's chief function (lines 85–93). Its use is a prerequisite for entry to the cornices where the 'knot' of sin (the debt of punishment and the attachment to sin) is untied by means of a universal rite (the seven P's) applied with absolute justice in proportion to the individual's past sins. It admits to the realm of satisfaction and pardon by opening the door to the merits of Christ's infinite act of satisfaction. In all these ways it reflects its equivalent in the earthly Church, and it is the silver key which needs special skill, wisdom, and mercy in its use. But in contrast to the keys of the earthly Church, the keys of Purgatory work in perfect accordance with each other and with the will of God. So here the silver key must and does turn cleanly in the lock together with the complementary and more precious golden key of access to purely spiritual benefits. The whole episode, from the angel's first challenge to Dante's act of submission, culminates in the image of two keys which in perfect harmony turn smoothly in the lock and open a great door to the spiritual world of remission and purification made accessible to man by Christ's Passion, the sevenfold realm of the Christian's final, perfect, and complete pardon or indulgence.

In this way, the angel's final warning to Dante against recidivism is invested with a tone of profound solemnity (*Purg.* ix. 131–2; cf. x. 5–6). The soul who is loosed from bonds of real or spiritual excommunication, who is repentant and free to enter the realm of final penance and complete pardon through the merits of Christ, is like the man who on earth is worthy of an authentic plenary indulgence, from which there should be no turning back. So he is reminded of St. Peter's warning to those who relapse: 'Their latter state is worse than their former. For it would have been better for them not to have known the way of justice than, after knowing it, to turn back from the holy law which was given to them.'[50] The two keys have opened a 'sacred door' ('porta sacrata'), founded on the precious Rock of Christ entrusted to St. Peter and his vicars as the foundation-stone of the Church. The door is a 'sacred church-door' ('regge sacra') leading both to the Church of the saved and to the kingdom of heaven.[51] Thus, by the power of the angel's keys, Dante has entered a new realm of full pardon. He dare not look back. Having passed through this door once, he must strive to conserve his right to enter again, definitively, after his death. If, after entering, he had looked back, he would have lost this right, and in that case:

> qual fòra stata al fallo degna scusa?   (*Purg.* x. 6)

(would there have been any excuse to equal such a lapse?).

7. *The Door*

With the opening of the door, the schematic nature of the episode and the complex series of theological allusions, made visual in the compressed account of the steps and the ritual of admission, reach a climax and resolution. The aural imagery which describes the opening of the door gives to the close of the canto a more elevated and mysterious tone and conveys the sense of an important and impressive experience and of Dante's subjective response to it. The two similes, one classical and one liturgical and musical, seem to indicate a greater involvement of Dante in his material, particularly by his resort to the uplifting and cathartic power of music in the final lines. Momigliano, for instance, who elsewhere refers to the coldness of the allegory, uses more enthusiastic terms to describe the lines about the door. He talks of the 'powerful sound' and 'biblical solemnity' of words which are a mixture of 'impetus and ecstasy', in which the person of Dante disappears, his subjective response being absorbed into the sound of the door and of the *Te Deum*; the canto ends with grandeur and harmony, 'with the impression of the interior of a church'.[1] Writing under the influence of Croce, he seems to be presenting this last section as some sort of 'poetic climax', the only real justification for the preceding sixty-three lines of 'non-poetry'. Apart from the 'rather forced' Tarpeian simile, which even Landino, in an age accustomed to decorative classicizing effects, found 'troppo anxia e curiosa' (too forced and bizarre), it seems as though the moral and theological allegory, hitherto so objectively described, gives way to a sense of liberation, subjective, lyrical, musical, and positive. By passing through the door, Dante enters a new world, and he can never look back. He has left the negative, waiting world of Antepurgatory; the obstacles to his entry have been removed by the prescribed ritual. Now he is free to enter a positive world in which the souls are educated, weaned from sin, and impelled to virtue by the 'whips' and 'bridles', and so are restored to pure love of the Supreme Good, to perfect liberty of will, and to the absolute innocence of Man before sin, original and actual, came into the world at all. Immediately after the opening of the door, the positive function of Purgatory is defined:

> Poi fummo dentro al soglio de la porta
> che 'l mal amor de l'anime disusa,
> perché fa parer dritta la via torta ... (*Purg.* x. 1–3)

(When we were within the threshold of the door which weans the souls from bad love, because it makes the crooked way seem straight ...).

And even though Purgatory is a place of penance for the remission of a debt, it is much more important to think of it in its positive aspect, as a place which guarantees eternal reward, as Dante very soon emphasizes to his reader:

> Non attender la forma del martíre,
> pensa la succession ...   (*Purg.* x. 109–10)

(Do not pay attention to the form of the torment; consider that which follows ...).

In terms of language and imagery alone, it can be seen that for Dante the door represents an important frontier, and his entry through it, as in the parallel episode of *Inf.* ix, is a critical stage in his journey. Outside the door is Antepurgatory, where the souls are bound, after death as in life, by a form of excommunication, and this bond can only be loosened by a welcome but unproductive statutory period of waiting; the keys which loose this bond and open the door admit the soul to a positive, active process of remission and education, the straight path to salvation. Outside the door, there is a world apparently subject to normal weather conditions, but within there is no rain or hail or snow, no dew or frost or clouds, no thunder, lightning, or normal earthquakes. The only earthquakes are those with a spiritual cause, when the mountain shakes with joy upon the liberation of a soul: 'When Israel went out of Egypt ... the mountains exulted as rams, and the hills as the lambs of the flock.'[2] Outside the door, time is closely linked to earthly time (*Purg.* iii. 136–41; iv. 130–2; xxiii. 83–4); within, there is a sort of time for the remission of temporal punishment, but it is much more vague (*Purg.* xxi.

67–8; xxii. 34–6; *Par*. xv. 92). Indeed, it is essentially different from earthly time and is particularly precious (*Purg*. xvi. 26–7; xxiv. 91–3). Like the earthquake, time in Purgatory is a spiritual factor, dependent on the soul's sense of liberation from cornice to cornice (*Purg*. xxi. 68–9). Above all, the door is an important frontier because it is both the door of Purgatory and the gates of heaven, the door to suffering with the guarantee of bliss, the door to both the Church Suffering and the Church Triumphant. The door marks a crucial stage in Dante's moral exodus and in the anagogical exodus of the saved soul from bondage to liberty, from Egypt to the new mount Sion, from this false and corrupt world to a spiritual world where every soul is a 'citizen of a true city' (*Purg*. xiii. 94–5).

The entire significance and symbolism of the door, with its resounding hinges and the hint that it is not opened regularly, give a sense of finality and uniqueness to the whole episode. Neither the angel's last words to Dante nor the description of the opening of the door fit the theme of ordinary confession and absolution. The Sacrament of Penance implies a continuous process of sin and forgiveness; it can, and indeed should, be repeated frequently. But Dante's presentation of the door of Purgatory as a symbol and as a crucial frontier, and his elevated and allusive language for this, the climax of the whole episode, indicates that the door should not be interpreted in the context of life on earth with the Sacraments, but should be seen as a symbol of a spiritual reality in the afterlife fundamental to the whole of the *Purgatorio*.

*   *   *

> E quando fuor ne' cardini distorti
> li spigoli di quella regge sacra,
> che di metallo son sonanti e forti,
>
> non rugghiò sí né si mostrò sí acra,
> Tarpëa, come tolto le fu il buono
> Metello, per che poi rimase macra.
>
> Io mi rivolsi attento al primo tuono,
> e 'Te Deum laudamus' mi parea
> udire in voce mista al dolce suono.
>
> Tale imagine a punto mi rendea
> ciò ch'io udiva, qual prender si suole
> quando a cantar con organi si stea;
>
> ch'or sí or no s'intendon le parole   (*Purg*. ix.
> 133–45)

(And when the angles of that holy door, which are of metal, sonorous and strong, were turned in the hinges, the Tarpeian did not roar so much nor seem so unwilling, when good Metellus was taken from it, so that then it was left empty. I turned, intent upon the first thunder, and I seemed to hear *Te Deum laudamus* in a voice mingled with the sweet sound. What I heard reminded me exactly of the impression which one often receives, when one is present at singing with organs, when now one hears the words, now not).

The clearest indication that Dante's mind is working on an elevated level is provided by that same classical allusion which Landino and Momigliano found so unsatisfactory. Dante says that, when turned,[3] the hinges of the door of Purgatory made a greater sound and appeared to be more resistant than the door of the Tarpeian treasury when, despite the opposition of the tribune Metellus, the public treasure of the Roman people was taken away by Julius Caesar.[4] The reference to Lucan's *Pharsalia* may seem at first sight to be a mere humanistic touch, a classical allusion made for its own sake, but in fact it is poetically and conceptually an integral part of the episode.

The poetic value of the simile depends upon two factors: it is a classical parallel, and it is phrased in the form, 'not so much did . . . as now . . .'. Dante's frequent use of classical similes can almost always be justified in one or both of two ways: either as a poetic device employed to make the reader juxtapose the two terms of the comparison, or as a way of heightening the description of an experience so as to increase its impact on the reader. In the first two *cantiche* alone, Dante uses the classics for the heightening of effect in the following cases: *Inf.* xvii. 106–14; xxv. 94–102; xxx. 1–21; xxxi. 4–6; *Purg.* xviii. 91–3; xxvi. 94–5; xxvii. 37–9; xxix. 95–6. The phrasing of this comparison—a form of hyperbole by means of a negative simile—is an example of a device which Dante uses very frequently indeed, and always in order to heighten the effect of remarkable experiences in the after-life, as in: *Inf.* xiii. 7–9; xv. 4–12; xvii. 16–18; xxi. 44–5; xxii. 1–12; xxiv. 85–90, 100–1; xxv. 19–20, 58–60; xxviii. 7–21; xxxi. 16–18; xxxii. 25–30; *Purg.* iii. 49–51; v. 37–40; vii. 73–8; xvi. 1–6; xxxi. 70–3. The following examples resemble the Tarpeian simile even more closely, in that they use the double heightening device of being at the same time classical comparisons and expressions in the form of *non sí . . . come* ...: *Inf.* xxix. 58–66; xxx. 22–3; xxxii. 130–2; *Purg.* xx. 130–2; xxiii. 25–7; xxviii. 64–6, 71–5; xxix. 115–20. One should note particularly the earlier example in *Purg.*ix (lines 34–42) and a related example in *Purg.* x. 32–3. These examples vastly outnumber any mere learned glosses from the classics which involve neither conceptual reference nor comparison. When Dante compares his experience or theme to some classical event, he is telling his reader that his experience in the afterlife exceeded even the greatest example taken from the great classical past, and this technique of classical allusion, used not just as evidence of learning and prehumanistic taste but with the precise poetic purpose of heightening the effect, is a vital part of Dante's presentation of a supernatural world, constructed by God and surpassing anything known on this earth, even in the days of classical gods and heroes. Examination of the relevant examples in the *Purgatorio* shows how the use of the double device plays a particularly important part in Dante's description of the marvels of the supernatural realm of Purgatory.

Of these many examples, one is particularly relevant in the context of aural imagery and the description of the opening of the door. In the *Inferno*, Dante compares the thunderous sound of the horn of the giant Nimrod to that of Roland at Roncesvalles:

> . . . io senti' sonare un alto corno,
> tanto ch'avrebbe ogni tuon fatto fioco . . .
> Dopo la dolorosa rotta, quando
> Carlo Magno perdé la santa gesta,
> non sonò sí terribilmente Orlando   (*Inf.* xxxi. 12–18)

(I heard a horn sound so loudly that it would have made any thunder sound faint . . . After the grievous defeat, when Charlemagne lost the holy army, Orlando did not sound his horn so fearsomely).

The effect of this reference to the greatest hero of the chivalric epics is to heighten the aural impression for the reader. Nimrod's horn-blast is louder and more fearsome than the greatest human equivalent.

It will be seen that the Tarpeian simile, both as a classical comparison and by the way in which it is phrased, is designed to convey a double heightening of the aural experience. Dante is asking his reader to believe that the great sound of the hinges of the door of Purgatory was greater than that made when the greatest treasury of the ancient world was opened, and that the initial resistance of the door of Purgatory was greater than that of the Tarpeian treasury as it resisted the violent depredations of the greatest of classical heroes. The double heightening device emphasizes the unique, super-human, even totally supernatural quality of the sound. To the careful reader the image acquired should form a tremendous prelude to the aural experiences which follow.

Apart from the poetic effect, one must also enquire if Dante wishes the reader to establish also a conceptual parallel between the two poles of the comparison. This is his normal technique in his use of classical similes. If one considers Dante's source, it may seem as if he is presenting Julius Caesar, founder of the Empire, as a robber, and a sacrilegious one at that. Such an interpretation would stress the element of resistance in the opening of the temple-door and would attach particular weight to the adjective 'good' which Dante applies to Metellus. However, it is hard to believe that Dante wishes us to view Caesar as a robber at this point; even if he does, there is no real problem, because for Dante not all Caesar's military activities were morally justified by his mission to found the Empire, and Caesar himself, like Virgil, the poet of the Empire, is in Limbo (*Inf.* iv. 123; xxviii. 97–102). The Empire, though apparently established by force of arms, was really founded by divine Providence (*Conv.* IV. iv. 8–14; *Mon.* II. i). Rather than stressing Caesar's crime, Dante wishes to stress the violent impetus of Caesar's actions, in conquering the treasury as in defeating Pompey's armies (*Purg.* xviii. 101–2). Dante is saying that, despite the resistance of Metellus and of the door itself, the Tarpeian treasury was in fact stormed by the irresistible impetus of the greatest of Roman heroes. What the simile heightens is this impression of the treasury-door resounding and giving way to Caesar's irresistible force. Lucan also emphasizes this aspect, presenting the event as yet another moment in the violent transition from Republic to Empire, when the treasure of the Republic passed to one man. Caesar, representing the new State, claims the wealth of the old State. Even Lucan, though he portrays Caesar as a ruthless general seeking gold for his greedy soldiers, plays down any element of sacrilege in the taking of the treasure; the only sacred thing in the story is the blood of Metellus, a tribune.[5] Dante likewise avoids any hint of presenting Caesar's act as sacrilegious, like the thefts perpetrated on sacred buildings by Heliodorus or Vanni Fucci.[6]

The possible anomaly of a sacrilegious Caesar, however, may have worried Benvenuto, for at this point he seems to imply that Caesar had the right to take the treasure because he was also the *Pontifex Maximus*. But it is superfluous to try to explain away something which Dante does not say, nor is it necessary to justify the simile by means of interesting but over-subtle parallels between the angel and Metellus and between Dante and Caesar. As Benvenuto says, Caesar's act was not sacrilegious, but the reason it was not sacrilegious is not Benvenuto's reason. It is because, in Dante's terms, the Tarpeian treasure was not sacred. The two poles of the comparison are in fact the two treasures: the treasure of Rome and the treasure of Purgatory. The Tarpeian treasury resisted loudly, but still it was conquered by the might and force of Caesar. The 'good Metellus', although presented by Dante perhaps more as a hero of liberty, an idealist who was dissuaded by the more practical Cotta, is more ambiguous in Lucan, who also describes him as 'pugnacious' and as inspired to bravery by love of gold, 'the vilest part of things'.[7] Dante's final words, moreover, stress the dramatic fact that the Tarpeian treasury was ultimately left bereft and desolate: 'per che poi rimase macra' (so that then it was left empty).

So Dante is referring to the tremendous treasure of Rome which passed away, leaving the treasury empty, for it was only an earthly treasure. Lucan himself, in the precise passage to which Dante refers, stresses not so much the sound of the doors as the enormous size of the treasure and the dramatic fact that it all passed into the hands of one man, Caesar:

> Protinus abducto patuerunt templa Metello.
> Tunc rupes Tarpeia sonat magnoque reclusas
> Testatur stridore fores; tum conditus imo
> Eruitur templo multis non tactus ab annis

Romani census populi, quem Punica bella,
Quem dederat Perses, quem victi praeda Philippi,
Quod tibi, Roma, fuga Gallus trepidante reliquit,
Quo te Fabricius regi non vendidit auro,[8]
Quidquid parcorum mores servastis avorum,
Quod dites Asiae populi misere tributum
Victorique dedit Minoia Creta Metello,
Quod Cato longinqua vexit super aequora Cypro.
Tunc Orientis opes captorumque ultima regum
Quae Pompeianis praelata est gaza triumphis,
Egeritur; tristi spoliantur templa rapina,
Pauperiorque fuit tunc primum Caesare Roma.[9]

(Then Metellus was taken away, and the temple lay open. Then the Tarpeian rock resounded and with loud clanging bore witness to the opening of the doors; then was brought forth the wealth of the Roman people, hidden in the depths of the temple and untouched for many years: treasure acquired from the Punic Wars and from Perses; the spoils of conquered Philip; gold which in his fearful flight the Gaul left, O Rome, to you; gold for which Fabricius refused to sell you to the king; all that you stored up, O customs of our frugal ancestors; all the tribute which the rich peoples of Asia sent and which Minoan Crete gave to conquering Metellus; all that Cato brought across the seas from Cyprus far away. Finally were brought out the riches of the East and the last treasure of captive kings which was borne first in Pompey's triumph. By sad plunder was the temple despoiled. Then for the first time was Rome poorer than a Caesar.)

Dante is saying that the door of Purgatory makes a greater sound because it is the door to an even greater treasure, which once acquired can never be stolen—the merits of Christ, by which man pays off his debt to God in Purgatory to which the angel holds the keys, and at the same time the 'eternal wealth' of Paradise to which St. Peter holds the keys (*Par.* xix. 111; xxiii. 133–9). The sacredness of this door is in fact emphasized (lines 130, 134), and since the treasury of Purgatory surpasses the greatest classical equivalent, it is in effect supernatural. The door leads to a spiritual *mons pietatis* (a pawnbroker's fund, literally 'a mountain of pity'), a supernatural treasure created by Christ's infinite act of satisfaction so that man can redeem the pledge of his soul by paying his debt to God with the money to make satisfaction, and through which man can

regain full use of the treasure of his free will and obtain the
supreme riches of heaven which, unlike earthly riches, are
increased the more they are shared (*Purg.* x. 108; xi. 88,
125–6; xv. 49–75; xix. 91–2, 140–1; xxx. 144–5; *Par.* v.
19–30; vii. 79–120). Unlike the treasure of Rome, which
passed away, this is not a corruptible treasure of gold and
silver but the lasting treasure of the precious blood of Christ;
it is the priceless treasure for which a man will joyfully sell all
that he has; it is the treasure which cannot perish or be stolen,
as is stated in the Gospel for Ash Wednesday: 'Do not store
up treasure for yourselves on earth, where rust and moth
consume, and where thieves break in and steal. Store up for
yourselves treasure in heaven, where neither rust nor moth
consume, and where thieves do not break in and steal. For
where your treasure is, there also is your heart.'[10]

Whilst the roaring sound of the door stresses the fact that
the treasure of Purgatory is enormous and superhuman, indeed
infinite and spiritual, the word 'acra' is more difficult to
interpret. The word is used only on one other occasion in the
Comedy with reference to the sharpness of the sword of
Beatrice's accusations (*Purg.* xxxi. 3). If in *Purg.* ix it is to
mean 'harsh', then it is a gloss by Dante on Lucan's phrase,
'with loud clanging'. At all events, it implies some element of
resistance in the hinges of the door. This accords perfectly
with Dante's presentation of the Tarpeian door, which un-
successfully resisted the violence of the great Caesar. But as
regards the door of Purgatory, it seems to imply that the door
is not opened easily or often. This detail is inexplicable in the
sacramental interpretation of the episode, for access to the
Sacrament of Penance is both easy and always available. The
present study, however, does allow at this stage at least a
partial explanation, and a further possibility will emerge later.
In its relationship to the angel's keys, which admit the soul to
the realm of final indulgence and salvation through the merits
of Christ, the initial resistance of the door stresses the unique
nature of the occasion: the individual soul has the opportunity
for complete pardon only once, and so he is solemnly warned
not to relapse. This is the main point of this crucial event in the
saved soul's anagogical exodus to God, and in the moral
message to the individual reader of the poem. One cannot

establish with any certainty whether Dante wishes to imply that the door creaks because the human race as a whole neglects to use it. *Purg.* x. 1–3, as has been shown, does not mean this, but even so such an interpretation would not be untypical of Dante, who elsewhere provides a bleak contrast between the small number of the saved and the innumerable souls on the banks of the Acheron (*Inf.* iii. 56–7; *Purg.* xii. 94–6). However, this does not quite fit in with the Tarpeian simile, which emphasizes that the long-shut Roman treasury was opened only once and by one man. The more obvious way of adapting the simile to the context of Purgatory is to infer that this door too has been shut for a long time and its treasures hidden away until the moment they are claimed by Dante on his journey; thus it would be a door which is only opened to an individual or to man in general on rare occasions or at infrequent intervals. The exact interpretation of the elusive word 'acra' remains open to discussion, but there can be no doubt that one of its functions is to stress the importance of this crucial frontier on the path to God, for the souls and for Dante. The door's roaring sound and resistant hinges together describe the powerful effect which the opening of the door has upon the soul and upon the exceptional pilgrim, Dante, at the unique and solemn moment when he enters the treasury to claim the pardon won for him by the merits of Christ.

Whatever the precise meaning of the word 'acra', the crisis of the first roar and of the initial resistance of the door gives way to, and indeed is fused with, the sweeter, more human sound of the *Te Deum*, and the whole episode is resolved by a hymn and by the beautiful musical image which evokes the sense that Dante is entering a vast church. With the opening of the door described through the simile of the treasury, the crisis of this stage in the journey, which has been represented by the ascent of the steps, the imposition of the seven P's, and the use of the keys, is concluded, and the *Te Deum* sums up and resolves this crisis, linking it with the forward-looking element of Dante's entry into a new realm and a new Church.

Benvenuto and Buti both associate the *Te Deum* with St. Ambrose's conversion of St. Augustine, and Buti adds that it is sung when a man enters religion. These examples are quite appropriate, but the *Te Deum* is more than this. Principally it is the Church's hymn of thanksgiving, sung on occasions of deliverance and victory and by pilgrims on their arrival in Rome. It is sung in Paradise when Dante emerges victorious from his examination in Faith by St. Peter (*Par.* xxiv. 113). Its main features are an expression of faith in the Trinity, belief in the Redemption ('having vanquished the sting of death, you have opened to believers the kingdom of heaven'), and the hope of salvation ('make us to be numbered with your saints in eternal glory'). The prayer which follows it in the liturgy concerns the infinite treasury of God's goodness which answers man's prayers and disposes him to the future rewards of heaven. It is as a hymn of faith, gratitude, victory, and deliverance that it accompanies Dante's entry into a treasury and the new realm which leads to Paradise. Dante enters the holy mountain to music and a hymn: 'Enter into his gates with praise, into his courts with hymns.'[11] And the sweetness of the music emphasizes the contrast with the parallel episode of the entry into hell, as Dante later says of Purgatory:

> Ahi quanto son diverse quelle foci
> da l'infernali! ché quivi per canti
> s'entra, e là giú per lamenti feroci   (*Purg.* xii.
> 112–14)

(Ah, how different are those gates from those of hell! For here one enters to songs, and down there to fierce laments).

*   *   *

Two problems emerge from the reading of lines 139–45: the exact nature of the aural image which Dante wishes to convey, and the identity of the singer or singers of the *Te Deum*.

The first problem arises from the fact that Dante mentions three aural impressions which may seem to conflict with each other. He describes the sound of the door as a roaring and as 'acra', which, as has been noted, may imply a harsh or creaking sound of resistance. Then he mentions the mysterious 'primo tuono', which can be interpreted as 'the first thunder' or as merely 'the first sound'. Finally, there is the 'sweet sound' which is compared to the sound of an organ.

Sapegno's notes say that these sounds are all different: the 'primo tuono' means merely the first sound which Dante is waiting to hear in Purgatory, and the 'sweet sound' is perhaps a real musical accompaniment to the hymn.[12] Barbi is accused of subtlety for arguing that the sounds all refer to the door.[13] However, there are good reasons for finding Sapegno's interpretation too subtle and indeed unconvincing, and some of the same arguments can be used against M. A. Buchanan's intermediate theory, in which the 'primo tuono' refers to the door, the 'voce' and the 'dolce suono' to a hymn sung by angels inside Purgatory.[14] Sapegno's reading ignores the most obvious and appropriate meaning of the word 'tuono' as 'thunder'; the word 'attento' comes to mean 'waiting', and this further weakens 'tuono' in that it refers to a sound which Dante has not yet heard but which, in some unexplained and extremely indeterminate way, he seems to be expecting; and the definite article in the phrase, 'mista al dolce suono', which Sapegno hints is dubious although it is in fact unimpeachable, certainly implies reference to a sound already mentioned.[15] This definite article has caused other critics some difficulty, even to the extent of suggesting altering the text to 'a dolce suono'. Scartazzini wanted to do so but was unable to justify the correction; he poured scorn on Vellutello's belief that the 'sweet sound' comes from the door, but his reviser, Vandelli, omitted this note and accepted Barbi's proposal that both 'the first thunder' and 'the sweet sound' come from the door.[16] Petrocchi dismisses Porena's correction of the text, which is justified on the grounds that the roaring of a door, which is unwilling to be opened, could not possibly be sweet.[17] To this one can only reply that the word 'dolce' does not mean 'soft', nor even necessarily 'harmonious', though this is implied, but it is basically an affective word, expressing the fact that the music is sweet to Dante's ears. In any case, the word is later clarified by being compared to organ music, and in Dante's day sweet organ music might well have been preceded by a creaking of the instrument, so that 'acra' and 'dolce' are not necessarily contradictory in this context. Finally, in Sapegno's interpretation the description of the sound of the door ends at line 136, and a curiously static effect results. Dante is just waiting for, and then hearing, a sound from beyond the door. The opening of the next canto ('Poi fummo dentro ...') is thus

very abrupt, and the noise of the door closing again (*Purg*. x.
4) becomes an isolated and rather arid reference back to the
last mention of the door thirteen lines earlier.

To follow Barbi and read the three sounds as stages in the
sound of the door opening seems the most simple and natural
explanation. It is the most obvious way of reading the two
definite articles in lines 139 and 141, and it restores full aural
value to the word 'tuono', which Dante uses to mean 'thunder'
in the very similar context of Nimrod's horn and to describe
the tremendous shout of the souls in the Heaven of Saturn
(*Inf*. xxxi. 12–18; *Par*. xxi. 142; cf. also *Inf*. iv. 2; *Purg*. xiv.
134; xxix. 152). It is natural to link 'the first thunder' with the
enormous roar with which the door, surpassing the roar of the
Tarpeian treasury, gives way. If the phrase 'il dolce suono'
also is referred to the sound of the hinges, not only is the
contrast between hell and Purgatory, between torment and
sweetness, continued in the description of the door (cf. *Purg*.
xii. 112–14), but also, more significantly, the hinges of the
door of Purgatory are deliberately contrasted with one of
their literary sources, the Virgilian doors of Tartarus, which
open:

> ... horrisono stridentes cardine[18]

(screeching on the horrid-sounding hinge).

Taking the three aural references together, the description
of the opening of the door is prolonged to the end of the
canto. First, the door 'roars' because, for the individual at
least, it is not opened easily or often. Although the word 'acra'
is somewhat indeterminate, one can, if one wishes, hear also
the initial creak of stiff hinges at this moment. The 'roaring' is
great, greater than that of the Roman treasury, and so its first
sound is compared to thunder ('il primo tuono'). As Dante,
listening attentively, turns to face Purgatory ('io mi rivolsi
attento al primo tuono'), and as the door continues to swing
open, the thunderous sound, mixed with the words of the *Te
Deum*, is described by the affective word 'dolce', not because
it is soft but because it is sweet to Dante's ears, denoting his
definitive release from one world and entry into a new realm.
The door itself resolves the crisis of its first roar of resistance

by providing sweet music, as of an organ. The hinges of this door are, in fact, harmonious hinges, like those which one can still see and hear today in the chapel of the Baptist in the Lateran.[19] Grandgent even cites at this point a passage from Keats which may well illustrate the effect for which Dante too was striving:

> Sounds Aeolian
> Breathed from the hinges, as the ample span
> Of the wide doors disclosed a place unknown ...[20]

The complexity of this aural experience thus requires the simile of the organ in order to be fully understood. The unusual sound of the hinges, loud but sweet, is mixed with the words of the hymn in exactly the same way as, on earth, an organ accompaniment often drowns the words of singers.[21] In this way, the whole passage acquires a poetic and psychological unity, in the continuity of the aural and musical imagery and in Dante's subjective involvement at this important moment of his release into a new world. Above all, it furnishes the dynamic impression of the door opening by degrees of sound, thus preparing us for the first line of canto x and for the description of the door resounding again as it closes.

The second problem in this passage concerns the source of the 'voice mixed with the sweet sound', the voice or voices which sing the half-heard words of the *Te Deum*. To this there is really only one answer—that Dante does not say who sings the words.[22] One naturally assumes that they are not sung by the souls in Antepurgatory, for the dream of the eagle, the intervention of Lucia, and Virgil's words (*Purg.* ix. 58) have stressed that Dante has left them far behind. Most commentators either ignore the problem or infer that the *Te Deum* is sung by all the souls on the cornices. For this, they refer to the *Gloria* which Dante hears on the cornice of the avaricious and which, with the miraculous earthquake, denotes that Statius has reached the moment of his release from the cornice and is spiritually ready to proceed upwards (*Purg.* xx. 136–44; xxi. 58–60, 70–2). Leaving aside the fact that a strict parallel here would require that the *Te Deum* be interpreted as coming from the souls left behind in Antepurgatory, the main weakness in this theory is the unjustifiable assumption that a mysterious detail of the entry into Purgatory can be explained on the basis of a different situation eleven cantos later, when Dante actually sees and hears the souls singing and is bewildered by the events until they are explained to him. In *Purg.* ix–x, there is no indication of who sings the words, nor is there any bewilderment or explanation or reference back. In fact, Dante seems almost deliberately to exclude linking the *Te Deum* with any of the souls, for there is a long climb and a whole canto before he meets any of them, and then they are saying the Lord's Prayer (*Purg.* x. 7–21; xi. 1–24). One may assume that the souls sing the *Te Deum*, but there is no justification for this in the text, at this point or later, and the certainty of some commentators is purely wishful thinking, for Dante is deliberately uninformative.[23]

Dante's use of the singular 'voce' does not exclude the plural sense of several voices singing in unison, but it is most naturally read as referring to one voice. If one assumes that the angel-doorkeeper sings the *Te Deum*, then a pleasant symmetry is formed between this and the Beatitudes pronounced by the angels of the cornices.[24] But once again, Dante does not say that the angel sings the words, and, had he wanted to do so, nothing could have been easier than in lines with such simple rhymes as those of lines 140–1.

One can therefore make no assumptions nor hope for a definitive solution. Dante has left the reader with a mystery, a disembodied voice or choir singing the *Te Deum*. Dante's language in fact suggests that the experience is mysterious and subjective. He does not say that he heard but that he 'seemed to hear' the words. He then goes on to explain this subjective experience by means of the simile of the organ. In other words, the reader needs this simile to understand exactly ('a punto') the marvellous experience of seeming to hear the disembodied words mixed with the sound of the door.

All this points to a new but not impossible conclusion, based on a straightforward and unprejudiced reading of the actual text. Dante wishes us to conclude that the voice is, literally, 'disembodied', and that the whole experience is essentially subjective. As in Dante's presentation of other marvels of Purgatory, the voice or voices are to be seen primarily as a subjective sense experience produced in some unexplained way by the door itself. Mysteriously, the sweet thunder of the hinges is transformed in Dante's ears ('mi parea udire') into the half-heard words of the *Te Deum* mixed with the rich accompaniment. In order to evoke the precise effect of this marvellous experience, Dante provides the reader with the simile of the organ accompanying a hymn:

> Tale imagine a punto mi rendea
> ciò ch'io udiva, qual prender si suole,
> quando a cantar con organi si stea   (*Purg.* ix. 142–4)

(What I heard reminded me exactly of the impression which one often receives, when one is present at singing with organs ...).

But, as in the terms of the organ and the singing, the words of the *Te Deum* are only partially audible, and the whole experience remains subjective and uncertain:

> ch'or sí, or no s'intendon le parole   (*Purg.* ix. 145)

(when now one hears the words, now not).

It is the phrase 'or sí, or no' (now yes, now no) which above all indicates this solution. It should be seen as an expression of subjective doubt, as equivalent to a 'perhaps', as in Dante's own phrase:

> e io rimagno in forse,
> che sí e no nel capo mi tenciona   (*Inf.* viii. 110–11)

(and I am left in doubt [a state of 'perhaps'], as 'yes' and 'no' struggle in my head).

This type of doubt is a man's half-incredulous response to a miracle. Dante is doubtful about the evidence of his own ears, just like:

> colui che cosa innanzi sé
> súbita vede ond'e' si maraviglia,
> che crede e non, dicendo "Ella è ... non è ..."
> (*Purg.* vii. 10–12)

(the man who suddenly sees something before him which makes him marvel, and he believes and does not believe, saying, 'It is ... it is not ...').

Above all, the phraseology of the whole simile recurs in the very next canto, in Dante's description of his first experiences of Purgatory, the miraculous 'speaking sculptures' of the first cornice. These sculptures are created by God, a greater craftsman than the greatest of human artists, greater than Nature herself (*Purg.* x. 32–3, 99; xii. 64–9). These sculptures are miracles not found on earth but unique to Purgatory:

> Colui che mai non vide cosa nova
> produsse esto visibile parlare,
> novello a noi perché qui non si trova   (*Purg.* x.
> 94–6)

(He who has never seen anything new created this visible speech, strange to us because it is not found here).

When Dante describes these sculptures, he stresses the subjectivity of his response by using the verb 'parea' (seemed) (*Purg.* x. 37, 58, 79, 83). The words he uses for the artistic form which skilfully evokes this subjective impression are 'imagine', 'imaginata', etc. (*Purg.* x. 39, 41, 62, 98). Moreover, these miraculous sculptures cause a conflict of belief, a conflict of 'yes' and 'no', between Dante's senses. When he looks at the sculpture portraying the Ark of the Covenant, his hearing and his sense of smell conflict with the evidence of his eyes that the sculptures are inanimate. Mysteriously and uncertainly, he 'seems' to hear the choirs singing and to smell the incense rising:

> Dinanzi parea gente; e tutta quanta,
> partita in sette cori, a' due mie' sensi
> faceva dir l'un 'No', l'altro 'Sí, canta'.
> Similemente al fummo de li 'ncensi
> che v'era imaginato, li occhi e 'l naso
> e al sí e al no discordi fensi   (*Purg.* x. 58–63)

(In front appeared people; and, divided into seven choirs, they all made one of my two senses say, 'No', the other, 'Yes, they are singing.' Likewise, at the smoke of the incense which was depicted there, my eyes and nose began to conflict with a 'yes' and a 'no').

The recurrence of such terms so soon after the episode of the door is surely important evidence that Dante wishes to convey the fact that the words of the *Te Deum* are of miraculous origin, and that they cause his senses and his mind to oscillate between certainty and doubt. The close of *Purg*. ix could thus be paraphrased:

Mixed with the sweet sound of the hinges, I received the impression of hearing (*mi parea udire*) the words of the *Te Deum*. The nature of the sense-experience conveyed and received (*imagine*) was exactly (*a punto*) the same as when one hears organs accompanying singing, and one oscillates between certainty and uncertainty as to whether one can hear the words or not (*or sí, or no s'intendon le parole*).

There are thus strong indications that Dante wishes to leave his reader with the feeling that this mysterious, disembodied voice is in fact one of the miracles of Purgatory, a subjective impression left by the music of the hinges, and explicable only by means of a direct, everyday parallel with earthly music and liturgy. As a miracle, it belongs to the supernatural laws of Purgatory, which began with the miracle of the reed and continued with the mysterious spiritual rules of the journey (*Purg*. i. 134–6; vii. 43–60; cf. xxvii. 74–5). As a wonderful subjective experience, it acts as a prelude to those other miraculous experiences of the first three cornices: the 'audible' sculptures, the invisible voices, and the interior visions (*Purg*. x. 31 ff.; xiii. 25 ff.; xiv. 130 ff.; xv. 85 ff.; xvii. 13 ff.). The music and the simile of the organ express the uplifting or cathartic experience of Dante's entry into a marvellous, divinely ordered realm. The sweet music is like that of an organ, and this organ music reflects God's artistry and plan (cf. *Par*. xvii. 43–5). But God is a greater craftsman than the men who make harmonious doors such as those in the Lateran. The music of this door is a miracle of Purgatory: it gives to the soul the impression of hearing also the half-distinguishable words of the *Te Deum*. As with the inexpressible music and half-heard words of the *Christus vincit* in the Heaven of Mars (*Par*. xiv. 121–9), so also is this episode concluded with a miraculous and uplifting musical experience.

The simile of the organ and the hymn made Buti think of a vast church and so conclude that Dante meant his Purgatory to represent the Church Militant in every aspect. But this is to belittle Dante's capacity for projecting his poetic imagination into the afterlife. All the references to the ceremonies, the powers, the authority, and the liturgy of the earthly Church must be seen as figures fulfilled in the next world and, in this way, elevated to their place in the journey and the poem. The ritual and the use of the keys represent primarily the removal of those obstacles which keep Dante outside the door not of the earthly Church but of Purgatory. The opening of the door and the marvellous music convey the importance of this unique moment, when Dante is admitted not to the earthly Church but to a new community altogether. The essential point is that he is entering a truly spiritual world, with its own 'religion', a 'true city', a 'holy flock' (*Purg.* xiii. 95: xxi. 41–2; xxiv. 73), not the Church Militant but the Church Suffering, which leads necessarily and inevitably to the earthly Paradise and to the Church Triumphant in the heavenly Paradise, when the last angel sings the words of Christ to the saved on the Last Day: 'Come, O blessed of my father, take possession of the kingdom prepared for you since the creation of the world.'[25]

Part III
Conclusions

1. *The Episode in Context*

Now that we have investigated the various details of the episode of the door of Purgatory, it is time to rebuild these fragments of Dante's design and present the episode as a single entity, remarkable for its cohesion in itself and in the context of the whole of the *Purgatorio*. In an episode which operates through a series of theological symbols, we have discovered some constant themes and patterns which define this crucial stage in Dante's journey and which are interwoven in a flawless unity. A modern critic, unable to accept the sacramental interpretation, suggested that the episode is written in an 'arbitrary sign-language' which 'may be blankly obeyed without full understanding or assent'.[1] Now, however, it is possible to replace the sacramental interpretation with one which is far from arbitrary or unintelligible but which is clear, coherent, and structurally necessary at this point in the *Comedy*. It is true that the episode is written in a sort of code, but the key to this code, the key of polysemy, has made it possible to meet the challenge which Dante here lays before the reader (lines 70–2), and so to define the elevation of theme and technique to which he refers. Now at last we can set the episode in its context as part of a canto which truly 'adumbrates the whole purgatorial process'.[2]

The episode of the door of Purgatory only makes sense when interpreted as an example of multiple allegory and polysemy. In this respect, the term 'polysemy' can be taken in its most restricted sense, as Dante's method of composition, and the reader's principle of investigation, of a single episode in the poem, but it will also be seen how, according to one of the fundamental axioms of structuralism, the polysemy of this one episode reflects the overall polysemy of the *Comedy* as

illustrated by the analysis of the psalm *In exitu* in the Epistle to
Can Grande.[3] According to the Epistle, '*polysemos*' means 'of
several senses', whilst the term 'allegory' is to be interpreted
freely, from the Greek *alleon* ('other', 'different'). Allegorical
senses are thus 'other' or 'alternative' or even perhaps 'alter-
nating' senses ('alterni sensus') which 'flow round' the literal
narrative (*Ep*. xiii. 7–8). Polysemy is, therefore, the concealing
of several 'other senses' in the same symbol or series of symbols.
Frequently in the *Comedy* it operates by what might nowadays
be called the even freer techniques of allusion or allusiveness,
but the episode of the door of Purgatory is such a clear
example of the juxtaposition and agglomeration of symbols
that it seems a good basis for testing the term 'polysemy' as it
works out in practice as the principal method by which Dante
covers his vast range of material. The symbols used in the
episode have a literal sense, as part of the narrative of a visit to
the afterlife, but they have taken with them into the afterlife
the multiple associations which their earthly equivalents
possess. Dante's symbols are an elevation and fulfilment of
these earthly symbols, and they are part of a world which is an
exemplum, with lessons to be read back to men who are still
living among the earthly symbols. The early commentators,
preoccupied with moral allegory and with Dante as a moral
symbol in his own poem, failed to appreciate his epoch-making
move away from the allegorical literature of univocal moral
abstractions and into the realm of anagogical or figural
realism, polysemy, and a complex system of reference back to
human affairs. Thus they formed the traditional interpretation
of the episode of the door, narrowing the whole meaning
down to the merely sacramental, which is, at most, a sub-
category of what the Epistle to Can Grande calls the moral
allegorical sense of a literal event or narrative. By discarding
this single, simple allegorical interpretation and by investigating this series of symbols one by one, it has been possible
to show that some of these symbols are polysemous and
allusive, and that the series as a whole alludes to several
important doctrines and themes. Moreover, there remains, as
will be seen, the possibility of yet another level of meaning in
the episode. *Purg*. ix can now be restored to its rightful place
in the anagogical scheme of the *cantica*, with levels of allegory

or 'other senses' which include the moral, the redemptive, the theological, the ecclesiastical and political, the reforming, and the personal.

Purg. ix is, in fact, one of the three pivots of the whole *cantica*. The other two turning-points, which also involve prophetic morning-dreams, are Dante's passage from the lower to the upper cornices and his entry into the earthly Paradise (*Purg.* xix. 1–69; xxvii. 91 ff.). The episode of the door belongs to this sequence. The old interpretation is, as has been seen, full of anomalies. By examining these, by taking into account the clear examples of polysemy (especially lines 97–8, 101–2, 115–16) and of ambiguity (lines 99, 111), and by relying almost exclusively on sources available to Dante and to his earliest readers – the Scriptures and St. Thomas, Virgil and Lucan, and the *Comedy* itself – it has been possible to arrive at a reading which provides ample evidence of a fundamental, though complex, unity of concept and symbol at this point in the poem. The reader can once again enjoy a certain liberty in the emphasis to be given to some of the details and their ramifications with regard to his or her appreciation of the *cantica* as a whole, but the convergence of so many themes in the episode and their relationship to the central facts of the *Purgatorio* provide the framework within which this right can be exercised.

The extraordinary fact about *Purg.* ix is this integrated theological framework which unites and supports the variety and complexity of the allusions. For example, by reallocating the symbols, one can, if one wishes, reintegrate the sacramental interpretation into the scheme. Although the strict, detail-for-detail allegory disappears, there is a clear reference to the ministry of the earthly Church and in particular to the duty of satisfaction to be paid off in proportion to past sins. But the episode is much more than this. In a brief and highly compressed series of images, clear, objective, and stylized, Dante has hidden a wealth of allusions which define the whole theology of Purgatory as the Church Suffering and as the realm of pardon or indulgence, the remission of temporal punishment after death. The three steps and the rite of submission denote the moral state required in the soul who is repentant and eager to journey to final salvation. The figure of the angel and the imposition of the seven P's define the nature and structure of the Church Suffering. The explanation of the function of the two keys clarifies the juridical and spiritual basis of the purgatorial process. Beneath these aspects of the Church Suffering, there lies a hidden polemic and admonition to the Church on earth. All these themes converge in the climax, the opening of the door, when the soul's state is resolved by a sense of liberation as he enters the new Church, the true door to heaven, to salvation, and to God.

In this sense the episode is clearly a turning-point in the *cantica* and in the poem. It is also an impressive example of the unifying powers of Dante's imagination in presenting his narrative of a fictional journey. It is obvious that the whole of *Purg.* ix, both in itself and in relation to the parallel episode of Dante's entry into the city of Dis in *Inf.* ix, is essentially a canto of transition. When, at the end of the canto, Dante describes the door through which he enters to join 'God's elect' (cf. *Purg.*xix.76), he is indicating that he has crossed an important frontier between a realm linked to earthly life and a realm which leads to the eternal spiritual treasures of Paradise. When the door closes behind him, the process of detachment from earthly things has truly begun, and the result of this is inevitable, for the ascent of the mountain and the erasing of the seven wounds attenuate the physical weight of Dante's body, so that eventually he rises above the earth altogether, 'transcending the weightless spheres', as swift as lightning and as naturally as fire itself strives upwards (*Par.* i. 91–3, 99, 139–41).

When we read *Purg.* ix, however, all this is yet to come. At this stage in the fictional journey, the reader is mainly required to link the episode of the door with what has gone before. In this respect also the unity of Dante's presentation of Purgatory is apparent. This can be illustrated by considering the three stages in the journey of the souls of the saved to God, from the mouth of the Tiber to Antepurgatory to the sevenfold realm above the door.

The curious device by which Dante describes the souls of the saved as travelling first to the place 'dove l'acqua di Tevero s'insala' (where the waters of the Tiber join the salty sea) is, first and foremost, as is stated, a deliberate contrast with the fate of the damned, who descend to the banks of the Acheron and are ferried across by the demon, Charon (*Inf.* iii. 85–93; *Purg.* ii. 100–5; xxv. 79–87). But whilst God's justice goads the damned and makes them eager to cross into hell (*Inf.* iii. 124–6), the souls at the mouth of the Tiber are liable to be punished by being required to wait before the angel-boatman will accept them. The reason why the angel 'several times' refused to allow Casella to embark is not immediately clear, but it is obviously an aspect of God's justice administered by the angel (*Purg.* ii. 95–7), excluding the soul temporarily from the path to salvation.[4] Moreover, the context (Casella's late arrival in Purgatory despite the indulgences available for the last three months), the fact that the angel's refusal is no 'outrage' to the soul, and the phrase 'chi ha voluto intrar' (whoever wanted to embark) might well indicate that the punishment depends on the will of the soul, as in Purgatory, and is in a sense self-inflicted. It may be some sort of punishment for tepidity, as for the *ignavi* on the banks of the Acheron in the 'vestibule' of hell (*Inf.* iii. 31–69), but in any case the method of punishment by waiting links these souls with the souls in Antepurgatory, condemned to exclusion from Purgatory because in life they delayed their repentance and the required acts of satisfaction. Now Casella and many other souls have been freed more speedily from this bond because their debt of punishment has been partially paid for them by a special application of the *suffragia mortuorum*, the indulgences of 1300. They have now entered upon a new and more positive stage in their journey to salvation, and their duty is to make haste to the mountain to start the process of remission, of 'sloughing off the old skin' which keeps them from seeing God (*Purg.* ii. 122–3). The fact that Casella and his companions, and Dante himself, are 'tardy spirits', easily distracted from this duty by the power of music, defines at the outset the opposition between earthly attractions and spiritual obligations in Purgatory (*Purg.* ii. 112 ff.). Several themes are mentioned which reappear in a different form in *Purg.* ix: God's justice, the doctrine of remission by indulgence, Purgatory as the place for casting off the remains of sin and travelling to God (*Purg.* ii. 94–9, 122–3; iii. 3).

In addition to these elements, Dante's description of the

journey to salvation shows that the reader is intended to link the angel-boatman and the angel-doorkeeper. They have similar duties. Both are ministers of God's absolute justice, one by controlling passage across the seas, the other by controlling entry to Purgatory proper. Both have the power to exclude certain souls. Moreover, both these angels share associations with St. Peter and the city of Rome. The boat which plies between the Tiber and the shore of Purgatory represents the redemptive link between the earthly Church, governed by the Pope, and the Church of Purgatory, guarded by the angel-doorkeeper, and the angel-boatman, described as the 'heavenly helmsman', also has duties analogous to those of St. Peter, 'the pilot of the Galilean lake',[5] the steersman of the bark of the Church (*Purg.* ii. 43; xxxii. 129; *Par.* xi. 119–20; *Ep.* vi. 1). In his boat sit 'more than a hundred souls', the first small community of the saved, travelling from one Church to another and singing the psalm *In exitu* to celebrate their exodus from bondage to liberty, from the 'Egypt' of this world to the new mount Sion and the Promised Land (*Purg.* ii. 45–8; cf. *Par.* xxv. 55–6).[6] By the agency of the angel-boatman and the angel-doorkeeper, the souls travel from the city which is the 'threshold of Peter'[7] to the diamond threshold of St. Peter's vicar in Purgatory, from Ostia Tiberina, the gateway of earthly Rome, to the door of Purgatory and so into a 'true city' and to that eternal Rome 'onde Cristo è romano' (whence Christ is Roman) (*Purg.* xiii. 95; xxxii. 102).

In this journey from one Church and one Rome to another, and in Dante's case from the anti-Church of Lucifer to the true Church built on the Rock of Christ and St. Peter, Antepurgatory forms a sort of Limbo or vestibule. Like Limbo, Antepurgatory is also a place without 'martíri' (torments), and there is a noticeable similarity in tone and setting between Limbo and the Valley of the Princes, together with a possible cross-reference in the rhymes which introduce the listing of the inhabitants as Dante sees them from a high place (*Inf.* iv. 28, 113–17; *Purg.* iv. 128; vii. 89–93). Antepurgatory is also like the steps or entrance to a church, for the souls there, like excommunicates or certain sinners under sentence of public penance in the earthly Church, must remain outside the Church Suffering, 'supplying time for time' on the slopes where they must wait (*Purg.* xxiii. 83–4, 89). They are either static or wander on the same level or perhaps can go downwards, but they cannot go upwards without the guidance of the sun, nor can they enter Purgatory without the permission of the angel-doorkeeper (*Purg.* iv. 128–9; vii. 52–60).

Purg. ix is the canto of transition between this negative world and the positive world of remission and ascent to the stars. The whole canto emphasizes the gulf between the two worlds and the enormous step which Dante is taking in his journey to God. However, the canto is also divided by Dante's address to the reader (lines 70–2) into two distinct parts, and such a clear division is unusual in the *Comedy*. It is evident that Dante wishes to contrast these two almost equal halves, and that what unites them in the same canto is Dante's desire, as in *Inf.* viii–ix, to stress the importance, the uniqueness, and the tremendous implications of this stage in his journey. The miraculously accurate dream of the eagle and the extraordinary intervention of a heavenly lady are a clear statement of this, but they are at the same time the prelude to the wonderful entry into the spiritual realms of Purgatory and Paradise. Only if the episode of the door is seen not as an anticlimax or an allegorical postscript but as the culmination of this miraculous, almost mystical, redemptive process can the canto be properly understood.

The clear division of the canto indicates also that the first half employs a technique which is to be contrasted with the method in which the themes of the second half are presented. The dream of the eagle is not intended to be analysed in the same way as the episode of the steps and the door. The dream is directly presented as miraculously 'divining' or intuitive of visions which are 'prophetic', that is, 'speaking for' God (*Purg.* ix. 16–18). Like the other two morning dreams, of which the last is also described as 'prophetic' in the sense of 'foreseeing' (*Purg.* xix. 1–33; xxvii. 91–114), the dream of the eagle is an insight into the truths of Dante's present situation at this stage in his journey, in relation to what has gone before and to what is to follow.[8] It is an interior, subjective experience which, in addition, miraculously reflects the simultaneous reality of Dante's ascent while he sleeps. The second half of the canto uses the opposite technique of describing external events and objects which reflect ideas, doctrines, and moral states. Nevertheless, the indications of polysemy are already apparent in the symbol of the eagle.

C. S. Singleton has shown how the eagle is connected with the Exodus, a theme which is fundamental to Dante's presentation of Purgatory (*Purg.* ii. 46) and indeed of the whole mystery of the Redemption which underlies the *Comedy* (*Ep.* xiii. 7).[9] The eagle is also traditionally the symbol of St. John (*Par.* xxvi. 53) and so could refer here to the works and example of the beloved disciple, and in particular to his Apocalypse, that long allegory or vision of the Church and the new Jerusalem which forms the basis of several elements in the episode of the door, in the general presentation of Purgatory as the antipodean mount Sion, and in the final scenes in the earthly Paradise (*Purg.* iv. 67–71; xxix. 92–105; xxxii. 109–60; xxxiii. 34–45). No reader of the *Paradiso* can fail to associate Dante's use of the symbol of the eagle with his presentation of Rome[10] and of divine justice (*Purg.* xxxii. 109–60; *Par.* vi; xviii. 107 ff.), and under both these aspects this eagle prefigures Dante's ascent to a new, spiritual Rome, to a realm of just but merciful punishment, and to a door through which only the just, who are saved, may enter: 'Who will ascend to the mountain of the Lord, or who will stand in his holy place? The man who is innocent in deeds and in purity of heart, who did not take his soul in vain nor swear to deceive his neighbour'; 'Open to me the gates of justice; entering them I shall praise the Lord; this is the gate of the Lord; the just shall enter therein.'[11] All these ideas can be traced in the symbol of the eagle which carries Dante upwards in his dream, while Lucia transports him physically to the door.

The principal redemptive significance of the dream is, however, more than this. According to legend, the eagle, like the phoenix, renews itself every ten years by soaring to the sphere of fire: 'Your youth shall be renewed as an eagle's.'[12] In this respect, it came to signify baptism and penance and, in general, regeneration and rebirth.[13] This is obviously the primary significance of the eagle in Dante's dream, for it seizes Dante up as Jove took Ganymede and carries him up to burn in the sphere of fire (lines 19–33). In his dream at least, Dante passes through the sphere of fire to the world beyond. Nowhere does

Dante expressly and unequivocally describe his physical passage through the sphere of fire as such, but his dream in *Purg.* ix certainly indicates that, morally and psychologically at least, the door and the seven cornices are between the sphere of fire and the sphere of the Moon. This too stresses that the whole episode marks a crucial frontier between earthbound Ante-purgatory and the weatherless world above, belonging partly to this earth and partly to the heavens. So, by means of a dream, Dante conveys the sense of regeneration by fire at this point in the poem, whilst reserving his actual physical regeneration by fire to the even more apposite context of the purging-away of lust and the refining of love in the flames of the final cornice.

The meaning of the dream of the eagle is, therefore, quite clear. Like Ganymede, Dante is being transported by a divine agency from earth to the realm of the divine, and the process involves a complete regeneration by fire. Ten years after Beatrice's death (*Purg.* xxxii. 2), her companion, Lucia (*Inf.* ii. 97–108; *Par.* xxxii. 137–8), carries Dante up to the door of Purgatory, and the event is miraculously expressed in the dream of the eagle and in the burning of Dante in flames which anticipate the image of ardour in the porphyry step, from which he proceeds to the spiritual world of Purgatory, to the 'temporal fire' of healing punishment, to the process of regeneration in love, and finally, through the 'refining fire' of the last cornice, to the 'ancient flame' of his own love (*Purg.* xxvi. 148; xxvii. 127; xxx. 48). The themes of love and rebirth by fire are here stated at the outset as the principal motifs of the rest of the *Purgatorio*.

After this oneiric experience of destruction and regeneration, Dante awakes pale and fearful, not knowing where he is. One is reminded of Vanni Fucci's confusion after he too has been incinerated and reborn like the phoenix (*Inf.* xxiv. 97–120). But whereas in the episode of Vanni Fucci Dante uses the similes of demonic possession or convulsions to describe the sinner's astonishment, here he employs an elevated comparison of himself to Achilles. The reference is to Statius's account of how Achilles, while sleeping, was carried by his mother to a new place, and he was never to return to Thessaly.[14] Dante also stresses that, from then onwards, Achilles' destiny lay elsewhere (line 39). The main purpose of the comparison is to describe Dante's extreme amazement when he awakes after his dream and finds himself in a new place, from which there must be no turning back. Statius describes Achilles' awakening thus:

> . . . pueri tremefacta quies oculique patentes
> infusum sensere diem. stupet aere primo,
> quae loca, qui fluctus, ubi Pelion? omnia versa
> atque ignota videt dubitatque agnoscere matrem[15]

(the boy's tremulous sleep and opening eyes sensed the inpouring day. He is astonished at the first light. What place is it? What sea is this? Where is Pelion? Everything he sees is different and unknown, and he does not at first recognize his mother).

The effect is of a transition to a totally different world. Dante's reaction is exactly the same: 'Non altrimenti Achille si riscosse' (In exactly the same way did Achilles wake) (line 34).

Not only does the Achilles simile express this psychological state and stress the absolute newness of the place, but it also links the dream miraculously to the situation, for Dante, like Achilles, has been transported, while asleep, to this new world by Lucia, the agent of heavenly aid at this crucial stage in his journey. Lucia, in some way not fully known to us, held some special personal significance for Dante either in his own life or in his relations with Beatrice. Her name is associated with light, and she herself is linked both with Beatrice and the Madonna; Dante is her 'fedele', her vassal or devotee, and her place in Paradise, diametrically opposite Adam, therefore corresponds, in the Christian half of the Rose, to that of St. Peter (*Inf.* ii. 94–108; *Par.* xxxii. 121–6, 133–8; *Conv.* III. v. 10 ff.).[16] In *Purg.* ix, she is a 'donna del ciel' (line 88), a heavenly emissary, who links the two halves of the canto by fulfilling the dream of ascent, carrying Dante up to the door, and by guaranteeing his special right to enter into the Church Suffering which leads to the Church Triumphant. Like the angel who, in the corresponding canto of the *Inferno*, is sent from heaven to enable Dante to enter into the city of Dis, she represents the unique nature of Dante's mission; here this is emphasized because, apart from St. Paul, he alone has been appointed to enter the gates of heaven twice (*Inf.* ii. 28–36; ix. 64–103; cf. *Par.* xv. 28–30).

Thus all the elements in this canto of transition reach their natural climax and resolution in the opening of the door. This is the culmination of the dramatic events which begin with the sleep of Dante burdened by his body (*Purg.* ix. 10) and end with his joyful entry into another world, a world of justice, purification, and the refining of love. The static, waiting, even nostalgic world of the souls in Antepurgatory is abandoned definitively, and Dante may never look back. Purgatory's positive and dynamic elements of ascent and liberation truly begin with the dream of the eagle, the climbing of the steps, and the opening of the door.

*   *   *

In its place in the narrative, therefore, the episode of the door is both important in relation to what has gone before and a vital turning-point which helps to define what is to come. Its most conspicuous feature is its extreme compression, the extraordinary economy of means by which Dante describes this crucial stage in his journey. This compression perhaps explains why the sacramental interpretation has rarely been questioned and why it has taken so long to elucidate a mere seventy-six lines of the *Comedy*. Yet we have seen how, almost unobtrusively, Dante has concealed important theological and moral concepts in this short account. In this way, he fulfils his promise to elevate not only his material but also his technique at this point (lines 70–2), and he achieves this aim by a method of polysemy which is simultaneously realistic narrative and multiple allegory, a perfect fusion of the 'allegory of the poets' and the 'allegory of the theologians' (cf. *Conv.* II. i. 4). Whereas in the *Convivio* the concept of the allegory of the poets allowed poems addressed to a lady to be interpreted philosophically, here in the *Comedy* theological truths have been transmuted into a series of striking and evocative poetic symbols.

In this way too, the episode fulfils the statement in the Epistle to Can Grande that the *Comedy* as a whole has a literal sense and is at the same time a multiple allegory. Indeed, this one important episode reflects the overall polysemy of the poem as illustrated in the Epistle, and it makes it clear that if the author of the Epistle was not Dante, he was at least some extraordinarily acute commentator. The Epistle illustrates the technique of multiple allegory based upon a literal sense by providing interconnected allegorical meanings of the psalm, *In exitu Israel de Aegypto* ('When Israel went out of Egypt').[17] This analysis is provided both as an example of the critical method required from the reader of the *Comedy*, and also as an invitation to the reader to connect the poem with the theme of the Exodus. With regard to these objectives, it affords three possible meanings of the literal story of the Exodus in relation to the poem. The 'allegorical' sense—which must here be interpreted as 'typological' or 'figural' in the strict theological sense of a relationship of prefiguration and historical fulfilment between events of the Old Testament and events of the New—is the Redemption of man by Christ, who was both the Paschal Lamb and the new Moses; his death and Resurrection led all mankind from the slavery of paganism and the Old Law to the freedom of grace and the spirit in the New Dispensation. The moral or tropological sense of the Exodus is man's journey in this life, when, following Christ, he fulfils the Redemption, firstly by passing through the waters of Baptism, and then in his moral life by travelling from the grief and misery of sin to a state of grace; this aspect can also be universalized in the sense that not just the individual Christian but also the whole earthly Church, Christ's Mystical Body, should move towards conformity with the person of its founder, fulfilling the Exodus and the Redemption in the desert of this life and building a new Jerusalem on earth.[18] The anagogical sense of the Exodus is the journey of the saved soul after death from the slavery of this corrupt life to the liberty of eternal glory. The concept of typological prefiguration connects all these senses: the literal Exodus prefigured the Redemption; Christ is the *figura* of the perfect Christian in his moral life; and the moral life of the Christian prefigures and determines his eternal fate after death and after the end of time.

Clearly these aspects of allegorical interpretation should not be seen as all present equally in the poem. The Christological allegorical meaning is not present at all, except in the sense that the Redemption is the precondition for the whole of Dante's journey, and that there is an indirect reference in the setting of the Christian Dante's journey into hell and up to Purgatory at the season of Christ's descent into hell and his Resurrection. The moral sense is directly present only in the figure of Dante, the living Christian, who is travelling from sin to grace in order to earn his own future salvation after death and as an *exemplum* to other living members of the earthly Church. But the anagogical sense of the Exodus is present in all the souls whom Dante meets in Purgatory, the realm in which his literal narrative in fact describes the exodus of the saved souls from earth to heaven, anagogically prefigured in the Exodus of the Israelites. Strictly speaking, of the three realms only Purgatory directly uses the theme of the Exodus. *Inferno* and *Paradiso* describe the two terms but not the actual exodus, for the souls there are not going anywhere. In the *Purgatorio*, however, the souls are truly making their ana-gogical exodus, as is stated at the outset and again when Statius, anagogically fulfilling also Christ's Resurrection, makes his 'exodus' to eternal glory, and the mountain exults (*Purg.* ii. 46–8; xxi. 7–10).

In this additional respect, therefore, the episode of the door of Purgatory represents a crucial frontier, the actual moment of Dante's moral exodus and of the soul's anagogical exodus to the path of salvation. At the point where the souls of the saved ascend to the 'martíri', the torments, the positive process of remission, Dante acquires heavenly aid, passes through a stage of moral awareness, and submits to a ritual which earns him access to this process for his own moral benefit, for his own salvation after death, and as a lesson to others. The moral and the anagogical senses come together in that a living member of the Church Militant is exceptionally entering that Church's ideal fulfilment in the afterlife, the Church Suffering. Moreover, the right to enter through the door, for Dante and for the souls, is based upon the precondition for all salvation and for the whole poem, the first allegorical meaning identified by theologians in the story of the Exodus, the Redemption of mankind through the Passion and the Cross, the infinitely precious merits of Christ's act of expiation and satisfaction for sin. Thus the theme of Exodus, which, from the passage of the souls across the seas, is presented as fundamental to the whole scheme of the *Purgatorio*, is also at the very source of Dante's account of his entry through the door which is founded on the precious Rock of Christ and which leads directly from an earthbound world to the penances of Purgatory and the liberty of Paradise. When, as a moral figure in his own poem, making a journey which should prefigure and guarantee his own final salvation after death, he passes through this door, he is passing definitively from the Egypt of this world to the freedom of the Promised Land, the new, unshakeable mount Sion, the heavenly Jerusalem (cf. *Par.* xxv. 55–6).

The scriptural texts upon which the episode of the door is based, and in particular the words of Christ, the founder of the Church, to St. Peter, his vicar, in Matt. 16:18–19, must likewise, as in the case of Psalm 113, be interpreted according to the anagogical sense as defined by theologians and exegetes. Together with the associated symbols used, they should be seen primarily as 'figures' to be projected into the real world of the afterlife, as elements in the final eschatological fulfilment of this life in the next. Thus the theologians' interpretations of Christ's charge to St. Peter and of such symbols as the Rock of the Church, the power of the keys, and the door of heaven are to be seen in their next stage of fulfilment, that is, in the context of the theology of the afterlife. The theology of the Church Militant is transferred to the plane of its own fruition, the Church of the souls who repented in life and who now suffer, doing penance for their sins, and who are also pilgrims travelling inevitably to eternal salvation. Moreover, the two Churches are connected not merely by mutual prayers (*Purg.* xi. 19–24, 31–6) but in a special way, unique to the *Purgatorio*, of prefiguration and fulfilment. This is because, as has been seen, Dante's Purgatory is based upon the concept of the remission of the *poena* due to sin, and thus penances performed in life will reduce the debt to be paid in the afterlife (*Purg.* xi. 72). In other words, the path of purification is a single, continuous road to be started in this life in the Church Militant and completed in the next in the Church Suffering. Dante's Purgatory, in describing how this path of penance and purification is continued and completed after death, is therefore the model for its commencement in this life.

This is the true relationship between the two Churches in Dante's poem. The Church of Purgatory is not an allegorical scheme but the authentic continuation and fulfilment of the earthly Church, and so indirectly it is also an *exemplum*, a portrayal of a truly spiritual pilgrim Church, praying, learning virtue, and doing penance, in the certain hope of salvation. The Church on earth, the door of heaven guarded by the Pope, was founded to redeem man in life. When man fails, or when man's natural love is led astray by the corruption of the Church and its leaders (*Purg.* xvi. 85 ff.), the Church Suffering, guarded by the angel-doorkeeper, completes the process of purification and redirection to God after death. Dante, the living man, visits this true Church in order to describe how it is theologically the completion, and poetically the model, of a purification which is often impeded or neglected in life because of sin, evil, and corruption. The lesson to the earthly Church is moral; the poetic method by which the lesson is transmitted is both anagogical and an *exemplum*. Dante, by describing the route of the soul's exodus after death 'from the slavery of this corrupt world to the freedom of eternal glory', is also describing the path of man's moral exodus or conversion in life 'from the grief and misery of sin to a state of grace' (*Ep.* xiii. 7). In this respect, however, the symbolism used in the episode of the door does not reflect merely the three broad categories of theological allegory described in the Epistle to Can Grande but assumes also a more specific political-ecclesiastical dimension, which is a poetic adaptation of Dante's technique of extracting political allegory from scriptural texts, as he does in presenting the concluding arguments of his *Monarchia* (*Mon.* III. iv–ix). Indeed, as has been seen, some of the texts so used are the same as those which underlie the episode of the door and its angelic doorkeeper, who bears one sword alone and who possesses the perfect power of the keys. This political level of allegory is not just a symbol or moral representation of this life, but it too is part of Dante's anagogical or figural world which is the fulfilment of this world. Projected into the afterlife, its lessons can then be read back to this life, 'a' vivi del viver ch'è un correr a la morte' (to those living the life which is a race towards death), in order to reform it, 'in pro del mondo che mal vive' (for the benefit of the world which lives evilly) (*Purg.* xxxii. 103; xxxiii. 53–4). In this way, the political-ecclesiastical allegory of the reformed, repentant, purely spiritual pilgrim Church of Purgatory, and its exemplary function as a model for the Church on earth, contains a hidden polemic and forms part of the fundamental purpose of the whole poem, which is to prick the consciences of sinners and reform society, especially at the top (*Par.* xvii. 124–42).

Thus our analysis of the episode of the door confirms the necessity to restore the *Purgatorio* to its proper place in that unified narrative about the afterlife which we call the *Divine Comedy*. Although in this episode Dante does not meet any souls of the saved, the symbols employed belong to the same world as those souls whom death and Dante's poetic imagination have projected from this life into the next. The *Comedy* describes a life prefigured and determined by this life. The landscapes and symbols are based on their earthly equivalents but are in fact supraterrestrial realizations of them, their 'fulfilment' as instruments of God's justice and eternal plan, just as the souls too are seen in an eternal context as the fulfilment, outside history, of their historical selves.

This coincides perfectly with the statement in the Epistle to Can Grande that the literal subject of the poem is 'the state of the souls after death, described simply', and allegorically its subject is 'man inasmuch as by his merits or demerits, through his free will, he is subject to the justice which rewards or punishes'; the form of the poem is 'poetic, fictional, descriptive, . . . and gives positive examples' (*Ep.* xiii. 8–9). If one removes the terrestrial allegory of the Sacrament of Penance from *Purg.* ix, these statements can be applied directly and without qualification to Purgatory. It is fully a realm of the afterlife and not just a symbol of this life. It is the intermediate realm of God's justice, mixing punishment with the certainty of eventual reward. It is the central section of a complete narrative fiction in verse and contains positive examples of human souls seen in the context of a redemptive process, and positive examples of the rites and penances by which alone the soul can be purified and can travel to God. These positive examples must then be read back into this life, not as allegories in the abstract but as true *exempla* from the anagogical world of the afterlife, and indeed in this respect also the *Purgatorio* occupies a unique position among the three *cantiche*. This is because, alone of the three realms, Purgatory is not eternal

(*Purg.* x. 109–11). The world Dante describes here is not the definitive fulfilment of this life, with souls already fixed in their eschatological state of damnation or bliss, but it is a gradual path of purification and learning, a way of being fulfilled, of travelling to final fulfilment in eternal happiness. So the examples of Purgatory are uniquely relevant to man's pilgrimage in this life, when he must use, train, and purify his free will with regard to his eternal destiny and subjection to divine justice after death.

The Epistle to Can Grande (15–16) also asserts that the whole poem belongs, not to speculative philosophy but to ethics, its purpose being 'to remove those living in this life from a state of misery and lead them to a state of happiness'. The *Purgatorio*, the central part, describes this very process, achieved by one living man visiting the afterlife; thus it too is central in relation to the ethical aims of the entire poem and to the achievement of man's double goal—happiness in this life and happiness in the next (*Mon.* III. xv). In describing a world which, ideally, fulfils this world and corrects its defects, and in revealing a moral itinerary to be started in this life so that there will be less to be completed in the next, the *Purgatorio* is a complex, practical *exemplum* and an essential component in the poem's definitive judgement on the results of evil and the corrective effects of the power of love in man and in society as a whole. Indeed, Purgatory beyond the door occupies a crucial position in Dante's call for personal and universal purification and reform, since it describes the only true path to temporal and spiritual felicity, to the earthly Paradise and the heavenly (*Mon.* III. xv .7), a path which consists of prayer and asceticism, of contented acceptance of suffering, of the study of virtue and hatred of vice, and of dedication to the service of transcendent love and to the laborious process of the healing of man's misguided and, on earth, no longer truly free will.

The function of *Purgatorio*, from canto x onwards, is thus to show man what justice and purification mean in this life by describing how Justice purifies men's souls in the next life, on the eternal level of God's plan. Purgatory, though not itself eternal, leads inevitably to eternal bliss. In Dante's projection of human affairs on to the screen of God's eternal judgement, the eschatological function of Purgatory is subsumed into that of Paradise. For eternity there is only good or bad, and thus all men who are not wholly bad in this life are redeemable through Purgatory after death. Because of the Redemption man can pay his debt to God, purge away the remains of sin, and be remade in love. This is the function of the dual process, negative and positive, a purging and a renewing, of Purgatory, and this is why, in the *Comedy*, the positive element predominates, for the second *cantica* presents the souls of men optimistically, on the road, despite their failings, to eternal bliss. This, fundamentally, is the reason why for Dante the door of Purgatory is also the gate of Heaven.

For the same reason, the dominant note of Dante's *Purgatorio* beyond the door is not penitential and backward-looking but one of hope, contentment, and ascent. Whilst the *Inferno* and the *Paradiso* show Dante's brilliant handling of the poetic equivalent of the *crescendo*, his spectacular manipulation of grades of evil or of bliss, the dynamics of the *Purgatorio* are more subtle, and over-insistence on allegory can and does destroy them altogether. The episode of the door has been a prime example of this danger. The narrative flow and realism of the *cantica* has been impaired, and critics, faced with the aridity of the sacramental interpretation, have been inclined to view the episode as a rather limp moment in Dante's inspiration or, worse still, as that critical *deus ex machina*, an 'artistic pause', designed merely to prepare the reader for good poetry to come.[19] This, of course, directly contradicts Dante's address to the reader in lines 70–2, where he tells us, in effect, that the episode is not a trough but a high crest of the waves over which the ship of his mind is sailing (cf. *Purg.* i. 1–2). As has been shown, the episode does indeed occupy a crucial place in the structure and dynamics, the themes and poetic presentation, of Purgatory, which is a dramatic and progressive story of a journey of ascent from Antepurgatory to the cornices to the earthly Paradise of innocence and liberty, through a process by which love is purified and the will is healed, so that the soul becomes able to ascend to the stars.

Once the theological allusions in the episode of the door have been identified, it can be seen that Dante has in fact both defined Antepurgatory retrospectively and described the start of the true purgatorial process. Instead of putting into the mouth of Virgil or some other soul a discourse on the basic theology of Purgatory proper, Dante has compressed it into a series of sense images, objectively described, a masterpiece of allusion and polysemy through the medium of a few bare essentials. Moreover, the visual treatment of the symbols, the elements of form and ritual, and the aural and musical imagery are the first expressions of patterns to be repeated on each of the cornices in the presentation of the penances, meditations, prayers, and hymns of the souls and the pardon administered progressively by the angels. The traditional theology of Purgatory has been absorbed into a concise poetic code which is developed and enriched in the progress through the seven cornices and which reaches its climax in the visionary, ritual-istic, and liturgical procession or triumph of the Church and Beatrice in the earthly Paradise, where the essential unity of the three Churches, on earth, in Purgatory, and in Paradise, is expressed by a similar use of allusive symbols concealing deep truths 'difficult to conceive' (*Purg.* xxix. 42).

By employing this technique in *Purg.* ix, Dante has been able to surmount an obstacle in his conception of Purgatory and of its place in the scheme of the *Comedy*. Traditionally, Purgatory was a negative place of punishment or testing by fire, the fires of hell and Purgatory being contiguous.[20] Dante wished not only to separate hell and Purgatory very clearly, to contrast them, to introduce a variety of penances, to add extra theological, moral, and liturgical elements, but also, ulti-mately, to present Purgatory as positive and redemptive. Thus, when the actual discourse on the theology of Dante's Purgatory occurs in canto xvii, he employs a different tech-nique, and there the theology is Dante's major contribution to the whole *cantica*—the crucial, positive, and all-pervading definition of love as the principle of action in man. Through Purgatory, the soul's rational or elective love and natural love are made absolutely identical and co-extensive, so that the soul regains complete liberty of choice which is also the innate natural love of the Supreme Good, the cause of the soul's existence (*causa efficiens*) and the goal of its return (*causa finalis*) (cf. *Purg.* xvi. 85–90). This doctrine is conveyed clearly in disquisitions from Marco Lombardo and Virgil on the relationship between corruption and free will, between natural and elective love, and between the three types of wrong love and the true love of God, Supreme Good and giver of complete happiness (*Purg*. xvi. 67–93; xvii. 91–139).

It can be seen that, in *Purg*. ix and *Purg*. xvii, Dante has selected two quite different techniques for expressing the theological structure of Purgatory. The contrast between these allows us to identify with certainty and clarity the nucleus of Dante's *Purgatorio* in canto xvii, a turning-point in the *cantica* and in the whole poem. The ascent of the steps indicates briefly the first move away from the traditional negative presentation of Purgatory as a place of fire and punishment, close to hell, and Purgatory is given an unmistakable positive dimension at the end of the episode, in the description of the opening of the door. All this is done rapidly and by means of allusion. *Purg*. ix in fact conceals theology in symbols, and to decipher it one needs some basic knowledge and the faculty of imaginative association. *Purg*. xvii, however, at the heart of the *Comedy*, expounds Dante's own theology of Purgatory, positive, redemptive, and based on love, and this is done openly and unequivocally by the use of didactic verse which appeals boldly to the reader's intellect and powers of logical reasoning. The compressed episode of the door foreshadows this doctrine, but because of the contrast in techniques it is itself overshadowed by those doctrines of love and free will around which the *Comedy* revolves.

Purg. ix has not been an easy canto to interpret. Indeed, Dante's choice of a compressed, allusive technique was designed as a test for the reader so that the episode might be comparatively unobtrusive in the context of the theology of Purgatory. Dante tells us so himself when he states that the episode of the door is not a simple allegory but a poetic challenge, and that the reader should not be astonished that he here intends to transmute complex theological material into complex and allusive poetic symbols, to adapt an elevated and difficult theme ('matera') to an elevated and difficult poetic technique ('arte'):

> Lettor, tu vedi ben com'io innalzo
> la mia matera, e però con piú arte
> non ti maravigliar s'io la rincalzo   (*Purg*. ix. 70–2)

(Reader, you can see clearly how I elevate my theme, and so do not be surprised if I reinforce it with greater art).

From the *Vita nuova* to the close of the *Paradiso*, the story of Dante's life and art consists in the constant elevation of theme and his perpetual search for more elevated poetic means adequate to express those themes. The first and most obvious example of this is provided by his description of his transition from his earlier love-poems to the new and more noble theme ('matera') of the praise of Beatrice; after some days in which he fears that this theme is too lofty for his powers, he thinks of a style addressed to noble ladies, discovers a felicitous first line, and composes the *canzone* 'Donne ch'avete intelletto d'amore' (Ladies who have understanding of love), the first poem in which he uses the technique later described by the words 'dolce stil novo' (sweet new style) (*V.N.* xvii–xix; *Purg.* xxiv. 49–57).[21] In the *Comedy*, by invocations to the Muses and addresses to the reader, he frequently refers to his search for words to express his difficult material, and the *Paradiso* in particular elevates this search into a constant affirmation, fundamental to the understanding of the whole *cantica*, of the inadequacy of poetic language and technique to express the 'transhumanized' experiences and themes of Paradise.[22]

The address to the reader in *Purg.* ix is part of this series. Dante is informing his reader that the episode of the door is another example of an important stage in his journey-poem, involving this double elevation of theme and technique. Moreover, there is a scriptural reference which forms a model for this constant thematic and poetic renewal in Dante's development. Though relevant to other works, particularly the *Vita nuova*,[23] it fits the episode of the door of Purgatory with a startling accuracy to be found nowhere else in Dante's writings. When he crosses the diamond threshold of Purgatory, he leaves hell and an earthbound world behind and enters a new, spiritual world. The threshold marks an important point of redirection in his journey to God (*Purg.* x. 1–3). To express this elevated theme, he embarks upon a new type of poetry which is to describe the positive and redemptive aspects of God's marvellous plan for humanity:

Eduxit me de lacu miseriae et de luto faecis. Et statuit super petram pedes meos: et direxit gressus meos. Et immisit in os meum canticum novum, carmen Deo nostro.[24]

(He has brought me out of the pit of misery and the mud of the dregs. And he has set my feet upon a rock and directed my steps. And he has put a new song into my mouth, a hymn to our God.)

2. The Door of Purgatory as the Door of Pardon

The solutions proposed have been based to a large extent upon an analysis and critique of the earliest commentators. The indications which they provide have not so much been contradicted as elevated and extended. The elements which they limit to the Sacrament of Penance and to the allegory of the perfect confessor require to be transposed to another level so that the references to the ministers and the powers of the earthly Church are seen as prefigurations of the higher ministry and greater powers of the angelic vicar of St. Peter, guardian of the community of the saved.

We can only speculate upon the reasons why the early commentators failed to comprehend the full implications of the episode. The chief reason is that, in accordance with contemporary techniques of allegorization, and probably with Lana's theory in front of them, they all had an *a priori* desire to explain Dante's poem on the basis of a single moral interpretation, retrievable by simple investigation of allegorical detail and citation of relevant authorities. This led them into difficulties precisely because, in the architectural setting and in the ritual, in the symbols and in the words of the angel, Dante is using a technique of multiple allegory which is polysemous both in the sense that it is a concatenation of allusive symbols and in the requirement that the textual allusions be explored, like the psalm *In exitu* in the Epistle to Can Grande, on several levels of meaning, primarily the redemptive, the figural-moral, the figural-anagogical, and the exemplary. Moreover, the extreme compression of the episode and the complexity of the theological references have concealed several of these levels of meaning. Dante's deliberate choice of an allusive technique to overcome the hurdle of the negative theology of Purgatory has perhaps been too successful. The theology itself is difficult, and even St. Thomas argues by metaphor and the 'allegory of theologians' when he describes *con-tritio*, the power of the keys, and the treasury of merit. He also tends to generalize in his use of important words such as *culpa*, remission, satisfaction, and the 'science of discernment', and close reading is necessary to uncover the essential distinctions. The commentators, by limiting their explanation of the keys to citing the authority of only one article of the *Summa theologica*, neglected to read on and so failed to detect Dante's masterly synthesis of the difficult doctrines of the power of the keys, of excommunication, and of indulgences, with the theology of the afterlife and of Purgatory as the Church Suffering.

Other possible reasons may be traced in the historical background against which the early commentaries were compiled. Dante, writing the *Purgatorio* in the second decade of the fourteenth century, planted all the allusions in the episode within the context of the year 1300. By the time the first commentaries came to be written, the political and religious situation was quite different. Boniface VIII was long since dead, and with him certain excessive claims had been prudently laid to rest. The Popes were long established in Avignon, and their absence from Rome may well have helped to conceal from the first commentators the papal and Roman symbolism associated with the threshold, the angel, and Dante's submission at the angel's 'holy feet'. Rome entered a period of neglect, and it is not known if the commentators went there or, if they did, as Benvenuto may have done, how much they could have known by that time of the traditional phrases and symbols applied to the city as the true home of the Popes and the goal of pilgrims.[1] Dante's *Monarchia*, the basis of much of this interpretation, had been attacked and condemned,[2] and to cite its authority might have led to accusations of heresy against both author and commentator. Finally, after Lana and, with apparently less conviction, Pietro di Dante had laid down the lines of the sacramental interpretation, the second half of the century, in the aftermath of the Black Death, was marked by an increased sense of guilt and doom.[3] As a result, the penitential and moral interpretation of *Purg.* ix would have seemed the most relevant and practical to commentators who believed, and rightly, that their duty was to convey to mankind the principles which Dante puts forward in his poem for the reform of the individual and of society.

There remains the ever present possibility that, in the episode of the door of Purgatory, Dante has concealed some personal reference now lost to us. As A. Vallone reminds us, the *Comedy* is almost certainly full of allusions to people, places, and events from Dante's own experience.[4] Images, words, and phrases could have occurred to him because of their associations with events he witnessed, places he visited, conversations or sermons which he heard. Although this proposition is undoubtedly true, it is a rather unstable foundation for literary criticism, since the critic runs the risk, on the one hand, of falling into the morass of the wholly fanciful or, on the other, of becoming enmeshed in the web of attempting to psychoanalyse a man who lived and died many centuries ago, in a world very different from ours. Moreover, Dante does not ask his reader even to try to unearth any totally personal references. Being personal and almost impossible to retrieve with certainty, they would be for him neither legitimate nor useful as elements in his universalizing poem. However interesting these may be to the student of the Unconscious, the critic's first task is to identify only those personal allusions which are manifestly related to the conscious universal themes of the poem and which can thus be seen to have been chosen by Dante because they are retrievable either by common knowledge or by a little research and deduction.

Bearing in mind these risks and limitations, we must now examine a further level at which the polysemy of the episode might operate, namely, the level of personal experience elevated to the status of a universal symbol, an *exemplum* or message, judgement, and call for reform. Continuing to investigate the episode by means of the joint method of logical deduction and association of images, we find that the conceptual and poetic framework of *Purg.* ix provides strong evidence of the existence of such a level of personal reference, which links it to a generally accepted event in Dante's life and to the universal structure of the poem. Dante has left enough clues for us to identify this additional figurative meaning without distorting the literal sense of the narrative or the theological and moral allegory which we have already identified.

Indeed, the coexistence of these various levels enriches the episode in a remarkable way. In the sense that they complement each other, neither is conclusive or definitive, and this is only right, for any definitive and univocal conclusion would ultimately be no better than the sacramental interpretation, since it would deny the principle of polysemy upon which the episode is based. The chief benefits of polysemy are in fact these: that, within the strict limits of the literal narrative, it is at all levels open to further connected interpretations, and that even the conclusions may remain open, and the reader retains a certain liberty to select a preferred interpretation, to make a personal response in matters of detail, emphasis, and allusiveness, and to add his or her own speculations according to taste. In a limited way, the reader has these liberties also in *Purg.* ix which, because it involves symbols and not personalities, is one of the purest examples of polysemy in the *Comedy* and as such is one of the simplest episodes technically, if not conceptually. This further possible level of polysemy not only explains this remarkable blend of simplicity and complexity but also allows us to trace the source of the whole episode in the unique mind of the man who wrote it.

*   *   *

In his commentary to the *Purgatorio*, A. F. Ozanam provides the traditional sacramental interpretation of the steps, the angel, and the door of Purgatory. Then, without further explanation, he adds:

The angel holds the keys of St. Peter, exercising the papal prerogative, and the holy door is a reminiscence of the Jubilee. We have studied a too little-known passage of the *Divine Comedy*, and in the scene which occupies the poet at the door of Purgatory we have discovered the memory of an important period in his life, his pilgrimage to the Jubilee of 1300 in Rome, the great change which took place in his soul, and from the tears of this glorious repentance we have seen an immortal poem emerge.[5]

The last part of this statement is highly questionable, but nevertheless the logic and imagery of *Purg.*ix compel us to examine this final possibility, at which Ozanam arrived apparently by intuition, namely, that in the episode of the door Dante is using symbols intimately connected with the

Jubilee of 1300, and that he wishes the careful reader to transpose the doctrines of that occasion to their place in his universalizing description of his journey through the afterlife in that same year. Such a possible additional level of meaning would act as a further unifying feature, binding together, within a personal though universalized context, the various theological concepts, the ritual intonation, and the poetic symbols in the episode, and linking it to the fact, clearly significant but rarely investigated, that Dante sets the journey described in the poem during that period of the Jubilee year in which the earthly Church recalled the central mysteries of the Redemption. The irksome ambiguity of the word 'acra' (line 136), implying that the door is not opened often, would thus be explained as a natural association of ideas in Dante's mind, and there would be one final reason why the early commentators failed to appreciate the episode, for the Jubilees of 1350 and 1390 took place in different circumstances, and in any case there never has been a Jubilee quite like the first one.[6]

The Jubilee of 1300 was unique in that it was the result of a spontaneous popular ferment, arising from the rumour that very special indulgences were available to those who visited the Apostles' shrines in Rome in that centenary year. Cardinal Jacopo Stefaneschi's eyewitness account relates how, on New Year's Day, great crowds flocked to St. Peter's, and how this popular credence so persisted that on 22 February Boniface VIII, with the Bull *Antiquorum*, published the nature of these indulgences, making them retroactive from the previous Christmas, which to the Curia, which reckoned the years *a Nativitate*, had in fact been the first day of the centenary year: 'To all who, in the present year 1300 just begun, from the last feast of the Nativity of the Lord, and in every future centenary year, visit the Roman basilicas of the Apostles Peter and Paul, being truly penitent and having confessed, we grant not merely a full and generous but the fullest pardon of all their sins.'[7] Romans were required to visit the shrines for thirty consecutive days, foreigners for fifteen. Giovanni Villani, another eyewitness, describes the crowds, the ceremony of venerating Veronica's veil on Fridays and feast-days, and the wealth which the Church and the people of Rome acquired during the Jubilee year.[8] Guglielmo Ventura, who made his pilgrimage just before the close of the Jubilee at Christmas 1300, also makes this last point, complaining about the high cost of living for visitors to Rome.[9]

Stefaneschi provides the fullest details concerning the events and the religious implications of that Jubilee year. His account is clearly inspired by a desire to show Boniface VIII as a great religious leader and so to rehabilitate his memory, and in this respect it is noteworthy that it is probably Stefaneschi whom Dante condemns for his divisive policies as 'leader of the Trasteverine faction', accusing him of grafting the late Pope's anger on to himself (*Ep*.xi.10).[10]

In describing the events of 1300, Stefaneschi tells the story of a priest who dreamt that the Madonna appeared to him and said: 'God in his mercy has granted indulgence to all, both living and dead.'[11] That the dead may be included in the indulgence may seem strange. God may pardon them, of course, but the Pope's jurisdiction over the dead is limited to his powers to define and administer the *suffragia mortuorum*, the remission of temporal punishment by the living for the dead. However, theologically, the proclamation of the Jubilee indulgences would benefit the dead at least indirectly, for the indulgences gained by the living could be commuted as *suffragia*, and all the superabundant indulgences would join the treasury of merit to speed up the salvation of the Church Suffering.[12] Indeed, Jubilee indulgences were officially declared to be transferable to the dead in 1525.[13]

The belief that the indulgences of 1300 did in fact assist the souls of the dead as regards Purgatory must underlie Dante's presentation of Casella's release from his punishment of waiting at the mouth of the Tiber. When Dante asks Casella why he has taken so long to reach the shore of Purgatory, he replies that he has been obliged, by the just will of the angel, to wait, and that this he accepted; the angel-boatman has taken up all those willing to embark 'for the last three months', i.e. since Christmas 1299, or at least since early January 1300 (*Purg*. ii. 94–102).[14] It may be noted here that, if Dante wished to place his descent into hell on 25 March 1300, rather than on Good Friday, the time elapsed since the start of the Jubilee is almost exactly three months. It has been suggested that the episode of Casella refers to the decree in which Boniface closed the Jubilee and declared that its benefits also applied to those who died with the intention of making the pilgrimage, but, as Moore has shown, this is not the case for

Casella, who clearly died and was refused entry into the boat 'several times' before the Jubilee indulgences took effect for him and released him from the ban.[15] In fact, Dante uses the example of Casella not only to show the absolute justice applied to the various stages of the soul's journey to salvation after death, but also to link the earthly Church and the Church of Purgatory by the themes of the Tiber, Rome, and universal pardon in 1300, and the passage shows that Dante accepted not only the basic theology of the occasion, but also the extended application of the Jubilee indulgences to the dead, their importance in the context of the Church Suffering, and Boniface's retroactive decree, making them valid from the previous Christmas.

The date of promulgation of the Bull *Antiquorum* is significant. Though in fact proclaimed at the Lateran, it is dated from St. Peter's 'octavo kal. martii. pontificatus nostri anno sexto', that is, 22 February 1300. This was the feast of the Chair of St. Peter at Antioch, one of the two feasts of St. Peter's Chair which were of special importance in expressing the unity of the Church under the Pope.[16] Reading back from Easter Sunday (10 April) in 1300, and bearing in mind the fact that in the Julian calendar 1300 was a leap-year, it can be seen that 22 February was also the Monday before Ash Wednesday, the beginning of Lent.[17] The day thus seems to have been chosen in order to regularize the indulgences in time for those who visited Rome for the Lent and Passiontide of that special year. The actual promulgation is recorded in a fragment of a fresco by Giotto, which shows Boniface VIII making the proclamation of the Jubilee from his loggia looking out from the Lateran Palace. The artistic treatment of the scene and the companion pieces, now lost, recall Boniface's imperial claims as the heir of Constantine: 'I am Caesar, I am the Emperor.'[18] Frugoni notes that the fact that no kings attended the Jubilee might be explained as due to the belief that kissing the Pope's foot could imply acknowledgement of such claims to temporal power.[19]

There is no record that Boniface VIII performed a ceremonial opening of a Holy Door, although a marble copy of the Bull *Antiquorum* was later set up next to one of the doors of St. Peter's, the door which is now used as a Holy Door for years of Jubilee. Nowadays, the Pope knocks three times on it with a silver hammer, singing: 'Open to me the gates of justice' (a text cited by Pietro di Dante with regard to the door of Dante's Purgatory).[20] The ceremony of opening a special door on the occasion of a Jubilee is documented from 1423 but probably started earlier, i.e. at the Jubilee of 1390 or before. There was a legend that for the second Jubilee of 1350 Clement VI had a vision of opening a door.

Another, more apposite legend concerning the origin of the ceremony of the Holy Door provides a most remarkable possible connection with *Purg.* ix. The story is related by Pero Tafur, who visited Rome in 1437, and it is repeated in substance in Giovanni Rucellai's description of Rome in 1449. Tafur's account runs as follows:

This church [i.e. the Lateran], it is said, was once the building in which Rome kept her treasure, and there is the Tarpeian door, which Caesar opened when he took the treasure, and which until then had always been locked. The Emperor Constantine, when he was converted to the Catholic Faith and gave the Patrimony of the Empire to the Church and endowed it, entreated Pope Sylvester to grant a bull for that door for the souls who entered by it, just as before had been granted for the lives of those who arrived there; it had been the case that any fugitive who arrived at the Tarpeian door could not be taken from it, no matter what crime he had committed; and this was out of reverence for the treasure which was there. And so the Pope gave it this concession, that anyone who entered by it should be absolved from stain and punishment (*á culpa é á pena*); but since many people were audacious enough to sin with the intention of being absolved at the door, the Pope sent for it to be locked and decreed that it should not be opened except every hundred years, and this was later reduced to fifty years, and then as the Pope should prescribe.[21]

Although it involves ignorance of the true location of the *Mons Tarpeia*, this legend, if it existed in Dante's time, would explain why his contemporaries believed that the Jubilee tradition was of very ancient origin, as the Bull *Antiquorum habet fida relatio* ('A trustworthy tradition of our forebears maintains') implies at the outset. In any case, it establishes an early link between the Jubilee, the Lateran, and the Tarpeian treasury. A curious historical fact – or perhaps a clear association of ideas with reference to the treasury of merit – also makes the same link. The church of S. Adriano in the Forum was once believed, inaccurately, to have been the Roman treasury;[22] when it was demolished, its ancient bronze doors were removed by Borromini to the main entrance of St. John Lateran.[23]

No doubt Ozanam's interpretation of *Purg.* ix was suggested by Dante's symbol of the 'holy door' which is rarely opened, but no direct connection between the door of Purgatory and the institution of the Jubilee ceremony of the Holy Door can be established. Undeniably, however, both derive from the same source—the doctrine of the treasury of merit.

As has been shown, this doctrine had been evolved by St. Albert and St. Thomas.[24] The treasury of merit, opened by the power of the keys, was used for dispensing indulgences, purely spiritual benefits which commuted the duty of making satisfaction for sin and so diminished the debt of punishment after death in Purgatory. However, by the time of Dante indulgences had often become something of a mere formality and, in particular, were frequently attached to rituals and purely exterior actions, such as the custom of kneeling before the penitentiaries in St. Peter's or visiting certain churches or the shrine (*limina*) of a saint, especially those in Rome.[25] It was this practice which had sparked off the rush to St. Peter's on the first day of the centenary year and through the ensuing months. Few people seem to have understood what an indulgence really was. Giovanni Villani makes the most common theological error, when he says that the Pope proclaimed a 'full and entire pardon of all sins . . . both of the stain and of the punishment (*di colpa e di pena*)'.[26] In fact, as has been seen, no one but God, not even Boniface VIII, can remove the stain, and even God cannot do so unless the sinner repents (*Inf.* xxvii. 100–20; *Mon.* III. viii.7). Nevertheless, in the popular mind, indulgences forgave the *culpa* of sins as well as diminishing Purgatory, and later pilgrims to Rome wildly exaggerated the benefits which could be acquired by visiting the churches and relics of that city. Spurious authorities for these excessive Roman indulgences in fact existed.[27] The fifteenth-century English pilgrim, William Brewyn, like Villani and Tafur, confuses the remission of the *culpa* and the *poena* by indulgences. Also for him the indulgences available in

Rome were truly spectacular, being graded, as often as not, in multiples of thousands of years of release from Purgatory. For instance, he believed that, at the showing of Veronica's veil, Romans acquired 6,000 years and foreigners 9,000 years of remission in Purgatory.[28] From this contemporary and later evidence it is easy to see why, amid the heady but mistaken fervour of that first Jubilee, Boniface VIII should have felt it necessary, for reasons of theological accuracy, of his own authority, and of public order, to invoke the correct doctrine of plenary indulgences, a prerogative of the papal power of the keys,[29] to set limits on their efficacy and availability, and to minimize the unfair advantage which Romans had over foreigners in gaining them.

However, the Bull *Antiquorum* does not directly clarify the doctrine nor remove the possible sources of misunderstanding and abuse, and it has sometimes been alleged that Boniface exploited the occasion to amass, not purely spiritual treasures, but real wealth in gold and silver.[30] Villani makes the point that the Church acquired great wealth from the pilgrims, and the manuscript of Stefaneschi's account gives the total amounts of 30,000 gold florins given by pilgrims at St. Peter's and 21,000 at St. Paul's.[31] Ventura paints a somewhat scandalous scene: 'The Pope gained from them [the pilgrims] incalculable wealth, because day and night two clerics stood at the altar of St. Paul holding in their hands rakes and raking in infinite money.' The Romans in general also seem to have exploited the pilgrims, as Ventura complains: 'For bread, wine, meat, fish, and oats, there was a good market; the inns were very expensive, so that my bed, and my horse's, on straw, and the oats cost me a *tournois* silver groat.'[32]

Whatever was in Boniface's mind at the time, Rome in 1300 must therefore have provided several examples of the chief dangers of the doctrine of indulgences: excessive and disproportionate claims made for them, and the narrow line which separates them from simony.[33] Nor is it likely that Dante, opponent of Boniface's divisive crusade against the Colonnas (*Inf.* xxvii. 85–111; cf. *Par.* xxvii. 49–51), would have approved of the Bull *Nuper per alias nostras litteras*, which specifically excluded that family, 'damned by us and rebels against us and against the Apostolic See', from participating in the centenary indulgences.[34] For all these reasons, it might well be said that the silver key of jurisdiction over plenary indulgences 'needs extreme skill and intellect before it unlocks' the treasury of the infinite spiritual merits of Christ (*Purg.* ix. 124–5).

Stefaneschi's style has been called obscure, indeed 'hieroglyphic' and 'barbarously involved',[35] but although his Latin is almost impossible to decipher with grammatical certainty, his exposition of the theology of the first Jubilee is generally fairly clear. There are several points of contact with the imagery of *Purg.* ix. The manuscript of his *De Centesimo seu Iubileo Anno Liber* ('A Book on the Centenary or Jubilee Year') contains a miniature showing St. Peter holding the keys and St. Paul with a sword, and Stefaneschi emphasizes the importance, in the Jubilee, of St. Paul, co-founder of the Faith and of the authority of Rome; for him, a pilgrimage to Rome is a visit to the 'threshold of Peter' or 'of Peter and Paul', or 'of the Apostles'.[36] These ideas, which, as has been noted, were traditional in pilgrim literature,[37] confirm the Roman associations of Dante's angel-doorkeeper, who bears both sword and keys, and who sits on the diamond threshold which is contrasted with the threshold of hell and heresy in *Inf.* ix, and which thus recalls the Rock of the Church, Christ, St. Peter, and the See of Rome. In terms of the Jubilee also, earthly Rome and the threshold of St. Peter's vicar in Purgatory are linked by the office of the angel-boatman, who administers the Jubilee indulgences to the dead. As has been seen, the two angels are linked in several ways, and this alone would indicate the possible existence of a reference to the Jubilee in *Purg.* ix.

It has been said that the doctrine of the treasury of merit was not fully worked out for the Jubilee of 1300.[38] However, this study has shown how the doctrine underlies the whole theology of indulgences and therefore of the plenary indulgence proclaimed in the Bull *Antiquorum*. Boniface VIII and his advisers must have known this, even though the Bull does not specifically mention it. Dante also could easily have discovered the correct doctrine of the Jubilee, at least by the time he came to write the *Comedy* in later years. Stefaneschi certainly uses the idea of the treasury in his description of the first Jubilee, and it was common knowledge by the second half of the century, for Matteo Villani's account of the Jubilee of 1350 ends: 'And so was celebrated this year of the holy Jubilee, the dispensing of the merits of the passion of Christ and of the merits of the holy Church, and the remission of sins of faithful Christians.'[39]

Although Stefaneschi, like others on the same subject, refers occasionally to the 'washing-away of sins', thus partially obscuring the essential distinction between the *culpa* and the *poena*,[40] he does put forward the correct theology of indulgences and of the treasury of merit with regard to the Jubilee of 1300. He states that the Jubilee was a way of making satisfaction for the *poena* of sins by the power of the keys and the authority of Peter and continues:

Profluens igitur cruoris eius haud incassum unda purpurei. salutare misterium in filios presulis dispositione agignente eos sibi sponsa impertiendum. ipsius thesaurum locuplectat. Thesaurus tuus thesaurus infinitus.

There follow the doctrines of the foundation of the Church, the power of the keys, and Christ's charge to St. Peter. Then he goes on:

Hiis ecclesie maximis inextimabilibusque gazofilatio referto. excellentium ipsum alia opulentant clenodia. Sanctorum siquidem lacrime. Iustorum penalitates. Martirum veneranda supplicia. Qui nedum sibi sed veluti ipsorum perfecta omnia fatiens communia caritas sancire. toti prodesse ecclesie congeriei decrevere.

His igitur romanus presul divina apostolorum suaque fultus auctoritate dispensat opes. has in filiorum alimenta distribuit. Qui fide recti spe longanimes capiti invicemque caritate vinciuntur. Quod apostolorum reverentiam hortari. populi necessitatem pulsare. actorem pietatis indulgere deum fatemur.[41]

Thus, to paraphrase rather than translate, the Jubilee indulgence was a plenary remission by the power of the keys, with which the Pope ('presul') dispenses the stream of Christ's purple blood ('cruoris ejus . . . unda purpurei'), a treasure which is infinite ('thesaurus tuus thesaurus infinitus'). The Pope has the power to administer the treasury ('gazofilatio') of the saints' tears, the tribulations of the just, the torments of the martyrs, etc. In other words, the plenary indulgence of 1300 depended on the merits of Christ's Passion and the treasury of superabundance. By these, therefore, the Roman pontiff, relying on the divine authority of the Apostles, and his own, dispenses riches; he distributes them as nourishment to his children, who are supported by faith, sustained by hope, and united to each other and to the head by charity. Thus we acknowledge that reverence for the Apostles exhorts, that the faithful must knock, that God grants indulgence to those who perform an act of piety.

It can be seen that this last passage implies the metaphor of opening a door: when the people knock, the Pope uses his keys to open the treasury of merit and distribute its spiritual riches. Stefaneschi uses the imagery of doors on three other occasions: in the year 1300 the door of heaven was open ('patet . . . regia celi'); the basilicas of the Apostles were also open ('delubra patentia'); and, in a sense, the year itself was a door, for Stefaneschi talks of its final days as 'the fortnight which closed the doors of the centenary (*centesimo valvas claudentem quindenam*)'.[42] Boniface's decreeing of the Jubilee, moreover, is valid, for the Church cannot err ('minime errasse') in granting indulgences.[43]

Finally, Stefaneschi summarizes the doctrine in one of his poems, 'A heroic song on the centenary or Jubilee (*De centesimo seu Iubileo Heroycum Carmen*)':

> Ne lacerent animos patet hiis nam[44] regia celi.
> Nec poterant auferre luem. sed gratia summe
> Sedis apostolice. christi subnixa cruori
> Purpureo. dispensat opes. quas vulnera christi
> Sanctorumque patrum sibi dant. tua crimina
> laxans.[45]

(Lest they should destroy their souls, the door of heaven lies open to them. Nor could they have cast off the disease. But the mercy of the supreme Apostolic See, resting on the purple blood of Christ, dispenses riches given to it by the wounds of Christ and of the holy fathers, and loosens your sins.)

Thus in Stefaneschi's account of the Jubilee of 1300 we find a startling convergence of themes present also in *Purg.* ix: the wounds and disease of sin (the second step), the purple blood of Christ (the third step), the powers of the Pope who bears the keys (the angel), the 'threshold of Peter' (the diamond threshold), the rite of requesting the pardon (Dante's submission), the relationship between the duty of satisfaction and the paying of a debt, the process of cleansing, and the gaining of full pardon (the seven P's), and the infinite treasury of merit (the Tarpeian simile). For Stefaneschi these elements ensure that the door ('regia') of heaven is open to men in a special way in the centenary year, that indeed the year itself could be considered an infrequently opened door to pardon and heaven. Dante also sums up these symbols and ideas with the concluding description of a rare, if not unique, event, the opening of a sacred door ('quella regge sacra') (*Purg.* ix. 130, 134). Later generations were to adopt the same symbol for the special years of Jubilee.

*   *   *

It seems quite possible, therefore, that Dante, having referred to the occasion of the Jubilee in *Purg.* ii, wishes to allude also to its doctrines in *Purg.* ix. This can only be confirmed if we can identify the reasons, poetic and doctrinal, personal and universal, behind this possible inclusion of a further level of polysemy in the episode of the door. The most obvious reason, of course, is that the whole poem is set during the principal religious and redemptive season of that unique centenary year which itself had such special religious and redemptive significance. Everybody knows this, and all can see the general universalizing symbolism implied in the whole description of Dante's journey because of the year and the season in which it is set. It is, as has been indicated, intimately connected with the various senses of the theme of Exodus, from the Redemption to the final journey to salvation, and with the moral exodus of Dante as an *exemplum* to his readers. Nevertheless, the details remain rather vague. Why precisely did Dante choose to underpin his great poem with the symbolism of that particular year of the Jubilee? The reasons are usually traced back to certain events in Dante's personal life in that year, but now, using *Purg.* ix as a key provided by the poem itself, we can identify some specific themes which link the personal and

universal significance of the year 1300 with Dante's presentation of his whole poem and of the *Purgatorio* in particular.

As regards the personal motive for the time-setting which
Dante chose for his poem, not only did this unique centenary
anniversary of the foundation of the Christian era coincide
with his reaching of the half-way point in the allotted span of
man's life (*Inf.* i. 1) and with a critical period in the relations
between Rome and Florence and in the events of his own life,
but it is also generally accepted that he visited Rome for the
Jubilee of 1300. Although he has eliminated any direct reference to this personal experience, it does seem one of the most
likely reasons for his choice. He had earlier shown interest in
the pilgrims who passed through Florence on their way to
Rome to see Veronica's veil (*V.N.* xl), and elsewhere he
refers several times to the Rome which a pilgrim would see.
He mentions the obelisk of St. Peter's in the *Convivio* (*Conv.*
IV. xvi. 6).[46] In the *Comedy*, there are various indications. To
convey an exact idea of the size of the giants in hell, he
describes the pine-cone, then in the forecourt of St. Peter's, as
if he had himself seen it (*Inf.* xxxi. 58–9). He refers to the sight
of Rome from Monte Mario, which was traditionally the place
from which pilgrims caught their first sight of Rome, and
where they would sing the hymn *O Roma nobilis* in praise of
the city of Sts. Peter and Paul (*Par.* xv. 109–10).[47] He evokes
the wonder with which the earliest pilgrims would have
regarded Rome in the days of its glory, after Constantine had
given the Lateran Palace to the Popes and had enriched the
shrines of the Apostles (*Par.* xxxi. 31–6).[48] He skilfully
describes the deep religious sensibilities of the pilgrim who
has travelled far to venerate the image of Christ impressed on
the veil of St. Veronica (*Par.* xxxi. 103–8). All these references
certainly seem to show that Dante himself visited Rome as a
pilgrim, and that he was impressed by the sight of Rome's
ancient glories and reacted especially to seeing pilgrims coming
from very distant parts of Europe. The chief source for presuming that Dante made his pilgrimage in the Jubilee year is
the famous simile by which he compares the movement of the
two groups of souls in the first *bolgia* of Malebolge to the
crowd regulations introduced on the Ponte Sant'Angelo during
the Jubilee (*Inf.* xviii. 28–33). This description, used precisely

for reasons of realism and immediacy, certainly seems to be that of an eyewitness and is corroborated by Giovanni Villani.[49]

If Dante did in fact make a Jubilee pilgrimage to Rome in 1300, then the connections between this and *Purg.* ix may be illustrated by Gregory Martin's account of the Jubilee of 1575, which shows how little the theology of the occasion changed after the time of Dante and Stefaneschi. Many of the details provided by Martin recall elements found also in *Purg.* ix: the frequent use of the phrase *limen Petri* for Rome; the doctrines of the treasury of merit, the keys, and the 'Pope's Pardon'; the symbolism of the number seven (the sevenfold washing of Naaman, the seven angels of the Apocalypse, the seven Gifts of the Holy Ghost, the seven years of penance in the early Church, the seven psalms and litanies on Rogation Days, and the seven churches to be visited by pilgrims to Rome, especially in Lent); the sackcloth or grey garb of some pilgrims; the rods of the Franciscan penitentiaries of St. Peter's; the custom of kissing the Pope's foot; the singing of the *Te Deum*; the warning against recidivism.[50] As in Dante's day, special crowd regulations were necessary to control access to St. Peter's: 'I nede not tel you here what a multitud of people folowe them foreward and backward, so great that if on one side of the brode Burgo were not for the goers forward, and the other for the returners backward, ther would be no passage.'[51]

The reasonable assumption that Dante took part in the Jubilee not only helps to explain the setting in time chosen for the whole poem, but also underlies the special relevance of Jubilee themes to his conception of Purgatory. The episode of Casella states this at the outset, whilst, as has been seen, the various elements are brought together in the episode of the angel and the door. The gathering of the souls of the saved at Ostia links earthly Rome with mount Purgatory; the episode of Casella links the special indulgence of 1300 with the process of the speedier remission of temporal punishment after death; and the whole episode of the door is full of symbolism relating to Rome, the Pope, and the doctrine of plenary indulgence. Many other details of the episode could be associated, if somewhat more conjecturally, with the Rome of pilgrims. The imperial stone of porphyry was associated with the baptism of Constantine and the tomb of St. Peter, and, as has been noted, there was a legend that Pope Sylvester divided the bodies of Sts. Peter and Paul on a porphyry stone.[52] Given the papal and Petrine symbolism of the angel-doorkeeper, Dante may even have wished, in his presentation of the seven angels who act as the doorkeeper's agents and ministers on the cornices of the Church Suffering, to allude to the ancient division of Rome, attributed to St. Peter and regularized by Sylvester and other Popes, into seven regions, each administered by a deacon on behalf of the Pope; this presumably underlies the medieval tradition, related by John the Deacon (*c*.1073), that only the Pope and the seven hebdomadary Cardinal Bishops were allowed into the sanctuary of the Lateran.[53] Whatever the validity of such additional details, the symbol of the door sums up all these Roman elements in the episode. The door leads to a 'true city' (*Purg.* xiii. 95), the sevenfold city of a penitential, pilgrim Church; it is also the gate of heaven, the entrance to the eternal Rome ruled by Christ (*Purg.*xxxii.102). In this way, at the very least, the door is linked to the fundamental pilgrimage symbolism of the *Purgatorio* and of the whole *Comedy*.

Dante and the souls of the saved are all pilgrims through Purgatory (*Purg.* ii. 63). In the case of Dante, this pilgrimage evokes a sense of nostalgia on the evening of the first day, before he enters through the door, but a feeling of joy on the morning of the last day, when, paradoxically, the pilgrim who is nearing the goal of his journey is in fact returning home, to the earthly Paradise, man's original home on earth, and then to the heavenly Paradise (*Purg.* viii. 1–6; xxvii. 109–11). From his arrival on the shore of Purgatory, and in a new and more positive sense after he has passed through the door of Purgatory and Paradise, Dante is travelling to his true home, and this journey is expressed as a pilgrimage from corrupt Florence to the eternal Rome. The pilgrim's goal is the magnificent sight of the Rose of the Blessed in the Empyrean Heaven:

> Se i barbari, venendo da tal plaga
> che ciascun giorno d'Elice si cuopra,
> rotante col suo figlio ond'ella è vaga,
>   veggendo Roma e l'ardua sua opra,
> stupefacíensi, quando Laterano
> a le cose mortali andò di sopra;

io, che al divino da l'umano,
a l'etterno dal tempo era venuto,
e di Fiorenza in popol giusto e sano,
   di che stupor dovea esser compiuto!
Certo tra esso e 'l gaudio mi facea
libito non udire e starmi muto.
   E quasi peregrin che si ricrea
nel tempio del suo voto riguardando
e spera già ridir com'ello stea,
   su per la viva luce passeggiando
menava io li occhi per li gradi,
mo su, mo giú e mo recirculando   (*Par.* xxxi.
31–48)

(If the barbarians, coming from the region which is covered each day by Callisto [the Great Bear] turning with her son whom she loves [Boötes], were astonished upon seeing Rome and her elaborate monuments, when the Lateran surpassed all mortal things; with what amazement must I have been filled, who had come from the human to the divine, from time to eternity, and from Florence to a just and sound nation! Indeed, between astonishment and joy, I desired neither to hear anything nor to speak. And like the pilgrim who rests, looking around the temple which he has vowed to visit, and who already looks forward to describing it to others, so did I allow my eyes to travel up through the living light, directing them through all the ranks [of the Rose of heaven], now up, now down, now moving round and round).

So at the end of his journey, Dante the pilgrim feasts his eyes on the temple he has vowed to visit, which is the Church of the Redeemed, the Heavenly City of the Bride of Christ, a holy nation, a true kingdom, a just Empire, ruled by God and by Maria Augusta (*Par.* xxx. 98, 122, 129–30; xxxi. 1–3, 25, 39; xxxii. 52, 61, 117, 119). Already he is thinking of how to describe it on his return from his pilgrimage to his earthly home (*Par.* xxxi. 45). And when he meets St. Bernard, who is to prepare him for his final visions of Mary and of God, Dante is like the pilgrim who has travelled from afar to Rome and now contemplates the chief object of his devotion:

   . . . colui che forse di Croazia
viene a veder la Veronica nostra,
che per l'antica fame non sen sazia,
   ma dice nel pensier, fin che si mostra:

"Segnor mio Iesú Cristo, Dio verace,
or fu sí fatta la sembianza vostra?"   (*Par.* xxxi.
103–8)

(the man who has come perhaps from Croatia to see our Veronica's
veil, and who has hungered to see it for so long that he cannot now
be sated, but, for as long as it is on show, he says in his thoughts: 'My
lord Jesus Christ, true God, were your features, then, so formed?').

Dante has reached the City which is both the new Jerusalem
and the new Rome. Its members are divided into the Jews who
believed in Christ to come and the Christians who believed in
Christ after his coming (*Par.* xxxii. 22–7). For both groups the
Rose represents the fruition of the redemptive work of Christ.
This work is now continued by his Church on earth, centred
on earthly Rome, and on the Last Day one Rome will send to
the other the fruits of the Redemption, as St. John Chrysostom
says: 'Think and tremble, what a sight Rome will see, when
Paul swiftly rises from that tomb with Peter and is taken up at
the coming of the Lord: what a rose Rome sends to Christ!'[54]

In this way, Dante's experience of a pilgrimage could be
seen also to be elevated to the level of an Exodus, an entry
into a Promised Land and to an eternal Holy City. Under one
aspect, his journey is an exodus and pilgrimage of a living man
from the Egypt of this world to a Holy Land and the new
Jerusalem (*Par.* xxv. 55–6). Perhaps it is that pilgrimage which,
because of Boniface's indifference, Dante was unable to make
in his real life (cf. *Par.* ix. 126, 136–8). Under another aspect,
it is also a transformation of a pilgrimage which he almost
certainly did make to Rome, and so he chose to express the
personal and the universal redemptive significance of the
poem, setting it also in the Jubilee year, as a journey from
earth to heaven, from time to eternity, from Florence to the
true 'Eternal City' of Paradise.

The idea that Dante's journey to the heavenly Rose represents a pilgrimage to Rome is, of course, shared by others,
and in particular by Demaray.[55] However, his premisses for
this conclusion are as distinct from those given here as is the
East from the North. For Demaray, the whole *Comedy* is a
representation of a pilgrimage to Jerusalem, Sinai, etc., as
gleaned from Dante's reading of pilgrim texts, and at the end

of the poem Dante arrives in Rome after travelling across the sea on his return from the Holy Land. The main difficulty in this theory is, of course, that, whilst there is some evidence that Dante made a pilgrimage from Florence to Rome, there is none at all that he ever made one to the Holy Land, which was in any case being forgotten and neglected by Boniface VIII in 1300 (*Par.* ix. 126, 137–8; xv. 143–4). Thus any use by Dante of pilgrim-text models is purely artificial and impersonal. Moreover, since in *Par.* xxxi Dante is quite clearly describing the *goal* of his pilgrimage, it is extremely improbable that he would express this in terms of a purely imaginary *return* journey to Italy from the Holy Land. Dante's goal is the heavenly Rome, and his return journey is his return to earth to tell us all about it (*Par.* xxxi. 45). By Dante's time a pilgrimage to Rome had replaced the circular journey to the Holy Land and back. Many of the chief relics from the Holy Land were in Rome, and Rome, especially the church of S. Croce in Gerusalemme, was the new Jerusalem for pilgrims.[56] Thus a pilgrimage to Jerusalem was already a model for one to Rome, and both were earthly figures of the journey to the heavenly Jerusalem and the heavenly Rome.[57] Dante absorbs this model, together with the biblical imagery of the Exodus, into the scheme of his journey to the anagogical world pre-figured by these earthly pilgrimages. In one sense he is a 'palmer', bearing, on his return to earth, the palm of knowledge which is the sign of his pilgrimage through the afterlife (*V.N.* xl; *Purg.* xxxiii. 78). Much more important, however, when he comes to describe the heavenly Rose, is the fact that he presents himself as a 'Romer' (*V.N.* xl), and in this he is probably transcribing the meaning of a real pilgrimage which he once made to a real goal, Rome. He does not say that he has arrived in this heavenly Rome from the East. Indeed, he specifically states that he has come from Florence (*Par.* xxxi. 39).

The themes of pilgrimage and of Rome, and particularly of a pilgrimage to Rome in the Jubilee year, are thus probably a personal reference and certainly an essential thread in the symbolic pattern of the whole poem as a journey and as an exodus. To this scheme Dante adds a further universal and redemptive level of meaning by his choice of the actual days of his journey, for these present him, the living Christian making his moral exodus in the poem, as a follower of Christ, the *figura* of the perfect Christian, in the exodus of his descent into hell and in his resurrection on Easter morning. In his personal moral life Dante fulfils what was itself the first fulfilment of the biblical account of the Exodus—the Redemption, when all mankind was led out from slavery to freedom.

In all these ways Dante is asking his reader to transpose the significance of the year 1300 of the Christian era into the context of a journey-poem which aims at universal meaning and at universal instruction and reform. The use of Jubilee symbolism in *Purg.* ix would indicate that this theme should be applied in a special way to the structure of Purgatory after Dante's entry through the door which leads to the straight path to God. In fact, there are three principal ways in which the year of Jubilee is linked to the universal redemptive message of the whole poem and especially of Purgatory above the door. These can be distinguished by an examination of the three terms used by Dante and his contemporaries to describe the importance of the year 1300: Pardon, Jubilee, and Centenary.

The word 'pardon' is used by Giovanni Villani, and, as has been seen, it was the normal word for indulgences in Dante's time (*Purg.* xiii. 62; *Par.* xxix. 120). The main precondition for the gaining of a plenary indulgence was that the recipient should have repented of all mortal sins, and also, normally, that he should have confessed. These are also the preconditions, required before death, for entry into Dante's Purgatory, and failure to effect formal reconciliation with God by confession and satisfaction before death must be expiated in Antepurgatory, outside the door, before admission to the realm of final indulgence. An indulgence on earth is a method of remitting the *poena*, the temporal punishment due to sin during life and after death. It is a participation in the treasure of the Church and so is not, of course, available to excommunicates. It is a dispensation of the merits of Christ and of the saints by the power of the keys. A plenary indulgence can only be granted by the Pope.

In *Purg.* ix Dante uses these ideas to present Purgatory above the door as the realm of final indulgence or the plenary remission of the *poena* still due to sin after death. The souls in Antepurgatory are temporarily 'excommunicated' and cannot be admitted to the realm of indulgence until their juridical bond has been loosened by their supplying 'time for time' outside the door (*Purg.* xxiii. 84). Then for them too, as for other souls, the angelic 'vicar of Peter' uses his keys to open a priceless treasury and admit them to the realm of full remission of the seven *Poenae*. In the episode of the door, therefore, Dante wishes us to conclude that this is the moment in his journey when he gains access to full pardon or 'plenary indulgence' on the cornices, and the setting of the poem in the year of full, universal pardon indicates that the doctrines described be applied to the destiny of the whole human race. Thus the word 'acra' implies the warning that such an opportunity for full and final pardon occurs only once in a lifetime for the individual, and only once in a century for mankind. Taken in conjunction with the warning against relapsing, it might also allude to the fact that few men gain this pardon definitively and without turning back, and this would make the word a brief but tragic reference, not just to human frailty, as Lana implies (cf. also *Purg.* xii. 94–6), but also to the general inefficacy of that first Jubilee.

The word 'Jubilee' allows us to apply the significance of the year 1300 more closely still to the general scheme of the poem and of the second *cantica*, for it is linked to the presentation of Dante's journey as an exodus from slavery and an acquisition of freedom (*Purg.*i. 71; ii. 46; *Ep.* xiii. 7). The term 'Jubilee' may not have been generally used in the year itself, though people did believe that there had been special Roman indulgences a hundred years earlier, and some leonine verses on the indulgences of 1300 contain the words: 'Annus centenus Rome semper est iubilenus' (The hundredth year in Rome is always Jubilee year).[58] However, despite the opening words of the Bull *Antiquorum*, tales of earlier Jubilees, and the evidence of one old pilgrim from Savoy that he actually remembered the Jubilee of 1200,[59] it is impossible to trace the origin of the Christian Jubilee tradition further back than the Jubilee of Boniface VIII and of Dante.[60] The first dated application of the word to the year 1300 occurs in Boniface's decree which closed the Jubilee on Christmas Day 1300: 'In addition, our lord the supreme Pontiff declares that this '300th Jubilee year (*annus iste iubileus trecentesimus*) is finished today and may not be extended to the year of the Incarnation according to some (*secundum quosdam*) but to the years of the Lord according to the rite of the Roman Church.'[61] The term must have come into general use fairly soon, for it is found in the *Inferno*, where it is used as if it were already a known term (*Inf.* xviii. 29), and it was later employed for doctrinal reasons by Stefaneschi in his *De Centesimo seu Iubileo Anno Liber* ('A Book on the Centenary or Jubilee Year'). Giovanni Villani may also have known it, although it occurs only in the chapter-heading and not in the text of the *Cronica*. After 1350 it became one of the accepted words for the event.[62]

Although associated with the idea of 'jubilation', the term does not primarily involve rejoicing. It derives from Leviticus 25, where, following the rule of the seventh or sabbatical year, it is decreed that after seven by seven years the fiftieth year shall be set apart for the remission of all debts, for the freeing of slaves, and for allowing men to return to their own lands again; it is contrasted with God's sevenfold punishment of sins. The Jubilee year was proclaimed by trumpets of horn (*yobel*).[63] The doctrine of the Hebrew Jubilee as a figure of reconciliation and liberation from sin was well known, and it presumably underlies such expressions as Stephen Langton's declaration that fifty years represents the number of remission, and the words of the early thirteenth-century hymn, 'Anni favor jubilaei poenarum laxat debitum' ('The favour of the Jubilee year loosens the debt of punishments').[64] The tradition of a Christian Jubilee every fifty years did not begin until the Jubilee of 1350, and then, after some oscillation between thirty-three (in memory of Christ's life) and twenty-five years for the Jubilee of 1390–1400, held during the schism from Rome, and the following one of 1423–5, the period between Jubilees was established as twenty-five years.[65] Clement VI's Bull *Unigenitus Dei Filius* of 1343 proclaiming the second Jubilee does not contain the actual word, but Clement used it in a letter.[66] Matteo Villani's account certainly draws out the figural parallel between the new fifty-year Christian Jubilee and the Hebrew Jubilee year, 'in which each man returned to his own true possessions; and the true possessions of Christians are the merits of Christ's Passion, through which we obtain indulgence and remission of sins'.[67] Another reason given for the reduction of the period to fifty years was to give everyone a chance to gain these special indulgences once in a lifetime, and in this last respect Frugoni cites the words of Mastro Bonaiuto with regard to Purgatory: 'Postpone this punishment until at least the Jubilee year goes by.'[68]

In general, therefore, the Hebrew Jubilee could be seen as a prefiguration of Christ redeeming and delivering man by his merits, and of special years in which these merits were made available for the remission of the *poenae* due to sin by means of plenary indulgences. Even with regard to the year 1300, before the Christian Jubilee was declared applicable every fifty years, Stefaneschi had described in quite close detail the scriptural and figural parallel between the Hebrew Jubilee and the special centenary indulgences of 1300, which, he says, gave man full remission of the debt of his sins, freed Christians from their enslavement to the devil, returned to man his stolen possessions of virtues, and so restored him to his true home, 'the house of his heavenly homeland and the family of the citizens on high'.[69] If Dante is using Jubilee symbolism in *Purg.* ix, he is asking his reader to regard the episode as a crucial moment when, at this one point in his lifetime, he enters into the treasury of pardon won by, and founded on, the merits of the Passion, and into the realm of the remission of debts, of the acquisition of liberty, of the regaining of virtues by the 'whips' and 'bridles'. He is embarking on the straight path which leads to his true home, to the family of God, to the true city of the faithful under Christ, to the eternal Jubilee of Paradise (*Purg.* x. 3; xiii. 94–5; xxxii. 101–2; *Par.* i. 92–3, 124–6; x. 49–50; xxiv. 43–4). In this sense also, the theme of liberty, which is fundamental to Dante's *Purgatorio* (*Purg.* i. 71; xxvii. 140), is contained in the theme of the Jubilee, and so both themes are closely linked with the figural analysis of the theme of the Exodus in the Epistle to Can Grande as applied above to the episode of the door of Purgatory which is also the gateway to Paradise.[70] Thus any reference to the Jubilee in *Purg.* ix would be, not a denial, but an enrichment of the basic figural and interpretative model upon which the polysemy of the whole poem, and especially of the *Purgatorio*, is based.

The full figural parallelism between the Hebrew and the Christian Jubilees, as described by Stefaneschi, may have been evolved after the event itself, to be sanctioned later in the century by the establishment of the fifty-year Jubilee. The unique feature of the first Jubilee was that it was a centenary occasion. This is what caused the spontaneous belief in the special indulgences and this is what Boniface VIII, appealing to the 'trustworthy tradition of our forebears', proclaimed in the Bull *Antiquorum*, even though we today have no solid evidence that these indulgences were customary in previous centenary years. One result of the belief that the year 1300 was a year of great religious importance was that there were increased calls for a Crusade, but these the Pope ignored.[71] Perhaps this fact allows us to see the theme of the Jubilee as another link between *Purg.* ix and Folchetto's condemnation of Boniface's neglect of the Holy Land in the corresponding canto of the *Paradiso* (*Par.* ix. 125–6, 136–8; cf. xv. 144).

Both the Jubilee itself, as a year of pardon, and Dante's choice of the Jubilee year for the setting of his poem derive from the obvious and fundamental fact that the year 1300 was a hundredth anniversary of the start of the Christian era and a bridge-year between one century and another. The word which Stefaneschi constantly uses is 'centesimo [anno]', and Dante uses the very same expression in that episode of the *Paradiso* which is parallel to the episode of the door (cf. also *Purg.* xxii. 93). In the Heaven of Venus, Cunizza tells Dante that Folchetto has left great fame behind him on earth:

> '. . . e pria che moia,
> questo centesimo anno ancor s'incinqua' (*Par.* ix. 39–40)

(and before it dies, this hundredth year will be multiplied five times).

The phrase is, of course, used as a method of hyperbole, to stress the permanence of Folchetto's renown. Later, Dante employs a similar, and connected, expression as a form of litotes, when Beatrice prophesies that God will restore goodness on earth 'before January leaves winter altogether, *per la centesima ch'è là giú negletta'*, i.e. because of the hundredth part of a day which was lost every year in the Julian calendar (*Par.* xxvii. 142–3).[72] Since January will therefore move away from winter by only one day every century, several millennia are implied. Both these references describe vast periods of future time, marked by the passage of those centenary years such as the one in which the poem is set. Yet the effect of each is contradictory. In *Par.* ix, Dante is referring to a hypothetical date in the distant, but real, future. In *Par.* xxvii, by mentioning an almost inconceivable span of time, he really means that the renovation of the world is not too far away.

There is, in fact, a strange ambiguity in Dante's presentation of the future. On the one hand, in the *Convivio*, while discussing the eternal and almost imperceptible motion of the sphere of the Fixed Stars, he talks as if the end of this motion were at hand: 'We are already in the last age of the world, and we truly await the consummation of the celestial movement' (*Conv.* II. xiv. 13). Since the sphere of the stars moved by only one degree every century, this is also a concealed reference to great spans of time marked by centenaries, and Dante believed that the motion of this sphere would never be completed in the sense of returning to the same point as at its creation (*Conv.* II. xiv. 11–12). Given Dante's sources, this whole passage implies that the end of the world is imminent.[73] Heaven is nearly full (*Par.* xxx. 131–2; xxxii. 38–9). On the other hand, he often refers, for reasons of rhetorical emphasis, to times in the very distant future (*Inf.* ii. 60; *Purg.* xi. 106; xiv. 65–6; *Par.* ix. 40; xxvii. 142–3).

This ambivalence underlies and is at the same time crystallized and given meaning in what may be called Dante's 'millenarianism', his sense of God's imminent retribution and regeneration of mankind. Probably under the influence of the 'prophetic spirit' of Joachim of Fiore (*Par.* xii. 140–2), and certainly in line with biblical prophecies of retribution, with the early Church's constant expectation of the Second Coming, and with the sense of imminent destiny contained in much apocalyptic literature, Dante's poem looks towards a new age, not far off, indeed to be accomplished in his own lifetime, when the wicked will be punished and the world renewed by a

Greyhound or a DXV, emissary of God (*Inf.* i. 101–11; *Purg.* vi. 100–2; xxiii. 98–9,110–11; xxxiii. 37–51; *Par.* xxii. 14–15). In this way, Dante judges the corruption of the past and present and creates his own ideal or myth of a new age close at hand. Such feelings and hopes would be many men's natural response to a centenary year, especially to one which followed a century so full of conflict and tension, of commercial progress together with calls for poverty and religious reform, as was the thirteenth century in Italy. Indeed, the whole movement which produced the Jubilee of 1300 was 'millenarian', imbued with Joachimite eschatology and Franciscan ideas.[74] Thus Dante's 'millenarianism', with all its hopes, its enigmatic presentation, and its ambiguity, can be seen, at least in part, as a literary elaboration and universal application of his own reactions to the centenary year in which the poem is set. Thus too does the theme of the Jubilee as a centenary underlie the eschatological impetus and the exemplary function of the whole poem, and particularly of Purgatory after the episode of the door, with its reformist elements, introduces the description of how man is purified and renewed and travels inevitably to salvation and beatitude.

At the beginning of the poem, Dante is in a dark wood, striving to climb a sunlit hill (*Inf.* i. 1–21). His initial personal situation is in tension between darkness and hope. In this way, writing in later years, he crystallizes his recollections of a year which was not only so fateful for the world and for himself, but was also a year in which one century, with all its burden of guilt, passed away, and another was ushered in, offering the hope of release. The rest of the poem describes how, since that first symbol of hope proved unattainable in terms of earthly life and normal earthly powers, escape was possible only with help and guidance to knowledge of the next life. Moreover, not only does Dante present this crisis in the context of the 1300th year from the Incarnation, but the actual day on which his journey through the afterlife begins is the 1266th anniversary of the Crucifixion (*Inf.* xxi. 112–14). From Boccaccio onwards, it has been thought likely that the date is intended to be, not Good Friday 1300 (8 April), but 25 March, the traditional date both of Christ's Incarnation and of his death, and the first day of the centenary year in the

Florentine calendar, which counted *ab Incarnatione* (cf. *Par.* xvi. 34–9).[75] The convergence of these exceptionally important centenary and religious events at the very source of the *Comedy* gives universal Christian, moral, and exemplary significance to the figure of Dante in his own poem and to his long journey from the dark wood, down into hell and then up through Purgatory to the living forest of the earthly Paradise, and thence to heaven and enjoyment of the fruits of the Redemption of all mankind. Dante makes his journey when the whole world should have been passing from darkness to hope, from death to resurrection, from sin to renewal in a new century.

If the world did not take this path, Dante himself did so, for the *Comedy* is the story of his journey from crisis to renewal, set in the centenary year of pardon, Jubilee, and the hope of a new age. After descending from the dark wood into hell, Dante emerges to climb another hill, the mountain of Purgatory, under the guidance of the sun.[76] The *Purgatorio*, from the scene on the shore before dawn, through the regenerating dream of the eagle and the entry through the marvellous door into a realm of remission, liberty, and the refining of love leading to the earthly Paradise, is the *cantica* which describes the stages of this personal and exemplary renewal. This, as Dante finally states, with triple insistence on the word 'new', is the essence of the *Purgatorio*:

> Io ritornai da la santissima onda
> rifatto sí come piante novelle
> rinovellate di novella fronda,
>   puro e disposto a salire a le stelle   (*Purg.* xxxiii.
> 142–5)

(I came away from that most sacred water, remade just as new plants renewed with new leaves, pure and prepared to ascend to the stars).

3. Dante's Two Journeys

On these three ever deeper levels, therefore, the symbolism of the year 1300 underlies the whole poem and, in a special way, the essential doctrines and imagery of the *Purgatorio*. Through the themes of pardon, liberation, and renewal, it can also be seen as a final unifying feature which draws together the universal and the personal elements, the theological, the moral, and the reforming aspects of the symbols of the three steps, the threshold, the angel bearing one sword and dressed in penitential garb, the rite of admission, and the keys which open a marvellous door to a true city and a new Church.

However, since an open-ended conclusion has been promised, it is legitimate to apply a little more logic to our hypothesis. If the assumption that *Purg.* ix contains Jubilee symbolism is correct, it is possible to formulate two further speculations, each of which is supported by other evidence, internal and external, though unfortunately always circumstantial. It is comparatively easy to connect the symbolism of the year 1300 with the Dante who is the protagonist of his own poem. Writing in later years, he looks back to that unusual and important year and requires his reader to make the necessary associations between it and his journey. What has never been done, and probably never can be done with certainty, is to establish a clear and direct link between the universal event and the personal life of Dante, not in later years, but at that particular time. Most people agree, tacitly perhaps and always on circumstantial evidence, that somehow the *Comedy* was born, not just from Dante's political experiences but also from his spiritual and moral situation in that Jubilee year, and that one important religious experience— more important in the basic pattern of the poem than the crisis in Florence or Dante's service as a Prior—was a pilgrimage to Rome sometime during the year. This experience can then be seen to underpin the general use of pilgrimage symbolism in the poem as a whole and in Purgatory in particular (*Purg.* ii. 63; viii. 1–6; xxiii. 16–21; xxvii. 109–11; xxxiii. 77–8).

There are thus two connected lines of enquiry. Firstly, since the *Comedy* is set, not on 1 May, nor on any other date critical in Florentine history, nor during Dante's Priorate, but around the end of March or the beginning of April in the year 1300, we may well be intrigued to know where Dante was at the time in the Jubilee year which he afterwards chose in which to encapsulate his life's experiences and provide a synopsis of his spiritual conversion. And secondly, it is perhaps of greater importance still to decide if Dante's spiritual conversion, as described in the poem, rests upon his experiences at the time of his Jubilee pilgrimage or if it was elaborated in later years, and specifically in and through the poem, or if indeed both these possibilities are in their different ways true.

*		*		*

The first line of enquiry, therefore, consists in examining any evidence for identifying the time of Dante's pilgrimage to Rome in 1300. It need hardly be said that, if it could be established with even the remotest degree of conviction that Dante was in Rome at the very time in which the *Comedy* is set innumerable threads in the pattern and imagery of the poem would be drawn together in a virtually indissoluble unity. Such a hypothesis might thus merit the sympathetic treatment of a proposition which, if not incontrovertibly demonstrated, is at least *ben trovato*.

As has been seen, the Bull *Antiquorum* was promulgated just before the beginning of Lent 1300. It invited non-Romans to visit Rome for fifteen days in order to claim the centenary plenary indulgence available at the shrines of the Apostles. The *Comedy* is set at the end of Lent, during the great religious festivals of that year, and at the time which for a Florentine would have been the start of the centenary year. The most direct clue in the poem to the possibility that Dante made his pilgrimage to Rome during this same, uniquely important period of the year arises from the tenses which he uses in his one direct reference to the Jubilee.[1] In describing the *bolgia* of the seducers and the procurers, he says that the two groups of sinners were moving in opposite directions:

dal mezzo in qua ci venien verso 'l volto,
di là con noi, ma con passi maggiori,
   come i Roman per l'essercito molto,
l'anno del giubileo, su per lo ponte
hanno a passar la gente modo colto,
   che da l'un lato tutti hanno la fronte
verso 'l castello e vanno a Santo Pietro,
da l'altra sponda vanno verso 'l monte
                              (*Inf.* xviii. 26–33)

(from the middle to this side, they were coming towards us; on the
other side, they were going in the same direction but with longer
strides; just as, because of the great multitude, in the year of the
Jubilee, the Romans have chosen a way of letting the people pass
over the bridge, for on one side they are all facing the castle and
going to St. Peter's, while on the other side they are going towards
the mountain).

In the middle of a passage written entirely in the *passato
remoto* and the imperfect, Dante changes abruptly to the
passato prossimo and the present, and so, whether deliberately
or unconsciously, he greatly heightens the immediacy of the
simile. He seems, in fact, to be referring to the crowds which
are flocking across the Ponte Sant'Angelo at the very same
time as he is visiting hell. Thus the crowds described are the
particularly great hosts of pilgrims who were in Rome for the
end of Lent in 1300. But since the realism and impact of the
whole simile depend upon Dante's desire to evoke graphically
a scene which he once witnessed, then if he saw that particular
'great multitude' and later remembered it so vividly, he must
have been there at that time too.

   If the episode of the door of Purgatory is now taken to
contain a less direct personal reference to Dante's participation
in the Jubilee, or a literary re-elaboration of it, then in the
colour of the angel's robe, in the public penance of exclusion
imposed on the souls in Antepurgatory, and perhaps also in
the seven signs of penance, another possible link can be traced
in Dante's mind between the Jubilee and the season of Lent,
and this explains why his picture of a repentant pastor and a
Church suffering for its sins in the centenary year is frequently
associated with various penitential texts and the liturgy of
Lent and Holy Week.[2] Moreover, since the angel who presides

over this rite of remission is an idealization of the Pope, and since in the scene Dante throws himself at the 'holy feet' of a truly spiritual vicar of St. Peter, it seems most natural to assume that Dante's memory of the Jubilee included also the sight of the worldly Boniface VIII receiving the homage of the faithful, and Dante himself may even have participated in the ceremony. Yet if Dante did see Boniface VIII during his pilgrimage to Rome in 1300, then he must have gone there either before Easter or at the end of the year, after his own Priorate and the other fateful events of that summer. Boniface in fact left for Anagni after the Easter festivities of the Jubilee year and did not return to Rome until October.[3]

The episode of the door, therefore, may well involve a blending of the themes of Jubilee and pilgrimage with that of Lent, and this would be a further enriching not only of the polysemy of the episode but also of its polemical intention. From these elements it can be inferred that for Dante Purgatory, which above the door consists in sevenfold penance and expiation, with prayers, psalms, rituals, and the whole liturgy of the Church Suffering, resembles and is the model for the season of Lent in an ideal earthly Church. In this way, the Church of Purgatory and the angel, its reformed 'Pope', might be an *exemplum* and an implicit polemic against the worldliness of the earthly Church and Boniface VIII during the great pilgrimage year of 1300, and specifically in the penitential season of Lent in that year. Again, this would involve assuming that Dante actually witnessed the divergence between the ideals and the reality of Lenten penances in the year of universal pardon.

The suggestion that Dante was in Rome towards the end of Lent, that is, around the end of March 1300, is not a new one,[4] but it is strange that the significance of this possibility with regard to the setting of the *Comedy* has been so generally ignored. The evidence has, of course, been slight, but now this study of *Purg.* ix has brought forward extra reasons for seeing the themes of Rome, the Papacy, the Jubilee, pilgrimage, and the season of Lent at the heart of the *Comedy*. Beneath these themes lies the fundamental model of the Exodus and the Redemption, commemorated by the principal festivals of the end of Lent, and with them can also be associated the important theme of Spring, the time of renewal, as presented at the beginning of the poem and in its two goals, the earthly Paradise and the heavenly (*Inf.* i. 37–43; *Purg.* xxviii. 143; *Par.* xxviii. 115–17). From being lost in a dark wood in Spring 1300, Dante travels to a living forest of perpetual Spring in the garden of Eden and then to the 'garden of the eternal gardener' (*Inf.* i. 1–6; *Purg.* xxviii. 1–2; *Par.* xxvi. 64–5).

Hitherto, it has been assumed that Dante made his Jubilee pilgrimage to Rome either just before Easter or at the end of the year, and that of these two possibilities the former is more likely. As Cosmo says, 'we may logically suppose that his pilgrimage took place before he assumed office'.[5] Indeed, shortly after Easter, during the Priorate of Lapo Saltarelli, the break between Rome and White Guelph Florence widened considerably, and the hostility and tension increased during the year, with the brawling on 1 May, the mission of the Cardinal of Acquasparta, and the events of Dante's own Priorate of June to August.[6] During their Priorates both Lapo and Dante earned the hatred of the Papal and Black Guelph factions, and in Dante's case this would seem to make a visit to Rome before Easter more likely than one later in the year.

Lapo Saltarelli was a Prior just before Dante took office. His name figures prominently on the same list of exiles as Dante's in 1302. It has, in fact, been suggested that Dante was in Rome at the same time as the Florentine embassy to the Pope in the second half of March and early April 1300, an embassy which included Lapo Saltarelli and other prominent White Guelphs.[7] Even though Lapo was a leader in the Florentine resistance to Boniface's ambitions in 1300, Dante's later judgement on him, shared also by Dino Compagni, is unreservedly hostile.[8] In the *Paradiso*, by contrasting him with Cincinnatus and by linking his name with that of a lady of accommodating manners and ill repute, Dante condemns Lapo's notorious venality and political corruption in terms which reveal the poet's special bitterness against a man who was an influential colleague in the year 1300 (*Par.* xv. 128). It is not impossible that Dante, whose political destiny, in terms of office, accusations of corruption, and exile, was so linked with Lapo's, but whose moral integrity and spiritual destiny were so different, was in Rome at about the same time in 1300.

This fascinating convergence of internal and external evidence does at least suggest the possibility that, on hearing of the proclamation of the Jubilee at the beginning of Lent, Dante decided to make his pilgrimage coincide with the Passiontide and the Florentine New Year. Officially or unofficially, he may have been there at the same time as the Florentine mission. All this would place the time of Dante's pilgrimage around the end of March, from about 25 March to Easter Sunday (10 April). In this way, his required fifteen days would include the Florentine New Year and all the major anniversaries and religious festivals of the end of Lent. This experience would then have provided him with strong personal motives in later years for choosing this period of this particular year as the setting for his poem of spiritual pilgrimage. Moreover, this part of the centenary year was not only critical for Florence and for Dante, but it was also still in and towards the end of his own thirty-fifth year. Thus the journey of which the goal and half-way point was Rome, undertaken to gain the life-giving pardon made available to all mankind, for once in each man's lifetime, during the centenary, still coincided exactly with his own situation, 'half-way through the journey of our life' (*Inf.* i. 1).

Another consequence of this hypothesis is that it ceases to be particularly important to establish whether Dante means to imply that his journey into hell begins on 25 March or on Good Friday, since the setting of the poem becomes an 'ideal time', based upon a real period of time in which both anniversaries of the Crucifixion were commemorated. The existence of this 'ideal time' might also explain another curious anomaly, which once upon a time led some critics to place the setting of the poem in 1301 rather than in 1300. This possibility, at which Boccaccio hints, is based upon astronomical details and on the improbability of Dante making such an elementary mistake as to regard the year 1300 as the first year of the new century rather than as the last of the old.[9] It thus seemed more logical to suppose that the *Comedy* is set around 25 March or Eastertide in the year 1301, that is, at the true moment of passing from one century to another in the Florentine calendar. This theory can easily be disproved by such facts as the death of Guido Cavalcanti, still alive at the time of the journey described in the poem (*Inf*. x. 111), but dead by the end of August 1300. Also, when Boniface VIII closed the Jubilee on Christmas Day 1300, he specifically and perhaps with deliberate hostility forbade that it should be extended to the following March, reckoning *ab Incarnatione* 'according to some' (i.e. the Florentines),[10] so that the reference in the episode of Casella to the Jubilee indulgences made available to all at the mouth of the Tiber for the past three months would simply not apply if Dante's journey were set in March 1301.[11] Yet in choosing his ideal period for the poem and in basing it on his experiences at the end of Lent 1300, Dante might well have noticed a strange anomaly, and this could account for the ambiguity of some of the astronomical references which has led to this double controversy on the date of Dante's journey.

Dante may in fact be aiming to create not only an 'ideal time' but also an 'ideal astronomy' precisely because he was aware of a contradiction in that centenary year between the Roman calendar and the Florentine. The matter is a little complicated. The Roman populace, which in effect declared the Jubilee, dated it *a Circumcisione*, i.e. from 1 January 1300;[12] Florentines would have dated it *ab Incarnatione*, i.e. from 25 March 1300; Boniface VIII, however, firmly dated it *a Nativitate*, from 25 December 1299, to 25 December 1300, which is the dating 'according to the rite of the Roman Church', not to be extended to the following March.[13] If one considers these facts, it is clear that in a calendar which reckons *ab Incarnatione* the centenary in terms of religious anniversaries really began on 25 March 1299, and ended on the same day in 1300. Or, to put it another way, Boniface's authoritative proclamation of the Jubilee pardon for the centenary year from the nativity of Christ, 1299, would by the same reckoning mean that the year which began in Florence on 25 March 1300, the anniversary of Christ's conception, was in religious terms really 1301. In these respects also, Dante's choice of setting for the poem can be seen to reflect an amalgamation of dates associated with the centenary and the principal mysteries of the Redemption. This also indicates that in some special way the period from 25 March to Easter in the year 1300 held a personal significance for him.

The main problem in supporting such speculations is that the

Comedy is not an autobiography but a universal poem. Dante did not consider it legitimate for a poet to talk about himself directly (*V.N.* xxviii; *Conv.* I. ii. 2; *Purg.* xxx. 62–3), and all the personal references in the poem are absorbed into a higher and more extensive scheme. This is what happens to Beatrice, especially at the moment of her apotheosis and appearance in triumph in the procession in the earthly Paradise, and even the highly personal theme of Dante's own exile is projected as an *exemplum* of the contingent elements in God's plan for men, as a general pattern of the relationship between the vicissitudes of fortune and the spiritual and, in this case, poetic destiny of the individual (*Par.* xvii. 13–27, 37–45, 94–9, 106–42). Thus we know a lot about Dante as a man, as a thinker, and as a poet, but little about the details of his life. If he was in Rome at the time he later chose for the setting of his poem, the last thing we would in fact expect would be that he would say so directly in that poem. However, from the *Vita nuova* we know that Dante's technique as regards the people, the places, the events, and even the spiritual experiences of his personal life was to blur them, to render them indeterminate, and so to capture their symbolic and universal essence. If we extend this principle, applied on a more complex level and in accordance with the technique of polysemy, to the *Comedy*, it follows that any personal references will have been chosen deliberately for their symbolic meaning, for Dante's inspiration is rarely, if ever, random, but that at the same time they will appear in oblique and indeterminate forms.

Now we know that the *Comedy* opens with Dante in danger of death 'su la fiumana ove 'l mar non ha vanto' (on the river where the sea cannot boast) (*Inf.* ii. 108). This highly elliptical phrase gives us, in some way or other, the topographical setting for the beginning of the poem. Boccaccio interprets the 'fiumana' as the rising waters of a river, more impetuous and dangerous than the sea.[14] However, in Dante, in Compagni, and in Boccaccio himself, the word 'fiumana' means merely 'river' and has pleasant connotations.[15] It seems likely, therefore, that Dante's phrase, 'su la fiumana', rather than meaning 'on [i.e. in] the flood' could equally and perhaps more accurately be interpreted as 'on the river', in the usual sense of 'on the bank of the river'. Benvenuto interprets 'fiumana' in this way and suggests that the whole phrase refers to the Acheron, which has no outlet to the sea. Boccaccio, though interpreting the phrase in a moral allegorical sense, sees it also as a topographical reference, for he says that this river is the 'horrible place where the author was attacked by the beasts'.[16] All this indicates that Dante, lost in the dark wood, is by some river to which he gives moral significance as a river where death threatens him, a river which is thematically linked with the dangerous, mortal waters of *Inf*. i. 22–7 and with the evil bank of the Acheron, river of death and damnation (*Inf*. iii. 107–8, 127). That it cannot actually be the Acheron is clear from the narrative of the beginning of the journey; only after his entry through the gate of hell and his encounter with the *ignavi* does Dante see the Acheron 'further on' (*Inf*. iii. 70–1).

The river where the poem begins can also be given symbolic meanings, as a river of sin or spiritual death, or as the baptismal Jordan of Dante's *descensus* and death to sin.[17] This last theory, which is Freccero's, means that the 'fiumana' is a real river, the Jordan, greater than Oceanus, to be interpreted as a symbol of Exodus and Baptism. Freccero's approach to the problem offers the only satisfactory way to a solution. If Dante is referring to a real river, which is then to be treated allegorically or symbolically, then the meaning may be obscure, but the poetic method and the phraseology are perfectly intelligible, logical, and typical of Dante. If, however, the phrase refers solely to a symbol of sin, evil, etc., it raises a host of problems and becomes on all levels quite impenetrable.

Firstly, why does Dante use the symbol of a river, whether in flood or not, for evil in the world? There is perhaps nothing against this if it is taken in isolation, but in fact the metaphor is immediately rendered unclear, as Benvenuto's comments show, by being duplicated in the symbolism attached to what is presented as a real river in the afterlife, the Acheron. Secondly, if the word 'fiumana' is taken as a pure metaphor, then what precisely is the meaning of the phrase 'ove 'l mar non ha vanto' (where the sea cannot boast)? The critics imply that the reference is to the real sea, which may threaten physical death but is less dangerous than sin and spiritual death. In this case, however, the relationship between a metaphorical danger (the river) and a real danger (the sea) becomes unclear, and the death which threatens Dante also becomes ambiguous, even though the context requires that it must be spiritual rather than, indeed as opposed to, physical death. In this sense, too, both the 'fiumana' and the sea become metaphors for danger, not for sin or evil, and the duplication of this metaphor could have been avoided by a phrase equivalent to 'in dangers worse than those of the sea'. However, as will be seen shortly, there is no justification in the text for introducing the idea of danger here, and in any case to say that spiritual damnation is worse than drowning at sea is, to put it mildly, rather trite. Thirdly, if it is now assumed that the sea is not the real sea but another metaphor, then what does it signify? It might symbolize something enormously evil, though in evilness inferior to the 'fiumana', but in this case the sea of moral evil duplicates the symbol of the river of moral evil; they are the same, but not equally the same, and there is no further basis for comparing the two. The sea becomes a sort of indeterminate nineteenth-century sea in which Dante would find drowning, not infinitely sweet, as did Leopardi in his sea,[18] but almost infinitely bitter in some obscure way, though falling just short of the bitterness of eternal damnation. In this interpretation, the phrase, 'ove 'l mar non ha vanto', is vague and purely rhetorical; it merely pads out the symbol of the river of great evil. Alternatively, and more logically, the opposition between the river and the sea implies that, if the river symbolizes evil, the sea symbolizes goodness, which cannot boast of any power over unrepented mortal sin, spiritual damnation, etc. Once again the relationship between the two metaphors becomes unclear; there is no obvious indication that the sea is to be interpreted as a symbol of good, and most readers of the *Comedy* would probably agree that, had Dante wished to convey this meaning, he would have written, 'on the river where grace, or love, or virtue, have no power'.

In other words, if both the river and the sea are metaphors, the result is either vague or repetitive. A metaphorical sea casts doubt upon the interpretation of the metaphor of the river, and vice versa. To break this vicious circle, one must presume that the sea is not a metaphor but the real sea, and in that case other problems arise which cast doubt upon the premiss that the river is purely a metaphor, and it becomes perfectly legitimate to ask: if a real sea, why not a real river? As Freccero says, 'a totally satisfying explanation would have to account for both the river and the sea on the same plane of reality'.[19] This is in fact the simplest of all solutions: the sea is the real sea, and the river is a real river, which Dante is using for the purposes of his allegory. Thus the reference to his own fight with death on its banks becomes some form of disguised, universalized, or allegorized personal allusion, and in order to identify this, all that remains is to identify the river—whether it is the Jordan or the Arno or some other river—by means of the phrase, 'ove 'l mar non ha vanto'. In this way, this curious, enigmatic allusion would have an initial literal meaning upon which the allegorical meanings depend, and its obscurity could have been deliberately designed to conceal a personal reference and to allow of further polysemy in its significance and interpretation.

The phrase is clearly an example of hyperbole, and it has a classical, almost Virgilian, ring. The precise meaning of this reference to some river 'where the sea cannot boast' is elusive, but there are three interconnected ways in which it can most naturally be read: as 'the river where the sea has no power'; as 'the greatest or proudest of waters'; and as 'the river which surpasses Oceanus', the 'sea which encircles the earth' (*Par.* ix. 84), and therefore 'the sea' by antonomasia.[20] Taking all these possible literal meanings together, there is only one river which Dante could, without ambiguity, call the safest, the greatest, and the proudest, the one which surpasses Oceanus.

In the first place, the obvious possibility that the 'river where the sea cannot boast' is primarily a safe river, a haven for sailors who have braved the perils of the deep, undoubtedly recalls the voyage of Aeneas to Italy (*Inf.* i. 106–8; ii. 13–27, 32), and in particular Juno's complaint that, though she has persecuted the Trojans over the whole sea, now 'they are hidden in the longed-for bed of the Tiber, safe from the sea and from me (*securi pelagi atque mei*)'.[21] So, of all the rivers known to Dante and his first readers, it is the Tiber, where Aeneas found shelter after all the dangers of the sea, which would best qualify for the description, 'where the sea has no

power'. Since, as has been seen, the metaphorical interpretations of the line involve seeing the river and the sea as
symbols of danger, it is clear that the most obvious meaning of
the phrase, 'ove 'l mar non ha vanto', excludes this entirely.
However, since Dante is indubitably in danger on the banks of
this river, it is perhaps worth noting that this opposite view of
the Tiber, not as safe but as more dangerous than the sea, also
occurs in Virgil, when the Sibyl addresses Aeneas as the man
who has undergone 'the great perils of the sea', adding, 'but
graver perils remain on land . . . I see wars, horrid wars, and
the Tiber foaming with much blood.'[22]

Secondly, as a consequence of the fact that it was a haven
for Aeneas, the Tiber is also described by Virgil as 'the river
which is the king of waters', 'the stream which is most pleasing
to heaven', the site of the greatest of cities, and thus, histori-
cally, the greatest and proudest of rivers.[23]

Finally, and above all, from the banks of the 'sacred Tiber'
spreads the great Roman Empire, which covers the earth and
which is bounded only by what Dante himself calls 'the useless
waves of Oceanus' (*Ep*. vii. 3; xi. 10–11; cf. also *Mon*. I. xi).[24]

If, therefore, *Inf*. ii. 108 is interpreted as meaning 'on the
banks of the Tiber', the phrase 'where the sea cannot boast'
becomes a marvellous example of connected layers of polysemy, moving from the simplest geographical and nautical
sense (the Tiber as safe from the sea) to a more literary and
hyperbolical sense (the Tiber as the greatest of waters) and
finally to elevation as an erudite classical allusion (the Tiber as
more important than Oceanus). What is more, the possibility
then arises that the word 'fiumana' is itself polysemous.
Although its basic meaning is 'river', as noted above, Dante
may also have wished to convey the idea of a torrential or
flooding river, and in this case the reference could still be to
the Tiber. According to Stefaneschi, Rome in 1300 had sufficient food for three months, but the 'unexpected influx of
pilgrims (*inopinus romipetarum concursus*)' brought the threat
of a food-shortage, and fears were increased when the Tiber
overflowed its banks a little. It is difficult to determine exactly
when this happened. The indications certainly point to some
time between March and May, and possibly around Easter,
for, after describing the solution of the problem with a good

harvest and the October rains, Stefaneschi seems to return to the question of the food-shortage when he says that the feast of Easter fell 'inter hec', i.e. 'in the meanwhile' or 'while these things were going on'.[25]

It is outside the scope of this study to investigate all the Roman associations of the beginning of the poem. Suffice it to note here that they include the contrast between the dark wood and the forest where Aeneas found the golden bough; the well-known theory that the wolf represents not only avarice but also papal Rome; the appearance of Virgil, poet of the Roman Empire, to save Dante from death on the banks of the river; and the definition of Aeneas' journey as the seal put by God on his mission to found Rome, the city of the Empire and of the See of Peter, together with the resultant image of Dante as a second Aeneas and of his mission as providential too, perhaps even specifically orientated towards the restoration of Rome's values as Empire and as true Church (*Inf*. ii. 13–27). All these would be confirmed by this hypothesis and identification of the mysterious river on whose banks Dante fought with death and where the poem begins. So too would be brought together at the very beginning of the poem two fundamental themes, of a journey and of Rome, and the journey itself, 'in the middle of the road of our life', ends in the dark wood on the banks of the Tiber and is replaced by 'another journey', willed by heaven like those of Aeneas and St. Paul, with Virgil through hell to Purgatory and the true 'door of St. Peter' (*Inf*. i. 1–3, 29, 35, 91–3, 112–20, 134; cf. also ii. 5, 13–36, 63, 120, 142).

If the literal narrative of the *Comedy* begins with Dante facing spiritual death on the banks of the Tiber, which is therefore symbolically an evil and sinful river, the poem makes it clear why, in order to conquer this evil, he must first cross another river, the real river of death, both physical and spiritual, the Acheron, and enter into hell, passing in *Inf*. ix through gates associated with heresy into the corrupt city and anti-Church of Lucifer. Then, on his emergence from hell, he learns of the Tiber under its good aspect as the divinely appointed centre of the earthly Church and as, in fact, the opposite of the Acheron, for now it is the river to which the souls of the saved travel on their way to Purgatory (*Purg*. i. 88;

ii. 103–5; xxv. 79–87). The Tiber as the river of sin and death in *Inf*. ii is 'redeemed' as the river of salvation in *Purg*. ii. In the same way, the gate of heresy and deliberate 'malizia' in *Inf*. ix is contrasted with the door of a true Church in *Purg*. ix, so that the lost 'diritta via' of *Inf*. i. 3 becomes the straight path to God up the crooked ways of the sunlit mountain (*Purg*. x. 3; cf. *Inf*. i. 18). Thus the possible presence of an oblique autobiographical reference at the beginning of the *Inferno* would establish a pattern of symbolism and universal reference for the rest of the poem. Dante's journey from Florence to Rome at the end of Lent 1300 is transformed, in the poem, into a journey first to hell and only afterwards to salvation.

*   *   *

This leads us to the second speculation, which can be taken in conjunction with the first one or independently. In a sense, it is perhaps more important, for it involves not just a hypothesis on a detail of Dante's life, but a fundamental question which underlies the rationale of the whole poem and of that Roman pilgrimage which, whenever he made it or considered making it, seems to have been in Dante's mind when writing the poem in later years. Ozanam deduces from the Jubilee symbolism in *Purg*. ix that Dante's pilgrimage to Rome in 1300 was a turning-point in his spiritual life, that the indulgence he gained marked the moment of his repentance, conversion, and re-generation and in this way became the stimulus for the writing of the poem. No one can deny this possibility except to point out that the opposite proposition is at least equally likely, if not more so. There is, moreover, an intermediate position: that Dante's Jubilee pilgrimage heightened his religious sense and, at the same time, his indignation against Boniface VIII.[26]

The *Comedy* is not in fact a poem which begins in darkness some time after the death of Beatrice in 1290 and reaches its resolution with the spiritual benefits which Dante acquired at the Jubilee of 1300. It is set wholly during the Passiontide and Easter of the latter year. This is the period, not of Dante's conversion, but of his crisis. This is the time when he is lost in the dark wood, attempting to climb a sunlit hill. In the Passion-tide of the Jubilee year, which was also his own thirty-fifth year, he finds himself and the world in darkness, fear, mortal bitterness, sleep, and falsehood (*Inf.* i. 1–12). Thus the poem begins, and upon this initial crisis the rest of the poem depends. Such a prologue can hardly be called a description of a man recalling his own religious conversion through a visit to a holy city, and setting his story at a time when that holy city was devoutly celebrating important religious festivals in a year of universal plenary Pardon.

There is enough evidence to suggest that a visit to Rome in 1300 would have had a profoundly negative effect on such a man as Dante. No Florentine White Guelph would have been favourably impressed by the sight of a Pope who was openly intriguing with the Blacks against their city.[27] Indeed, Dante shows that he was fully aware of Boniface's machinations precisely at the time in which the poem is set, around Easter-time in 1300, and later he was to see how this particular period of papal intrigue was to lead to his own exile. Ciacco prophesies to him that within three years the Blacks will prevail, 'with the force of one who is manœuvring now (*con la forza di tal che testé piaggia*)', and Cacciaguida also tells him that his exile is already being plotted by someone in Rome, the city of simony, 'where Christ is bartered all day long' (*Inf.* vi. 67–9; *Par.* xvii. 49–51). Especially at Eastertime, therefore, only a fortnight before Boniface's counter-attack to Lapo Saltarelli's more or less open denunciation of the Pope's intrigues against Florence, the Whites had ample cause to view the man, his motives, his ambitions, and indeed the whole city of Rome with deep suspicion.

There were other grounds too, besides the political, for reacting against Rome in that year. Giovanni Villani says that on his pilgrimage he saw 'Rome in her decline' and makes a special point of mentioning the vast wealth which the Church accumulated through the Jubilee.[28] Villani's impressions of the glories of ancient Rome were a stimulus to his sense of history, but his impressions of contemporary Rome were undoubtedly negative, for, he says, he then returned home to write, not about decadent Rome, but about rising Florence— a contrast which Dante also makes, giving it a further anti-Florentine twist, in *Par.* xv. 109–11. Indeed, Villani, when writing this chapter as a sort of second prologue to his

Chronicle may well be following Dante in his mention of his Jubilee pilgrimage as a negative inspiration for his work, and in condemning at this point the avarice of Rome.[29]

All that is known of Dante's opinions on avarice, on Rome, and on Boniface VIII indicates that he would have deeply disapproved when, during the Jubilee, a time for dispensing spiritual riches, he saw vast amounts of money being collected, even by priests with rakes, at the shrines of St. Peter and St. Paul, saints who came to Rome 'thin and barefoot, begging their food from any house' (*Par.* xxi. 127–9). If he was actually in Rome for Holy Week itself in 1300, he would have seen the Pope, not doing penance, nor recalling the Passion and Resurrection of Christ with true devotion, but using the occasion to celebrate the knighting of his nephew.[30] Dante would probably have felt the same disgust as Jacopone da Todi, who describes the scene in these words of bitter condemnation addressed to Boniface VIII:

> O pessima avarizia,—sete enduplicata,
> bever tanta pecunia,—non esser saziata;
> non ce pensavi, misero,—a cui l'hai congregata:
> ché tal la t'ha robbata—che non te era en pensiere.
>
> La settimana santa,—che onom stava en planto,
> mandasti tua fameglia—per Roma andar al salto,
> lance andar rompendo,—facendo danza e canto;
> penso ch'en molto afranto—Dio te degia punire.
>
> Entro per santo Petro—e per Sancta sanctoro
> mandaste tua fameglia—facendo danza e coro:
> li peregrini tutti—scandalizati fuoro,
> maledicendo tuo oro—e te e tuo cavalliere.[31]

(O most wretched avarice, doubled thirst, drinking up so much money without ever being sated. Wretch, you did not think for whom you were amassing it, for one you did not think of has stolen it from you.

In Holy Week, while everyone was mourning, you sent your household skipping through Rome, jousting with lances, dancing and singing. I believe that God must punish you with great affliction.

Between St. Peter's and the 'Holy of Holies' [in the Lateran], you sent your household, dancing and singing. All the pilgrims were scandalized and cursed your gold and you and your knight).

If, when writing *Purg.* ix in the context of Lent and Easter in the year 1300, Dante had in mind the theology of authentic plenary indulgences, the real meaning of the Hebrew Jubilee, and the theme of renewal in a new century, mixed in his memory with such scandalous scenes of worldliness, avarice, and irreligion at the heart of the Church, then the full contrast and polemic implicit in the episode can easily be established. The angel-doorkeeper, with the sword of spiritual power alone, in poor and penitential garb, is the vicar of St. Peter whom Dante did not see in the Rome of Boniface VIII. The 'holy feet' at which Dante makes his submission are not those objects of homage which Boniface used to exploit his office, and which are therefore destined to writhe and burn in hell in the *bolgia* of the simoniacs (*Inf.* xix. 52–7, 76–8; *Par.* xxx. 148). The door which the angel opens with his perfect keys does not lead to the worldly treasure amassed by a Pope who claimed to be also Caesar, but it is built on a priceless rock and leads to a treasury greater than Caesar's, the eternal treasures of Purgatory and Paradise. In other words, the spiritual pardon which the angel administers is that which Dante failed to gain on his pilgrimage to venal Rome in 1300.

When, in later years, in his poem, Dante emerges from hell to Purgatory on Resurrection Day and enters through the door of pardon on the following morning, this is his journey of escape by 'another way' (*Inf.* i. 91–3), the spiritual journey which he did not make in Rome in the Jubilee year of 1300, but the one he elaborated later as an alternative path leading out of the dark wood of that Passiontide in the Jubilee year. Prevented from reaching the sunlit hill in the Lent of the year 1300, he travels in his poem to another mountain, and his climbing of this mountain is both a spiritual ascent of the mountain of true pardon and a poetic conquest of the Christian Mount Parnassus (cf. *Purg.* xxviii. 139–41; xxix. 40; xxxi. 141; *Par.* i. 16–17). In the course of this ascent, Dante passes through an important stage in his narrative, in his spiritual pilgrimage, and in his poetic development, when, carried up to it by Lucia, he enters through a sacred door to claim—for the first, but with the help of Beatrice and Mary not the last, time (*Par.* xxxi. 85–90; xxxiii. 34–9)—the imperishable and inalienable treasures of a restored Rome and of a truly spiritual Church.

Notes

1 For summaries of this tradition, see *La Divina Commedia*, ed. G. A. Scartazzini, Leipzig, 1875, vol. ii, in notes to the episode; D. Bulferetti, *La porta del Purgatorio dantesco*, Brescia, 1903, 48–55.

2 See especially *La Divina Commedia di Dante Alighieri col comento di G. M. Cornoldi*, Rome, 1887, note to *Purg.* ix. 115; J. S. Carroll, *Prisoners of Hope: An Exposition of Dante's 'Purgatorio'*, London, 1906; P. Ghignoni, 'Alla soglia del Purgatorio (canto IX)', *Il giornale dantesco*, xxiv (1921), 213–16; D. L. Sayers, *The Divine Comedy: Purgatory*, Penguin Books, 1955 (Introduction and notes); P. Conte, *Il canto IX del 'Purgatorio'* (Lectura Dantis Romana), Turin, 1965; E. Raimondi, 'Analisi strutturale e semantica del canto IX del *Purgatorio*', *Studi danteschi*, xlv (1968), 121–46 (see also id., *Metafora e storia*, Turin, 1970, 95–122).

3 A. Momigliano (*La Divina Commedia*, Florence, notes to *Purg.* ix. 70–2, 100–2, 103–5) is ambiguous: the episode is a 'preambolo solenne, il quale . . . è, se non poesia, utile accorgimento retorico', and the somewhat 'baroque' imagery of the steps is an example of 'la freddezza della minuta allusione allegorica'; on the other hand, 'questa seconda parte del canto è d'inusitata altezza', 'una delle prove piú ardue superate dalla superba fantasia e dalla superba coscienza di Dante'. G. Lesca, *Il canto IX del 'Purgatorio'* (Lectura Dantis), Florence, 1919, does his best to see some 'poetry' in the episode, whilst K. Vossler, *Medieval Culture: An Introduction to Dante and his Times*, transl. W. C. Lawton, London, 1929, 319–20, who uses the word 'presumably' of the sacramental interpretation, prefers to see the symbols of *Purg.* ix as mysteries, veils, ambiguous and obscure, but picturesque and brilliant.

4 J. D. Sinclair, *The Divine Comedy: Purgatorio*, Oxford, 1971, 128–9.

5 See G. Di Pino's *lectura* in *Nuove letture dantesche*, Florence, vol. iv (1970), 35–56.

6 See especially C. S. Singleton, '*In Exitu Israel de Aegypto*', in J. Freccero (ed.), *Dante: A Collection of Critical Essays*, Englewood Cliffs, 1965, 102–21; also, for additional points, L. Ricci Battaglia, 'Polisemanticità e struttura della *Commedia*', *Giornale storico della letteratura italiana*, clii (1975), 161–98.

7 See G. Padoan, 'Il Limbo dantesco', in *Il pio Enea, l'empio Ulisse*, Ravenna, 1977, 103–24, with relevant references; E. Raimondi, 'Rito e storia nel I canto del *Purgatorio*', in *Metafora e storia*, 65–94; A. Pézard, 'Le chant premier du *Purgatoire*', in V. Vettori (ed.), *Letture del*

'*Purgatorio*', Milan, 1965, 29 ff.; M. Bambeck, 'Dantes Waschung mit dem Tau und Gürtung mit dem Schilf', *Romanistisches Jahrbuch*, xxi (1970), 75–92.

8 See F. Forti, 'Il dramma sacro della *mala striscia*', in *Magnanimitade: Studi su un tema dantesco*, Bologna, 1977, 83–101 (originally in *Giornale storico della letteratura italiana*, cxlvi, 1969, 481–96).

9 The close connection between public responsibility and private morality and piety was at the basis of medieval doctrines of the ideal king; see E. M. Peters, 'I principi negligenti di Dante e le concezioni medioevali del *rex inutilis*', *Rivista storica italiana*, lxxx (1968), 741–58.

10 *Inferno*, ed. N. Sapegno, Florence, 1955, note to *Inf.* viii.

11 Whether the Epistle is by Dante, as seems most likely, or not, its contemporary or near-contemporary evidence for the interpretation of the poem cannot be ignored.

12 *Par.* ii. 11; see also D. J. Ransom, '*Panis angelorum*: A Palinode in the *Paradiso*', *Dante Studies*, xcv (1977), 81–94; P. Armour, 'Matelda in Eden: The Teacher and the Apple', *Italian Studies*, xxxiv (1979), 13, n. 19.

13 The phrase 'andar dinanzi' implies that the reference here is to the angel-doorkeeper, into whose presence Dante must enter, rather than to the angel-boatman, who arrives more or less fortuitously at the time Dante is on the shore. But the two angels are closely connected, as will be seen, and both could be involved in this reference.

14 *Purg.* xxviii. 127–30; xxxi. 94–105; xxxiii. 91–9; cf. *Inf* xiv. 136–8. See also P. Armour, '*Purgatorio* XXVIII', in D. Nolan (ed.), *Dante Commentaries*, Dublin, 1977, 138; id., 'Matelda in Eden', 19, 21, 23.

15 See P. Armour, 'The Theme of Exodus in the First Two Cantos of the *Purgatorio*', in D. Nolan (ed.), *Dante Soundings*, Dublin, 1981, 59–99 (on 'anagogical' meaning 'ad superiora ducens', see p. 96, n. 16).

16 *S. Th. III Suppl.* Q.4, a.3, *contra*.

17 *S. Th. III.* Q.84, aa.2–3; Q.86, a.6, concl.; Q.90, a.1, ad 2.

18 Bulferetti (p. 72) realized this and offers a historical explanation.

19 See St. Albert, *Comm. in IV Sent.*, Dist. 17, A. a.1 (ed. Borgnet, xxix, 657 ff.); *S. Th. III.* Q.84, a.5; *III Suppl.* Q.6, a.1.

20 *S. Th. III Suppl.* Q.4, a.3, concl.

21 Ibid., resp.; ad 2.

22 Armour, 'The Theme of Exodus', 87.

23 See pp. 64–5.

24 F. Fergusson, *Dante's Drama of the Mind: A Modern Reading of the 'Purgatorio'*, Princeton, 1953 (repr. 1968), 42–3.

PART II: INVESTIGATIONS

1. *The Three Steps*

1 On the general possibility of irretrievable personal allusion and of multiple readings in the *Comedy*, see A. Vallone, 'Il Dante perduto', *L'Alighieri*, xi (1970), no. 2, 3–8.

2 St. Thomas uses the etymology of the word *con-tritio* as a metaphor for the breaking of the stony heart; to *con-tritio* (true sorrow) is contrasted *at-tritio* (imperfect sorrow due solely to fear of hell) (*S. Th. III Suppl.* Q.1, a.1, resp.; a.3; cf. also *S. Th. III.* Q.85, a.5).

3 Shame is principally a part of contrition; according to Chaucer's Parson, it is the first of the six causes which move a man to contrition ('Parson's Tale', 8). It is also an element in oral confession, indirectly associated with satisfaction also in that the shame of confessing one's sins diminishes the temporal punishment due to them (*S. Th. III Suppl.* Q.7, a.1, 4; Q.10, a.2). For Dante shame is a subsidiary aspect of the process of purgation from lust (*Purg.* xxvi. 81).

4 Though see also the anonymous *Chiose sopra Dante*, Florence, 1846, 338–41. The *Chiose Cagliaritane*, ed. E. Carrara, Città di Castello, 1902, dispense with sacramental contrition and confession and stress the element of satisfaction in the last two steps, following the recognition of sin (the first step) (p. 63).

5 Landino follows Buti in this analysis and self-contradiction; see *Comento di Christophoro Landino Fiorentino sopra la Comedia di Danthe Alighieri poeta fiorentino*, Florence, 1481, comm. to *Purg.* ix.

6 See Sapegno's notes to *Purg.* ix. 94, 98, 100, 103, 108.

7 G. Rossetti, *Comento analitico al 'Purgatorio' di Dante Alighieri*, ed. P. Giannantonio, Florence, 1967, 62.

8 Ibid., 65, 69–71. For another historical explanation (that the steps represent three stages in the history of man before Christ founded the Church), see *La Divina Commedia*, ed. C. H. Grandgent, revised by C. S. Singleton, Harvard, 1972, 389.

9 U. Foscolo, sonnet, 'A Firenze', line 6; *Dei sepolcri*, line 174.

10 M. F. Rossetti, *A Shadow of Dante*, London, 1894, 112.

11 J. Ruskin, *Modern Painters*, part v, cap. 8, par. 15, n.

12 See also Ghignoni, 213–14, and M. Scarpini, 'I gradini della porta del Purgatorio', *La Rassegna*, xlvii (1939), 199.

13 Domenico di Michelino, 'Dante and his Poem' (Florence, Duomo). See also P. Brieger, M. Meiss, and C. S. Singleton, *Illuminated Manuscripts of the 'Divine Comedy'*, Princeton, 1969, vol. ii, 352–5.

14 Biblioteca Laurenziana, MS Laur. Tempi, 1, c.32.

15 S. Aglianò, *lectura* of *Purg.* ix, in G. Getto (ed.), *Letture dantesche*, Florence, 1964, 864.

16 G. Fallani, *lectura* of *Purg.* ix, in *Lectura Dantis Scaligera: Purgatorio*, Florence, 1967, 300; see also id., *Dante poeta teologo*, Milan, 1965, 144–5. Compare *Enciclopedia dantesca*: 'Purgatorio' (the steps are three aspects of contrition after confession).

17 F. D'Ovidio, *Nuovi Studii Danteschi: Il 'Purgatorio' e il suo preludio*, Milan, 1906, 424, n.1 (on other elements in the episode, see 210–11, 322–7, 519–22). See also A. Franz, 'Dante zitiert. II', *Deutsches Dante-Jahrbuch*, xxix–xxx (1951), 49–50.

18 *Aen*, vi. 573 (for other reminiscences, see vi. 548–9, 552, 555–6, 569, 635–9).

19 Ezek. caps. 40–4, especially 40:2, 22; 43:1, 4, 25–6; 44:1–3.

20 Heb. 12:18–28.

21 *Chiose sopra Dante*, 338. E. Aroux, *Dante hérétique, révolutionnaire et socialiste*, Paris, 1854, 169, interpreted the steps as faith, hope, and charity; this is dismissed by Scartazzini (note to *Purg.* ix. 94), but see Raimondi, 'Analisi strutturale' (p. 139 and n.1) on Rabanus Maurus's interpretation of the Temple steps in Ezekiel, with regard to the 'merits of the virtues' and the *tres thalami* of faith, hope, and charity.

22 Compare Vellutello's explanation that the steps represent the three conditions required before entering the presence of a priest: purity of conscience, contrition, and the firm intention to reform (*La Comedia di Dante Alighieri con la nova espositione di Alessandro Vellutello*, Venice, 1544, comm. to *Purg.* ix). See also Bulferetti, 57–8; Ghignoni, 213–14; Scarpini, 198–9; Conte, 20–1; R. Dragonetti, *Dante pèlerin de la Sainte Face* (Romanica Gandensia, xi), Ghent, 1968, 147 and n. 1.

23 Prov. 18:17; cf. 2 Cor 13:5; Jas. 1:23–5. Compare Ariosto, *Orlando furioso*, x. 59 (on the diamond walls of the castle of Logistilla: 'mirando in esse,/l'uom sin in mezzo all'anima si vede;/vede suoi vizii e sue virtudi espresse,/. . . fassi, mirando allo specchio lucente/se stesso, conoscendosi, prudente'). See also Raimondi, 'Analisi strutturale', 140.

24 *Inf.* iii. 29; v. 89; vi. 10; vii. 103; cf. *Purg.* i. 129; xi. 30 (compare the liturgical phrase 'caligo peccatorum').

25 Ezek. 36:26; Luke 8:6; St. Ambrose, 'Prayer I before Mass'.

26 Pss. 101:5; 142:6.

27 Luke 11:24.

28 Joel 2:13.

29 Ps. 37:6; cf. also Isa. 1:6; Jer. 30:12.

30 Luke 11:17–18.

31 *Telluris alme conditor*, lines 9–10.

32 Pss. 50:5; 37:18–19; Rom. 7:22–5.

33 Chaucer ('Parson's Tale', 8–15) discusses these four motives for contrition, together with others which are also appropriate in the context of Dante's *Purgatorio*: disdain for sin, remembrance of good, and the hope of forgiveness, grace, and salvation.

34 *S. Th. III Suppl.* Q.6, a.1, ad 1; Q.7, a.1, 4; Q.10, a.2, concl.

35 *S. Th. III.* Q.85, a.5; *III Suppl.* Q.1, a.2, 2; a.3, concl.

36 *S. Th. III.* Q.85, a.5, resp.; *III Suppl.* Q.7, a.1, ad 2; Q.10, a.4, ad 1; Chaucer, 'Parson's Tale', 6, 11, 12.

37 Apart from 2 Macc. 12:46, the principal scriptural text concerning the existence of Purgatory was 1 Cor. 3:12–15, on the testing by fire of all men's works; this was glossed by St. Augustine and St. Gregory with the comment: 'in the same fire gold is reddened and straw is consumed; thus in the same fire the sinner is burnt and the saved soul is purged'; from this, St. Thomas concludes that the fires of hell and of Purgatory are contiguous (*S. Th. Appendix*, Q.2, aa.4–6; *Art. 2 de Purg*, a.2, *contra*; *III Suppl.* Q.15, a.2, ad 2). Since only four of the twenty or so distinct punishments in Dante's hell involve fire, it is clear that the contrast between the 'eternal fire' and the 'temporal fire' in *Purg.* xxvii. 127 requires the word 'foco' to be taken as a metaphor for punishment in general. For the theology of Purgatory, see *P.L.* ccxx, Index 130, cols. 249–56; also, as a general study, Fallani, *Dante poeta teologo*, 101–93.

38 *S. Th. III*. Q.87, a.2, resp.; *III Suppl*. Q.9, a.1; Q.14, aa.2–4.

39 Heb. 9:14, 22; Apoc. (Rev.) 22:14.

40 *Missale Romanum*, Prayer II before Mass.

41 For Ghignoni, sorrow gets its expiatory power from the Cross of Christ (the second step), and pardon comes from the merits of Christ's blood (the third step). Conte (p. 21), though missing an essential connection, correctly speaks of Christ's blood, 'sul quale poggia tutta la Chiesa militante e trionfante'.

42 Fallani in *Lectura Dantis Scaligera*, 301–2.

43 Ibid., 301. On solemn and public penance, see *S. Th. III Suppl*. Q.28; Chaucer ('Parson's Tale', 4) distinguishes three types of penance: solemn (imposed for infanticide and sins which caused public scandal, and consisting in being excluded from the church in Lent and performing public penance), common (enjoined on groups of people, as, for example, pilgrimages), and private (imposed in confession).

2. *The Angel-Doorkeeper*

1 Isa. 6:6–7.

2 *De coel. hier*. caps. 7, 13; *De div. nom*. cap. 4, par. 22 (*P.G.* iii. cols. 210, 230, 273–6 (note), 299 ff., 723–4; for John Scotus Erigena's transl., see *P.L.* cxxii, cols. 1052, 1061 ff., 1141).

3 *S. Th. Appendix*, Q.2, a.3, resp.; ed. of Nicolai, Sylvius, Billuart, and C.-J. Drioux, Paris, 17th ed., vol. viii, 169, n.1

4 See Matt. 25:34.

5 See *Inf*. vii. 37–48; xv. 106–14; xix, *passim*; xxiii. 103–8; *Purg*. iii. 124–35; vi. 91–6; xvi. 97–129; *Par*. ix. 127–42; xi. 124–40; xii. 82–93, 112–26; xxi. 103–5; xxii. 73–96; xxvii. 40–60; xxix. 103–26.

6 On the problem of bad priests, see *S. Th. III Suppl*. Q.8, a.4, 5; Q.19, aa.5–6; Q.22, a.3; Q.26, a.4.

7 See A. R. Bandini, 'St. Peter's Gate', *Italica*, xli (1964), 36–40.

8 Cornoldi and Ghignoni both mention papal authority here, but only in the context of the Sacrament of Penance.

9 See especially E. Auerbach, 'Figura', in *Studi su Dante*, Milan, 1967, 174–221; J. Chydenius, 'The Typological Problem in Dante', *Commentationes Humanarum Litterarum* (Societas Scientiarum Fennica), xxv, no. 1, Helsingfors, 1958 (1960); Armour, 'The Theme of Exodus'.

10 See Lactantius, *P.L.* vi, cols. 801–3 (and notes), 1012–13 (on the concept of a temporal fire punishing the just after death until—and this was not considered orthodox—they went to heaven on the Last Day).

11 *Aen*. vi. 258; *Inf*. iii. 88–99; v. 16–24; vii. 1–15; viii. 81–130; ix. 64–106; xii. 63 ('Ditel costinci; se non, l'arco tiro'); *Purg*. i. 37–48, 52–4, 65–6, 82.

12 Compare *Inf*. xxvi. 137–41 and *Purg*. i. 131–6; *Purg*. xix. 110–14 and xxii. 32–6; *Purg*. xxi. 95–9 and xxx. 44–8; *Purg*. xi. 29–33 and *Par*. xv. 89–93. See also M. Marti, *Poeti del dolce stil nuovo*, Florence, 1969, 98–101, esp. 99, n.1 (on Guinizzelli and the rhyme 'marche/imbarche' in *Purg*. xxvi. 73–5).

13 See J. A. Scott, 'The Rock of Peter and *Inf*. xix', *Romance Philology*, xxiii (1969–70), 462–79.

14 See M. Maccarrone, '*Vicarius Christi*', *Lateranum*, Ann. xviii (1952), caps. 5–6; id.. 'Papato e impero nella *Monarchia*', in *Nuove letture dantesche*, vol. viii (1976), 259–332.

15 G. Rossetti, 71.

16 *P.L.* xxii, col. 355.

17 *De cons. phil.*, Book 3, Metr. 12, lines 44–6, 55–8 ('But let a law govern the favours, decreeing that when he leaves Tartarus he is forbidden to turn his eyes . . . For he who is vanquished and turns his eyes back to the tartarean cave loses the greatest thing he is taking, when he looks on hell'); Gen. 19:26; cf. Luke 17:31–2.

18 Luke 9:62.

19 2 Pet. 2:20–2; cf. Prov. 26:11.

20 Matt. 16:19; John 18:10–11; see *Brewer's Dictionary of Phrase and Fable*: 'Peter, St.'

21 *Comm. in Matt.* 26: 'Converte gladium tuum in locum suum'; cf. Matt. 26:52; John 18:10–11; Gen. 3:24; Eph. 6:17.

22 See also Honorius (*P.L.* clxxii, cols. 1263–4, 1266–7).

23 Heb. 4:12.

24 See F. Gregorovius, *History of the City of Rome in the Middle Ages*, vol. i, transl. Mrs G. W. Hamilton, London, 1900, 106.

25 See Pietro di Mallio, in R. Valentini and G. Zucchetti, *Codice topografico della città di Roma*, Rome, vol. iii (1946), 384, 421; also vol. iv (1953), 80; William Brewyn, *A XVth Century Guide-Book to the Principal Churches of Rome*, transl. C. Eveleigh Woodruff, London, 1933, 8, 26, 29, 37; Gregory Martin, *Roma Sancta*, ed. G. Bruner Parks, Rome, 1969, 27–9.

26 *P.G.* lx, cols. 678, 680.

27 The Bull *Unam sanctam* of 18 November 1302 (see *Les Registres de Boniface VIII*, ed. G. Digard *et al.*, fasc. 13 (Paris, 1921), no. 5382, cols. 888–90).

28 Luke 22:38; see also St. Bernard, *P.L.* clxxxii, cols. 776–7; M. Maccarrone, 'Il terzo libro della *Monarchia*', *Studi danteschi*, xxxiii (1955), 5–142, especially 60–71.

29 See *Inf.* xix. 90–9, 106–8, 115–17; *Purg.* vi. 91–6; xvi. 94–114, 127–9; *Par.* vi. 94–111; xvi. 58–66; xxvii. 139–41.

30 See especially Ps. 68:12; Jonah 3:4–10; 1 Macc. 3:47.

31 See also Joel 1:13; 2:17.

32 Jonah 3:4–10.

33 Antiphon for Ash Wednesday; see Joel, 2:12–13.

34 Ps. 102:14–15; cf. Ps. 89:4–10 and *Purg.* xi. 115–17.

35 See Job 27:16–17.

36 Blessing of the Ashes, Prayer 2. For Conte (p. 22), the robe is 'quella sembianza di cose caduche'.

37 See R. Manselli, 'Dante e l'*Ecclesia spiritualis*', in *Dante e Roma*, Florence, 1965, 131, n. 31.

38 Matt. 16:19; John 21:15–17; St. Bernard, *P.L.* clxxxii, col. 751.

39 See *The Catholic Encyclopedia*, New York, 1913–22: 'Communion of Saints'; also *S. Th. II-i*, Q.102, a.4, ad 3; *III*, Q.8, a.1; a.4, resp., ad 2;

Q.49, a.1, resp.; Q.80, a,4, resp.; Q.83, a.4, 3, ad 3, ad 9; *III Suppl.* Q.19, a.3, resp.; Q.71, a.1, resp.; a.2, resp.; a.9, resp.; a.10, 3; a.13, resp.; a.14, ad 2. The main link between the Church Militant and the Church Suffering consisted in the *suffragia mortuorum* (2 Macc. 12:46; St. Bonaventure, *Breviloquium*, ed. Bougerol, part 7, p. 76), that is, the Masses, prayers, and penances performed by the living who are good (*S. Th. III Suppl.* Q.71, a.3; cf. *Purg.* iv. 133–4; viii. 72) on behalf of the dead, and they were not a lifting but a commutation of divine justice (*S. Th. III Suppl.* Q.71, a.6, ad 1; cf. *Purg.* vi. 37–9).

3. *The Diamond Threshold*

1 The most natural reading is undoubtedly that 'che' defines the 'soglia', not the angel, and that Dante, who has just described the stones of the three steps, is here describing the stone of the threshold, which is the climax of the ascent and a fundamental symbol for the rest of Purgatory (*Purg.* x. 1–3).

2 Apoc. (Rev.) 21:10–20.

3 Ps. 117:22; Isa. 28:16; 50:7; 1 Cor. 10:4; 1 Pet. 2:4–8; St. Augustine, *P.L.* xxxv, col. 1774; *Mon.* III. x, xv. See also *Dante Alighieri's Göttliche Comödie: II. Das Fegefeuer*, transl. Philalethes, Leipzig, 1868, 94 ('the diamond threshold . . . obviously signifies the precious merits of Christ'); M. F. Rossetti, 112–13 ('The adamantine threshold-seat [stands revealed] as the precious merits of Christ the Door, Christ the sure Foundation and the precious Corner-stone'); Raimondi, 'Analisi strutturale', 137, n.1.

4 Matt. 16:17–19; John 21:15–17; St. Augustine, *P.L.* xxxv, col. 1444; St. Thomas, *Comm. in Joann.* 21.

5 St. Augustine, *P.L.* xxxv, col. 1973; C. Sommier's prolegomenon to Anastasius Bibliothecarius, *P.L.* cxxvii, cols. 937–70 (esp. art. 1); St. Thomas, *Comm. in Matt.* 16. For Ghignoni, the diamond threshold is the perpetuity of the Church.

6 St. Jerome, *Comm. in Ev. Matt.*, *P.L.* xxvi, col. 122; St. Bruno, *P.L.* clxv, cols. 213–14; St. Thomas, *Comm. in Matt.* 16. D. Heilbronn, 'Dante's Gate of Dis and the Heavenly Jerusalem', *Studies in Philology*, lxxii (1975), 167–92, sees the parallels but draws the very peculiar conclusion that Dante's entry into lower hell is 'indirectly an entry into the Heavenly Jerusalem' (p. 186).

7 The angel's shining sword of the true Faith also forms a contrast with the image of the heretic as a sword distorting the light of the Scriptures (*Par.* xiii. 128–9). Since Baptism admits man to the Christian Faith and the Church, the theological image of the Church as a door supports Petrocchi's reading of 'porta' in *Inf.* iv. 36, despite A. Pézard's objections ('La *porte* de la foi?', in *Dans le sillage de Dante*, Paris, 1975, 502–16).

8 See also the fourth responsory for Holy Saturday ('Today our Saviour broke the gates and locks of death. He has indeed destroyed the cloisters of hell and overturned the forces of the devil'). Above the mosaic of the

Last Judgement in the basilica of Torcello, there is a representation of Christ trampling on the burst doors of hell and scattering its keys.

9 See the commentaries of Momigliano, Sinclair, Sapegno, etc.

10 A. J. Butler, *The 'Purgatory' of Dante Alighieri*, London, 1880, 113.

11 S. Battaglia, *Grande dizionario della lingua italiana*, Turin, 1970: 'Disusare'.

12 Cf. Matt. 7:13–14; 19:24; Mark 10:25; Luke 18:25.

13 The 'limen' or 'solium' of a saint was the burial-place, and the 'limen confessionis' was the place where pilgrims visited the shrine. The threshold of St. Peter's in Rome was known as the 'solium Apostolicum', and access to it was through a portico known as 'Paradise'. St. Thomas uses the word 'limina' for shrine, and for St. Gregory the phrase 'limina Apostolorum' was a metaphor for Rome; the phrases 'threshold of Peter', 'of Peter and Paul', 'of the Apostles' became traditional in the literature of pilgrims to Rome. See St. Paulinus, *P.L.* lxi, cols. 214–15, 656 (line 377), 848–9 (nn. 39–40), 924 (n. 304); St. Gregory, *P.L.* lxxvii, cols. 718, 1245 and n. *a*; Anastasius Bibl., *P.L.* cxxvii, col. 352; *S. Th. III Suppl.* Q.71, a.10, resp.; Petrarch, *Ep. Metr.* II, 1, line 71 ('ad limina Petri', viz. St. Peter's; cf. line 28: 'ad limina Rome'); Gregory Martin, 19, 26, 223; E. R. Barker, *Rome of the Pilgrims and Martyrs*, London, 1913, 93, n.1; also Paul VI's Bull, subtitled 'Apostolorum limina', of 23 May 1974, proclaiming the Holy Year of 1975.

4. *The Rite of Submission*

1 Cf. Matt. 7:7–8, 13–14, 21; Luke 11:9–10; 13:23–5; *Purg.* xii. 94.

2 *P.L.* xxii, cols. 355–8.

3 See especially Ps. 50 and *Purg.* xxxi. 98.

4 *La Commedia secondo l'antica vulgata*, iii, 150.

5 St. Albert, ed. Borgnet, xxix, 639. The Latin phrase is 'dimitte nobis debita nostra' (forgive us our debts) (cf. *Purg.* x. 108). For the use of the Lord's Prayer in Purgatory, see *Purg.* xi. 1–21.

6 See Fallani, *Lect. Dantis Scal.*, 299.

5. *The Seven P's*

1 See M. Barbi, *Problemi di critica dantesca*, Florence, 1965, i, 229. For the view that only Dante is marked, see C. S. Singleton, *The Divine Comedy*: *Purgatorio*, Princeton, 1973, ii, 189, 503–4.

2 For St. Thomas, the *poenae* of Purgatory are proportional to past sins in two ways: 'the severity of the punishment corresponds to the quantity of the guilt, its duration to the extent to which the *culpa* has taken root in the subject' (*S. Th. Appendix*, Q.2, a.6, ad 1).

3 Ezek, 9:2–6; Apoc (Rev.) 7:2–14; 13:1, 16–17; 14:9, 11; 15:1, 6–8; 16:1 ff.

4 G. R. Sarolli, 'Noterella biblica sui sette P', *Studi danteschi*, xxxiv (1957), 217–22; see also V. Capetti, 'I sette P', in *Illustrazioni al poema di Dante*, Città di Castello, 1913, 199–206. Cf. St. Jerome, *Comm. in Ezech.*, *P.L.* xxv, cols. 85–9.

5 F. Riccardi del Vernaccia, *Lezione sopra i sette P. ricordati da Dante nel canto IX del Purgatorio*, Florence, 1837, 13–16; Capetti, 204–5, n.2; A. Medin, 'Le stimate di Dante', *Atti del R. Istituto Veneto di scienze, lettere ed arti*, lxxxviii (1928–9), 761–9; *La Divina Commedia*, ed. J. A. Carlyle, T. Okey, and P. H. Wicksteed, London, 1933, and the Temple Classics ed. of the *Purgatorio*, London, 1933 (note to *Purg.* ix. 112); Raimondi, 'Analisi strutturale', 141; *La Divina Commedia*, ed. D. Mattalía, Milan, 1960. For a possible classical reminiscence, see D'Ovidio, 310.

6 Lev. 26:21–5; 4 Kgs. (2 Kgs.) 5:10, 14; Ezek. 43:25–6; Apoc. (Rev.) caps. 13, 15, 16; Matt. 18:21–2; Luke 4:27.

7 *Breviloquium*, ed. Bougerol, part 5, pp. 60, 62, 70–3. St. Bonaventure's scheme, somewhat different from Dante's, may be represented thus:

Sin	Gift	Virtue	Beatitude
Pride	Fear of God	Temperance	The poor in spirit
Envy	Piety	Justice	The meek
Wrath	Knowledge	Prudence	Those who mourn
Accidie	Fortitude	Fortitude	Those who thirst for justice
Avarice	Counsel	Hope	The merciful
Gluttony	Intellect	Faith	The pure in heart
Lust	Wisdom	Charity	The peaceful

8 *Aen.* vi. 569; *Purg.* iv–vi; see D'Ovidio, 404–5.

9 G. Rossetti, 66.

10 See also Riccardi del Vernaccia, 10, 13–16 (P is for *Penitenza*); L. Filomusi Guelfi, 'La struttura morale del *Purgatorio* dantesco', *Il giornale dantesco*, v (1898), 371 (P is for *Piaghe*).

11 *S. Th. Appendix*, Q.2, a.1, 3; a.4, resp.

12 For this reason, Bulferetti interpreted P as *Peccavi* (p. 60); see also B. Stambler, *Dante's Other World: The 'Purgatorio' as Guide to the 'Divine Comedy'*, New York, 1957, 130.

13 Ps. 31:1.

14 *S. Th. III Suppl.* Q.30, a.1, 2.

15 Ibid., Q.1, a.1.

16 Ibid., Q.4, a.3, concl., resp., ad 3.

17 Ibid., Q.8, a.7; Q.10, a.3; Q.14, a.2; a.3; Q.15, aa.1–3. On the ascetic aspect of Purgatory, see P. Perez, *I sette cerchi del Purgatorio di Dante*, Turin, 1865, 9–18.

18 On Purgatory as fire, as school, as place of asceticism and testing, see R. Palgen, 'Il quadruplo Purgatorio', *Convivium*, xxxii (1964), 3–23.

19 *S. Th. III Suppl.* Q.5, a.2; Q.6, a.1, resp.; Q.8, aa.1–3; Q.11, a.3; Q.71, a.5, ad 5; *Appendix*, Q.2, a.1, 2; a.4; *Art. 2 de Purg.* a.1, resp., ad 2.

20 *S. Th. III Suppl.* Q.12, aa.1–3; Aristotle, *Eth.* ii. 3.

21 See C. S. Singleton, 'Campi semantici dei canti XII dell'*Inferno* e XIII del *Purgatorio*', in *Miscellanea di studi danteschi*, Genoa, 1966, 17–22.

22 *S. Th. III Suppl*, Q. 21, a. 1.

23 Ibid., Q.10, a.2, ad 2; *Art. 2 de Purg.* a.1, resp.

24 *Aen.* vi. 569.

25 See pp. 33–4.

26 See *S. Th. III Suppl.* Q.7, a.1, 4; St. Albert, vol. cit., 687 ff.

27 Deut. 25:2; *S. Th. III*, Q.88, a.3, *contra*; *Appendix*, Q.2, a.1, 2 (also a.6, 1).

6. *The Keys*

1 Matt. 16:19.

2 John 21:15–17; St. Thomas, *Comm. in Joann*. 21; *S. Th. III Suppl.* Q.17, aa.1–2.

3 *Comm. in Evang. Matt.* (*P.L.* xxvi, col. 122). On this idea, see also J. A. Watt, 'Dante, Boniface VIII and the Pharisees', in *Post Scripta: Essays on Medieval Law and the Emergence of the European State in Honor of Gaines Post*, ed. J. R. Strayer and D. E. Queller (*Studia Gratiana*, xv), Rome, 1972, 201–15.

4 St. Bonaventure, *Brevil.*, part 6, cap. 10; St. Thomas, *Comm. in Matt.* 16.

5 Apoc. (Rev.) 4:1.

6 Isa. 22:22; Matt. 16:18–19.

7 *S. Th. III Suppl.* Q.17, a.3, ad 2.

8 St. Albert, vol. cit., 771.

9 Ibid., 770.

10 *S. Th. III Suppl.* Q.17, a.1, ad 3. St. Thomas must, of course, mean eternal punishment here as well as temporal, but, since God alone saves the contrite man from hell, the Church's keys merely confirm the removal of the obligation to eternal punishment. Since St. Thomas held that the fires of hell and of Purgatory were contiguous (*Art. 2 de Purg.* a.2, *contra*; also *S. Th. III Suppl.* Q.15, a.2, ad 2), he assigns to the Church's keys the more direct power of controlling the duty of temporal punishment in life (satisfaction) and in Purgatory. In this respect, the key of hell is a subsidiary aspect of the key of heaven, and a further implicit parallel can be traced between the gate of hell opened by the heavenly messenger in *Inf.* ix and the door of heaven opened by the angel's keys in *Purg.* ix.

11 *S. Th. III Suppl.* Q.17, a.1, 3, ad 3. Ruskin, not realizing that in the medieval tradition both St. Peter's keys were for opening heaven, compares Dante unfavourably with Milton who, in *Lycidas* (lines 110–11), presents St. Peter with a golden key, to open heaven, and an iron key, presumably to lock up the false shepherds (*Sesame and the Lilies*, I, 24).

12 Apoc. (Rev.) 4:1; John 10:7–9.

13 *S. Th. III Suppl.* Q.18, a.1; also *Comm. in Joann.* 20.

14 *S. Th. III Suppl.* Q.18, a.2; also *Comm. in Matt.* 16.

15 St. Albert, vol. cit., 659.

16 *S. Th. III Suppl.* Q.18, aa.3–4.

17 Ibid., Q.17, a.3, ad 2.

18 Ibid., QQ.19–24.

19 Ibid., Q.19, aa.3, 5, 6.

20 Ibid., Q.19, a.3; Q.20, aa.1–3; Q.21, a.1; Q.22, a.1; Q.40, a.4; St. Bonaventure, *Brevil.* part 6, cap. 10, 6.

21 *S. Th. III Suppl.* Q.22, a.1; Q.24, a.1, resp.

22 Ibid., Q.22, a.1, ad 2.

23 Ibid., Q.24, a.1, ad 2.

24 Ibid., Q.21, a.2, resp.; Q.22, a.1, *contra*.

25 Rom. 12:14; *S. Th. III Suppl.* Q.21, a.2, ad 1.

26 See the commentaries of Momigliano ('nodo' = 'matassa') and Mattalía to *Purg.* ix. 124–6; see also Sapegno's note to *Inf.* x. 95 (where the glossing of 'inviluppata' as 'ravviluppata' strengthens the idea of the 'nodo' as a tangle).

27 Compare the use of 'groppo' as 'knot' in *Inf.* xi. 96 and perhaps xiii. 123. In *Inf.* xvi. 111, 'aggroppata' ('bound in a knot') is to be distinguished slightly from 'ravvolta' ('tangled') (see the commentary of U. Bosco and G. Reggio, Florence, 1979). Compare also the similar images in *Par.* xv. 146; xxxi. 90; xxxii. 49–51.

28 St. Thomas, *Comm. in Matt.* 16; *S. Th. III Suppl.* Q.24, a.1, ad 2.

29 St. Thomas, *Comm. in Matt.* 16; see also St. Cyprian and St. Augustine (*P.L.* iii, cols. 1159–60; xxxv, cols. 1967–8, 1973; also cxxvii, cols. 937–70).

30 *P.L.* clxxxii, col. 751.

31 *S. Th. III Suppl.* Q.20, aa.1–2; Q.40, a.6.

32 *S. Th. II-ii*, Q.88, a.12, resp.; see Sapegno's notes to *Purg.* ix. 117, 119, 121, 124; *Par.* v. 56.

33 *S. Th. III Suppl.* QQ. 25–7; cf. Q.27, a.4, ad 3.

34 G. Villani, *Cron.* viii. 36; A. Potthast, *Regesta Pontificum Romanorum*, Graz, 1957, ii, no. 23981 (of 28 September 1294).

35 *S. Th. III Suppl.* Q.25, a.1, resp.

36 St. Albert, vol. cit., 848.

37 *S. Th. III Suppl.* Q.25, a.1, ad 2; a.2, 5.

38 Ibid., a.1, concl.; Q.27, a.1, resp.

39 St. Albert, vol. cit., 848.

40 *S. Th. III Suppl.* Q.26, especially a.3, concl.

41 *Brevil.* part 6, cap. 10, 7 (ed. cit., 116–17).

42 *S. Th. III Suppl.* Q.25, a.2, ad 1.

43 Ibid., Q.25, a.3.

44 See also M. Aurigemma, 'Manfredi e il problema delle indulgenze', in U. Bosco (ed.), *Dante nella critica d'oggi*, Florence, 1965 (for *Cultura e scuola*), 545–6, especially 545, n.2.

45 'The Pardoner's Tale', in *The Canterbury Tales*, text of W. W. Skeat, OUP, repr. 1958, 289.

46 *S. Th. III Suppl.* Q.71, a.6, ad 3; a.14, concl.; cf. 2 Macc. 12:46.

47 *S. Th. III Suppl.* Q.71, aa.9–10. Aurigemma seems to confuse indulgences with the *suffragia mortuorum*, a much wider category which may include indulgences.
48 *S. Th. III Suppl.* Q.71, a.3 (cf. *Purg.* iv. 133–4; viii. 72); a.6, ad 1 (cf. *Purg.* vi. 37–9); St. Bonaventure, *Brevil.* part 7 (ed. cit., 76).
49 *Aen.* vi. 376.
50 2 Pet. 2:20–2.
51 The word 'regge' refers primarily to a church-door (see Barbi, i, 222–3), hence here to the Church Suffering, but its derivation (from *regia*) does not exclude reference to a royal door, hence also to the kingdom of heaven.

7. *The Door*

1 Momigliano's notes to *Purg.* ix. 133–6, 145; also Lesca, 15.
2 Ps. 113:1, 4, with regard to *Purg.* xxi. 43–57 (and cf. xxviii. 102); see also Perez, 25, n.3; Armour, 'The Theme of Exodus', 88.
3 For the word 'distorti', see Mattalía's commentary; see also *Purg.* xi. 108; *Par.* xvii. 81.
4 *Phars.* iii. 112–68.
5 Ibid., iii. 123–5, 130; vii. 758.
6 *Purg.* xx. 113 (cf. 2 Macc. 3:7–40); *Inf.* xxiv. 138.
7 *Phars.* iii. 114, 118–21, 137–40, 145–52.
8 Cf. *Purg.* xx. 25–7.
9 *Phars.* iii. 153–68.
10 Matt. 6:19–21; 13:44–52; 1 Pet. 1:4, 18–19.
11 Ps. 99:4.
12 Sapegno's notes to *Purg.* ix. 139–40; see also Raimondi, 'Analisi strutturale', 145, n.2; Conte, 24–5; H. Gmelin (ed.), *Die Göttliche Komödie: Kommentar*, ii ('Der Läuterungsberg'), Stuttgart, 1955, 172.
13 Barbi, i, 223, 247–8; Bosco and Reggio, *Purgatorio*, pp. 148–9, 162; G. Tròccoli, *Il Purgatorio dantesco: Studio critico*, Florence, 1951, 83–4, n.2.
14 M. A. Buchanan, 'At the Gate of Purgatory', *Italica*, xxv (1948), 6–7.
15 Petrocchi, *La Commedia secondo l'antica vulgata*, iii, 153–4.
16 Scartazzini, note to *Purg.* ix. 141; Scartazzini, revised by G. Vandelli, Milan, 1914, note to *Purg.* ix. 139–41.
17 M. Porena (ed.), *La Divina Commedia*, Bologna, 1955, note to *Purg.* ix. 141.
18 *Aen.* vi. 573.
19 Bulferetti, 62–3; M. Apollonio, *Dante* (Storia letteraria d'Italia), Milan, 3rd edn., 1965, ii, 35.
20 'Lamia', i. 386–8; Grandgent, note to *Purg.* ix. 144.
21 G. Fallani (*La Divina Commedia*, Messina–Florence, 1969, note to *Purg.* ix. 144) interprets 'organi' not as the instruments but as the *organum*, a method of singing by doubling the melody in octaves, fourths, or fifths. This, however, loses the parallel of *voce-suono/cantar-*

organi and with it the main point of the simile—to explain why the words are only half-heard; see also Bosco and Reggio, note to *Purg.* ix. 144.

22　D'Ovidio (pp. 271–5), though opting for the souls, finds the singing mysterious.

23　See Lana, the Ottimo, and Buti; also Sinclair, Porena, and U. Bosco, *Dante: Il Purgatorio*, Turin, 2nd edn., 1967, 77.

24　See Benvenuto; also Mattalía and Conte, 25–6, n.1 (citing Torraca).

25　Matt. 25:34; *Purg.* xxvii. 58.

PART III: CONCLUSIONS

1. *The Episode in Context*

1　Fergusson, 38.

2　Ibid., 44.

3　M. Corti employs a distinction between 'micropolisemia' and 'macropolisemia', which could be applied here (*Principi della comunicazione letteraria*, Milan, 1976, 108; also 94).

4　On the problem, see L. Peirone, 'Casella', in the *Enciclopedia dantesca*. S. Pasquazi, 'Dove l'acqua del Tevero s'insala', in *All'eterno dal tempo*, Florence, 1972, 275–81, discusses whether the delay is a 'pre-antipurgatorio' or a '*post-mundum*'. See also below (pp. 146–7).

5　The phrase is Milton's (*Lycidas*, line 109). Benvenuto calls the boat '*navicula Petri*', a metaphor for the Church.

6　See Singleton, '*In Exitu Israel de Aegypto*'.

7　See 'The Diamond Threshold', n.13.

8　See also G. P. Norton, 'Retrospection and Prefiguration in the Dreams of *Purgatorio*', *Italica*, xlvii (1970), 351–65; C. Speroni, 'Dante's Prophetic Morning-Dreams', in R. J. Clements (ed.), *American Critical Essays on the 'Divine Comedy'*, New York–London, 1967, 182–92.

9　Singleton, '*In Exitu*', 120–1; cf. Exod. 19:4; Deut. 32:11; Isa. 40:31. See also Raimondi, 'Analisi strutturale', 130–2.

10　See Capetti, 'Di una relazione simbolica tra i due monti Ida nel poema dantesco', in *Illustrazioni*, 47–52.

11　Pss. 23:3–4 (cf. 14:1–4); 117:19–20 (cited by Pietro di Dante here).

12　Ps. 102:5.

13　See 'Il libro della natura degli animali', in C. Segre and M. Marti, *La prosa del Duecento*, Milan–Naples, 309–10. See also L. Marin, 'Essai d'analyse structurale du chant IX du Purgatoire, v. 1–73', in *Psicoanalisi e strutturalismo di fronte a Dante*, Florence, 1972, ii, 183–216.

14　*Achilleid*, i. 228–41.

15　Ibid., 247–50. Dante's phrase, 'li occhi svegliati', indicates that he knew the reading 'oculique patentes' (see O. A. W. Dilke's edn., Cambridge, 1954; R. J. Deferrari and M. C. Eagan, *A Concordance of Statius*, Hildesheim, 1966, under 'pateo'). Momigliano and Sapegno, however, cite another reading ('oculique iacentis').

16　See E. Moore, 'Santa Lucia in the *Divina Commedia*', in *Studies in Dante: Fourth Series*, Oxford, 1917, 235–55.

17 Ps. 113. For fuller discussion of this in relation to the figural inter-pretations of the *Comedy* of Auerbach, Chydenius, Charity, etc., see Armour, 'The Theme of Exodus'.

18 On the typology of the Church in its various stages of fulfilment, and of Jerusalem, the Paradise, and the Bride, see especially Chydenius, *passim*. The identification of references to the Church Suffering in *Purg.* ix, and the fact that the relationship of the Church Militant to the Church Suffering is one of prefiguration and fulfilment, fill in this stage in Chydenius's argument and lead, inescapably, to an application of the figural interpretation to the hitherto neglected second *cantica*.

19 See in particular Momigliano's rather ambiguous approach (notes to *Purg.* ix. 70–2, 100–2, 103–5) with his reference to his own notes to *Inf.* xxv. 94–102.

20 *S. Th. Appendix*, Q.2, aa.4–6; *Art. 2 de Purg.* a.2, *contra* (with references to St. Augustine's and St. Gregory's interpretation of 1 Cor. 3:12–15); *S. Th. III Suppl.* Q.15, a.2, ad 2.

21 See K. Foster's introduction in K. Foster and P. Boyde, *Dante's Lyric Poetry*, Oxford, 1967, i, xviii ff.

22 Cf. *Inf.* ii. 7–9; ix. 61–3; xxxii. 1–12; *Purg.* i. 7–12; viii. 19–21; ix. 70–2; xxix. 37–42; *Par.* i. 10–36; ii. 1–18; x. 26–7; xviii. 82–7; xix. 7–9; xxii. 112–23; xxiii. 22–4, 55–69; xxiv. 25–7; xxx. 16–36, 97–9; xxxi. 136–8; xxxiii. 55–75, 106–8, 121–3, 142.

23 See D. De Robertis, *Il libro della 'Vita Nuova'*, 2nd edn., Florence, 1970, 119.

24 Ps. 39:3–4.

2. *The Door of Purgatory as the Door of Pardon*

1 On Benvenuto's possible visit, see *Enciclopedia dantesca*: 'Benvenuto'.

2 See Boccaccio, *Vita di Dante*, 26 and *Trattatello in laude di Dante*; also *Enciclopedia dantesca*: '*Monarchia*: Fortuna'.

3 See G. Barraclough, *The Medieval Papacy*, London, 1968, 154.

4 See 'The Three Steps', n.1.

5 A. F. Ozanam, *Le Purgatoire de Dante*, in *Œuvres complètes*, 2nd edn., Paris, 1862, ix, 168–9; cited also by W. W. Vernon, *Readings on the 'Purgatorio' of Dante*, London, 1889, i, 224.

6 See above all A. Frugoni, 'Il Giubileo di Bonifacio VIII', *Bullettino dell'Istituto Storico Italiano per il Medio Evo*, lxii (1950), 1–121; also Gregorovius, vi, part 1, 321–7; C. Carboni, *Il Giubileo di Bonifazio VIII e la 'Commedia' di Dante*, Rome, 1901, 44 ff., 105; R. Morghen, 'Il giubileo del 1300', in *Medioevo cristiano*, Bari, 1951, 304–26; id., *Bonifacio VIII e il Giubileo del 1300 nella storiografia moderna*, Rome, 1975; E. Duprè Theseider, *Roma dal Comune di Popolo alla Signoria Pontificia (1252–1377)* (Storia di Roma, xi), Bologna, 1952, 337–52, 618–24; V. Bo, 'Piccola storia degli Anni Santi', in *Storia e topografia dell'Anno Santo*, Vatican City, 1974, 19–74; J. Sumption, *Pilgrimage*, London, 1975, 231–42; A. Stickler, *Il Giubileo di Bonifacio VIII: Aspetti giuridico-pastorali*, Rome, 1977.

7 The Bull 'Antiquorum habet fida relatio', in Potthast, no. 24917; full text in *Les Registres de Boniface VIII*, fasc.v (ed. G. Digard), Paris, 1890, no. 3875, cols. 922–3; *Iacobi Sancti Georgii ad Velum Aureum Diaconi Cardinalis de Centesimo seu Iubileo Anno Liber*, ed. D. Quattrocchi, *Bessarione*, vii (1900), 299–317; A. Frugoni, 'Riprendendo il *De centesimo seu Iubileo anno liber* del cardinale Stefaneschi', *Bullettino dell'Istituto Storico Italiano per il Medio Evo*, lxi (1949), 163–72. On Stefaneschi, titular Cardinal of S. Giorgio in Velabro and patron of Giotto, see I. Hösl, *Kardinal Iacobus Gaietani Stefaneschi*, Berlin, 1908; Gregorovius, v, part 2, 629–30, 657; A. Frugoni, 'La figura e l'opera del cardinale Jacopo Stefaneschi (*c.* 1270–1343)', *Rendiconti dell'Accademia Nazionale dei Lincei*: Classe di scienze morali, storiche e filologiche, Ser. VIII, v (1950), 397–424; G. Marchetti Longhi, *Gli Stefaneschi*, Rome, 1954, 52–5.

8 *Cron.* viii. 36.

9 'Memoriale Guilielmi Venturae civis Astensis', cap. 26, in L.A. Muratori, *Rerum italicarum scriptores*, Milan, 1727, xi, cols. 191–2.

10 See A. Frugoni, 'Dante, *Epist.* XI, 24–5', in *Studi in onore di Alfredo Schiaffini* (*Rivista di cultura classica e medioevale*, vii), 1965, 477–86; O. Capitani, 'Una questione non ancora chiusa . . .', *Annali della Scuola Normale Superiore di Pisa*, iii (1973), 471–85.

11 Stefaneschi, 307.

12 See G. Fallani, *Dante autobiografico*, Naples, 1975, 130.

13 Bo, 48; also Fallani, *Dante poeta teologo*, 140–1.

14 See A. Camilli, 'La Bolla giubilare di Bonifacio VIII, le indulgenze per i defunti e il ritardo di Casella', *Studi danteschi*, xxx (1951), 207–9; A. Pézard, 'Le chant deuxième du Purgatoire', in V. Vettori (ed.), *Letture del Purgatorio*, Milan, 1965, 51–5.

15 E. Moore, 'The Date Assumed by Dante for the Vision of the *Divina Commedia*', in *Studies in Dante: Third Series*, 1903, 154–7; for the decree, see Stefaneschi, 316–17.

16 Stefaneschi, 301; see also D. Balboni, *La Cattedra di S. Pietro*, Vatican City, 1967.

17 Ash Wednesday was the first bissextile day (VI kal. mart.); Potthast misdates no. 24921, which in a leap year would correspond to our 26 February.

18 C. Mitchell, 'The Lateran Fresco of Boniface VIII', *Journal of the Warburg and Courtauld Institutes*, xiv (1951), 1–6; L. Vayer, 'L'affresco del Giubileo e la tradizione della pittura monumentale romana', in *Giotto e il suo tempo*, Rome, 1971, 45–59.

19 Frugoni, 'Il Giubileo', 77, 102; Duprè Theseider, 348.

20 See p. 126; also *The Catholic Encyclopedia*: 'Jubilee, Holy Year of: Ceremonial of the Jubilee'.

21 Pero Tafur, *Andanças é Viajes*, ed. M. Jiménez de la Espada (Colección de Libros Españoles Raros o Curiosos, viii), Madrid, 1874, 28; G. Rucellai, 'Della bellezza e anticaglia di Roma', in Valentini-Zucchetti, iv (1953), 405–6; see also Buchanan, op. cit.; Gmelin, 172. C. Pietropaoli's theory (*Il Giubileo nella 'Divina Commedia'*, Lanciano, 1900) that the door is the Holy Door of St. Peter's is dismissed as 'bizzarra' by D. Consoli in the *Enciclopedia dantesca*: 'Porta'.

22 Martin, 55.

23 S. Carletti, 'I luoghi santi di Roma', in *Storia e topografia dell'Anno Santo*, Vatican City, 1974, 100.

24 *Comm. in IV Sent.* Dist. 20, E. a.16 (vol. cit., 848); *S. Th. III Suppl.* Q.25, a.1.

25 Frugoni, 'Il Giubileo', 30–44; Fallani, *Lect. Dantis Scal.*, 299; see also *S. Th. III Suppl.* Q.25, a.2, ad 4; Q.71, a.10, resp.; John the Deacon, 'Liber de Sanctis Sanctorum', Pietro di Mallio, 'Opusculum Historiae Sacrae', and the fourteenth-century 'Memoriale de memorabilibus et indulgentiis quae in urbe romana exsistunt', in Valentini-Zucchetti, iii (1946), 333–4, 385, and iv (1953), 78–88. There are many examples of the granting of indulgences for visits to churches or shrines during the pontificates of Celestine V and Boniface VIII; two of the nearest to the Bull of the Jubilee are of 26 December 1299 and of April 1300 (Potthast, nos. 24895, 24948). Sometimes indulgences granted were excessive; Celestine V, for example, granted one of 2000 years and 2000 quarantines to his own monastery of S. Spirito de Sulmona for Christmas, and Boniface VIII, on coming to power, reduced this to the standard seven years (Potthast, nos. 23975, 23977, 24004, 24040).

26 *Cron.* viii. 36.

27 Valentini-Zucchetti, iii, 334, n.1.

28 Brewyn, pp. iv, 7–8, 56, 59.

29 *S. Th. III. Suppl.* Q.26, a.3.

30 Frugoni, 'Il Giubileo', 116–20; see also C. T. Wood, *Philip the Fair and Boniface VIII*, New York, 2nd edn., 1971, 41.

31 Stefaneschi, 306; see Frugoni, 'Il Giubileo', 119, and R. Davidsohn, *Storia di Firenze*, Florence, 1960, iv, 125–6.

32 Ventura, loc. cit.

33 *S. Th. III Suppl.* Q.25, aa.2–3; cf. *Par.* xxix. 118–26.

34 The Bull is published in Stefaneschi, 315–16 (dated 22 February) and Potthast, no. 24922 (dated 1 March).

35 Quattrocchi in Stefaneschi, 298; Gregorovius, v, part 2, 630.

36 Stefaneschi, 299 (n. 2), 305, 307, 308, 313–14.

37 See pp. 45–6, 58.

38 T. S. R. Boase, *Boniface VIII*, London, 1933, 232.

39 *Cron.* i. 56.

40 Stefaneschi, 308, 309.

41 Ibid., 310–11.

42 Ibid., 314, 304.

43 Ibid., 312.

44 For 'nam' (Quattrocchi) perhaps read 'iam'.

45 Stefaneschi, 314.

46 See the edn. of G. Busnelli and G. Vandelli, revised by A. E. Quaglio, Florence, 1964, part 2, 200, n.6.

47 For this and other details concerning pilgrims to Rome, see *The Oxford Book of Medieval Latin Verse*, Oxford, 1959, 140; A. Greco, 'Roma negli scrittori dell'età di Dante', in *Dante e Roma*, Florence, 1965, 250; Frugoni, 'Il Giubileo', 91 ff.; Sumption, 220–36; Boase, 231 ff.; Gregorovius, v, part 2, 557–65; G. Petronio, *Bonifacio VIII*, Lucca,

1950, 16–17, 47; the catalogue of the *Mostra di Bonifacio VIII e del primo Giubileo*, Rome, 1950, 70.

48 See Sapegno's note to *Par.* xxxi. 35. For Constantine and Rome, see the *Liber Pontificalis* (*P.L.* cxxvii, cols. 1511–28) and L. Ropes Loomis (ed.), *The Book of the Popes*, New York, 1916, 41–72; also Gregorovius, i, 90–116.

49 *Cron.* viii. 36; see Frugoni, 'Il Giubileo', 107.

50 Martin, *passim*, especially 220 ff.

51 Ibid., 91.

52 See *P.L.* cxxvii, cols. 1515–18; 'The Angel-Doorkeeper', n.25.

53 *P.L.* cxxvii, cols. 368–74; Barker, 10; Carletti, 120–1; Valentini-Zucchetti, iii, 344–5.

54 *P.G.* lx, col. 678; for associations between the Rose and the Jubilee, see Martin (quoting Carlo Borromeo), 28, 225; W. and T. Parri, *Anno del viaggio e giorno iniziale della 'Commedia'*, Florence, 1956, 53–7; on Jerusalem and the two Romes, see Duprè Theseider, 345; H. Rheinfelder, 'Il mito di Roma in Dante', in *Nuove letture dantesche*, vi (1973), 281.

55 See Fallani, *Dante autobiografico*, 129–30; J. G. Demaray, *The Invention of Dante's 'Commedia'*, Yale UP, 1974, 177–184; also id., 'The Pilgrim Texts and Dante's Three Beasts', *Italica*, xlvi (1969), 233–41; 'Pilgrim Text Models for Dante's *Purgatorio*', *Studies in Philology*, lxvi (1969), 1–24; 'Patterns of Earthly Pilgrimage in Dante's *Commedia*: Palmers, Romers, and the Great Circle Journey', *Romance Philology*, xxiv (1970–1), 239–58.

56 Frugoni, 'Il Giubileo', 78–83; Chydenius, 71–3.

57 Chydenius, 51–86, 103–5, 107–8, 120.

58 Frugoni, 'Il Giubileo', 90; Duprè Theseider, 344–5; Bo, 19–28.

59 Stefaneschi, 300, 305, 314.

60 Frugoni, 'Il Giubileo', 4–12, 26–9.

61 Boniface's 'Gratia non bullata', in Stefaneschi, 317.

62 M. Villani, *Cron.* i. 56.

63 Lev. 25:8–11, 13, 28, 39–41; 26:24, 28.

64 *P.L.* cxc, col. 421; Frugoni, 'Il Giubileo', 5–7.

65 Bo, 29–48.

66 Sumption, 237; Frugoni, 'Il Giubileo', 12.

67 *Cron.* i. 29.

68 Frugoni, 'Il Giubileo', 11, 109; id., 'Il carme giubilare del "Magister Bonaiutus de Casentino" ', *Bullettino dell'Istituto Storico Italiano per il Medio Evo*, lxviii (1956), 247–58 (citation on p. 257).

69 Stefaneschi, 309.

70 For these connections, see also Carlo Borromeo's homily on the Jubilee of 1575: 'So shal we al celebrate the holy yere in holy maner, and by the grace of God do workes worthy to bring us to the perfect and everlasting Jubilee, that is, the most perfect deliveries from all the miseries of this present life, and the possession of the infinite and eternal joyes of our heavenly inheritance in Paradise' (Martin's transl., 229).

71 Boase, 237–8; Frugoni, 'Il Giubileo', 68–70.

72 See B. Andriani, 'La centesima negletta', *Studi danteschi*, xlviii (1971), 83–103. The Gregorian Calendar corrected the error by making only every fourth centenary year a leap year.
73 See *Il Convivio*, ed. cit., part 1, 221–3; also Sapegno's note to *Par*. xxx. 132.
74 Frugoni, 'Il Giubileo', 17–19; Duprè Theseider, 339. On the general presence of apocalyptic and millenarian elements in Dante, see N. Mineo, *Profetismo e apocalittica in Dante*, Catania, 1968, 90–101.
75 Boccaccio, *Esposizioni sopra la Comedia di Dante*, ed. G. Padoan, Milan, 1965, 25, 78; Moore, *Third Series*, 146; Sapegno's note to *Inf*. i.1.
76 See C. Hardie, 'The mountain in *Inf*. i and ii, the Mount Ida in Crete, and the Mountain of Purgatory', *Deutsches Dante-Jahrbuch*, xlvi (1970), 81–100.

3. *Dante's Two Journeys*

1 Moore, *Third Series*, 159–60, makes the point without drawing further conclusions.
2 See pp. 49–50, 65–6.
3 Stefaneschi, 303; Boase, 237.
4 Moore, *Third Series*, 159.
5 U. Cosmo, *A Handbook to Dante Studies*, transl. D. Moore, Oxford, 1950, 59.
6 G. Villani, *Cron*. viii.38–41; D. Compagni, *Cron*. i.22–3; Davidsohn, iv, 141 ff.; P. Villari, *The Two First Centuries of Florentine History*, transl. L. Villari, London, 1895, ii, 144 ff.; G. Holmes, 'Dante and the Popes', in C. Grayson (ed.), *The World of Dante*, Oxford, 1980, 19–28.
7 P. Bargellini, *Vita di Dante*, Florence, 1964, 123; L. Giambuzzi, *Cronache degli Anni Santi*, Rome, 1975, 14; see also Davidsohn, iv, 138–9; Boase, 248.
8 *Cron*. ii. 10, 22; see I. Del Lungo, *Dino Compagni e la sua Cronica*, Florence, 1879, ii, 512–14.
9 Boccaccio, *Esposizioni*, 150 (but see 20, 352); P. Fraticelli, *Storia della vita di Dante Alighieri*, Florence, 1861, 282–5, 296–7; F. Angelitti, 'Sulla data del viaggio dantesco', *Atti dell'Accademia Pontaniana*, xxvii, no.7 (1897); W. and T. Parri, op. cit.; for discussion, see Moore, *Third Series*, 146–7 and notes; M. A. Orr, *Dante and the Early Astronomers*, London, revised edn., 1956, 275–88; A. Vallone, *Dante* (Storia letteraria d'Italia), Milan, 1971, 281–2; R. Orengo, *Note polemiche sui riferimenti astronomici della 'Divina Commedia'*, Riva Ligure, 1974. P. Boyde, *Dante Philomythes and Philosopher: Man in the Cosmos*, Cambridge, 1981, 163–5, draws the somewhat different, but closely related, conclusion that Dante is creating 'an "ideal" Easter Week, in an ideal universe, with an ideal calendar, such that in the year 1300 Good Friday fell on 25 March' (p. 164).
10 Stefaneschi, 317.
11 See also Moore, *Third Series*, 154–9.

12 Stefaneschi, 300.

13 Ibid., 317.

14 *Esposizioni*, 125; see also Buti, vol. i, 74.

15 *Purg.* xix. 101; *Par.* xxx. 64; Compagni, *Cron.* i. 26; *Decameron*, vi. 4; for other examples, see Battaglia, *Grande dizionario*: 'Fiumana'.

16 *Esposizioni* (see n.14).

17 J. Freccero, 'The River of Death: *Inf.* ii.108', in S. B. Chandler and J. A. Molinaro (eds.), *The World of Dante*, Toronto, 1966, 25–42.

18 'L'infinito', line 15.

19 Freccero, 31.

20 See also *Conv.* III. v. 9 ff., with Lucan, *Phars.* ix. 624–5 and iv. 334; *D. V. E.* I. viii; *Par.* xii. 49–51.

21 *Aen.* vii. 303–4. The context and phrasing of Juno's speech justify interpreting 'securi' as 'safe' (rather than as 'unconcerned') and so it would probably have seemed in Dante's day; in any case, the difference is unimportant for our purposes.

22 *Aen.* vi. 83–7.

23 Ibid., viii. 64–5, 77; see also *P. Vergili Maronis Opera*, ed. J. Conington, London, 1871, iii, 90–1 (note to *Aen.* viii. 77).

24 See also *Aen.* i. 286–7; *Phars.* viii. 797–9.

25 Stefaneschi, 303; Duprè Theseider, 351.

26 U. Cosmo, *Vita di Dante*, revised B. Maier, Florence, 1965, 73–7; Carboni, 57. One of the many weaknesses of W. Anderson's *Dante the Maker*, London, 1980, is the sheer assumption that Dante, back in Florence, had a vision of the Trinity at Eastertime in 1300; though neither hypothesis can be proved or disproved, the logic of the poem makes it perhaps on balance more likely that, around the end of Lent in 1300, Dante felt himself to be the furthest possible distance away from God.

27 Del Lungo, i, part 1, 185; Petronio, 17 ff.; G. Levi, *Bonifazio VIII e le sue relazioni col comune di Firenze*, Rome, 1882, 39–45.

28 *Cron.* viii. 36.

29 G. Aquilecchia, 'Dante and the Florentine Chroniclers', *Bulletin of the John Rylands Library*, xlviii (1965–6), 30–55 (see id., *Schede di italianistica*, Turin, 1976, 45–96).

30 G. Caetani, *Domus Caetana*, Sancasciano Val di Pesa, 1927, i, part 1, 136–7; Boase, 237, 243.

31 'O papa Bonifazio—molt'hai iocato al mondo', lines 63–74, in the version of the *editio princeps* (*Jacopone da Todi: Le Laude secondo la stampa fiorentina del 1490*, ed. G. Ferri, 2nd edn. revised S. Caramella, Bari, 1930, 129–30). The textual tradition for line 74 is confused, oscillating between use of the singular 'tuo cavaliere', 'l tuo cavalieri' etc., and the plural 'cavalieri', 'tuo' cavalliere', etc. (see *Le Satire di Jacopone da Todi*, ed. B. Brugnoli, Florence, 1914, 319). F. Mancini's edn. of *Le Laude*, Bari, 1974, gives 'to cavalieri' (p. 250), with the variant 'to cavaliere' (p. 618), noting that the word 'cavaleri' is normally singular in Jacopone (p. 689). G. Contini's edn. of *Poeti del Duecento*, Milan–Naples, 1960, ii, 142, gives the apparent plural 'cavalieri' in rhyme with

'pensieri', 'ponire', 'gaudere' (*rima siciliana*). However, the general rhyme-scheme of the passage suffers less distortion in Ageno's reading of 'tuo cavalire', although this obvious singular is then interpreted as a plural, 'i tuoi cavalieri' (*Jacopone da Todi: Laudi, Trattato e Detti*, ed. F. Ageno, Florence, 1953, 232). Ageno also mistakenly interprets the *Sancta Sanctorum* as 'the innermost part of St. Peter's' (note to line 71), whereas it is in fact the papal chapel of S. Lorenzo, once part of the Lateran, now in a separate building nearby at the top of the *Scala Santa*. This chapel dates from Constantinian times but was remade and beautified by Nicholas III; its name derives from its many relics, its portrait of Christ once attributed to St. Luke (or described as *acheropita*), and an inscription over the altar: 'there is no holier place in the whole world (*non est in toto sanctior orbe locus*)'. Jacopone is therefore referring to a scandalous festive procession of the Pope's family and retainers between St. Peter's and the Lateran during Holy Week. Ageno notes that 'this is perhaps an allusion to some feast celebrated in the Jubilee year' (note to line 68), but, by interpreting the word 'cavalire' as a plural, she misses Boase's point (pp. 237, 243) that this is a reference to the knighting of Boniface's great-nephew, Roffredo (Loffredo) (see also Duprè Theseider, 360–1). The imprisoned Jacopone's knowledge of this event which so scandalized the pilgrims can easily be traced, for it formed part of Pietro Colonna's testimony at the trial of Boniface's memory in Avignon (Caetani, 136).

Bibliography of Works Cited

AGENO, F. (see Jacopone da Todi).

AGLIANÒ, S., 'Il canto ix del *Purgatorio*', in G. Getto (ed.), *Letture dantesche*, Florence, Sansoni, 1964, pp. 849–68.

ALBERT, St., *Commentarii in Quartum Librum Sententiarum*, in id., *Opera omnia*, ed. S.-C.-A. Borgnet, Paris, Vivès, 1894, vol. xxix.

ANDERSON, W., *Dante the Maker*, London, Routledge and Kegan Paul, 1980.

ANDRIANI, B., 'La centesima negletta', *Studi danteschi*, xlviii (1971), pp. 83–103.

ANGELITTI, F., 'Sulla data del viaggio dantesco . . .', *Atti dell'Accademia Pontaniana*, xxvii, no.7 (1897).

ANONIMO FIORENTINO, *Commento alla Divina Commedia d'Anonimo Fiorentino del secolo XIV*, ed. P. Fanfani, Bologna, Romagnoli, 1868.

APOLLONIO, M., *Dante* (Storia letteraria d'Italia), Milan, Vallardi, 3rd edn., 1965.

AQUILECCHIA, G., 'Dante and the Florentine Chroniclers', *Bulletin of the John Rylands Library*, xlviii (1965–6), pp. 30–55 (also in id., *Schede di italianistica*, Turin, Einaudi, 1976, pp. 45–72, with Italian transl., pp. 73–96).

ARIOSTO, L., *Orlando furioso*, ed. L. Caretti, Turin, Einaudi, 2nd edn., 1971.

ARISTOTLE, *The Nicomachean Ethics*, London, Heinemann–Cambridge, Mass., Harvard UP, 1947.

ARMOUR, P., '*Purgatorio* xxviii', in D. Nolan (ed.), *Dante Commentaries*, Dublin, Irish Academic Press, 1977, pp. 115–41.

——, 'Matelda in Eden: The Teacher and the Apple', *Italian Studies* xxxiv (1979), pp. 2–27.

——, 'The Theme of Exodus in the First Two Cantos of the *Purgatorio*', in D. Nolan (ed.), *Dante Soundings*, Dublin, Irish Academic Press, 1981, pp. 59–99.

AROUX, E., *Dante hérétique, révolutionnaire et socialiste*, Paris, Renouard, 1854.

AUERBACH, E., 'Figura', in id., *Studi su Dante*, Milan, Feltrinelli, 1967, pp. 174–221.

AURIGEMMA, M., 'Manfredi e il problema delle indulgenze', in U. Bosco (ed.), *Dante nella critica d'oggi*, Florence, Le Monnier for *Cultura e Scuola*, 1965, pp. 540–50.

BALBONI, D., *La Cattedra di S. Pietro*, Tip. Poliglotta Vaticana, 1967.

BAMBECK, M., 'Dantes Waschung mit dem Tau und Gürtung mit dem Schilf', *Romanistisches Jahrbuch*, xxi (1970), pp. 75–92.

BANDINI, A. R., 'St. Peter's Gate', *Italica*, xli (1964), pp. 36–40.

BARBI, M., *Problemi di critica dantesca*, Florence, Sansoni, 1965, vol. i.

BARGELLINI, P., *Vita di Dante*, Florence, Vallecchi, 1964.

BARKER, E. R., *Rome of the Pilgrims and Martyrs*, London, Methuen, 1913.

BARRACLOUGH, G., *The Medieval Papacy*, London, Thames and Hudson, 1968.

BATTAGLIA, S., *Grande dizionario della lingua italiana*, Turin, UTET, 1970.

BENVENUTO DA IMOLA, *Benvenuti de Rambaldis de Imola Comentum super Dantis Aldighierij Comoediam*, Florence, Barbèra, 1887.

(BIBLE) *Biblia Sacra Vulgatae Editionis*, Tournai, Desclée Lefebvre, 1881.

BO, V., 'Piccola storia degli Anni Santi', in *Storia e topografia dell'Anno Santo*, a cura del Comitato Centrale per l'Anno Santo, Vatican City, 1974, pp. 15–93.

BOASE, T. S. R., *Boniface VIII*, London, Constable, 1933.

BOCCACCIO, G., *Decameron*, ed. V. Branca, Florence, Le Monnier, 1965.

——, *Esposizioni sopra la Comedia di Dante*, ed. G. Padoan, Milan, Mondadori, 1965.

——, *Trattatello in laude di Dante*, in id., *Opere in versi*, etc. (La letteratura italiana: Storia e testi, vol. ix), ed. P. G. Ricci, Milan–Naples, Ricciardi, 1965, pp. 565–650.

——, *La vita di Dante Allighieri* and *Il Comento*, ed. G. Milanesi, Florence, Le Monnier, 1863, 2 vols.

BONAVENTURE, St., *Breviloquium*, ed. J.-G. Bougerol, Paris, Éditions Franciscaines, 1966.

(BONIFACE VIII) *Les Registres de Boniface VIII*, ed. G. Digard *et al.* (Bibliothèque des Écoles Françaises d'Athènes et de Rome, Ser. 2, vols. iv, 5 and iv, 7), fasc. 5 (Paris, Thorin, 1890) and fasc. 13 (Paris, Boccard, 1921).

BOSCO, U., *Dante: Il Purgatorio*, Turin, ERI, 2nd edn., 1967.

——, and G. REGGIO (eds.), *La Divina Commedia*, Florence, Le Monnier, 1979.

BOYDE, P., *Dante Philomythes and Philosopher: Man in the Cosmos*, Cambridge UP, 1981.

208   *The Door of Purgatory*

(BREWER) *Brewer's Dictionary of Phrase and Fable*, revised by I. H. Evans, London, Cassell, 1971.

BREWYN, W., *A XVth Century Guide-book to the Principal Churches of Rome, by William Brewyn, c. 1470*, transl. C. Eveleigh Woodruff, London, Marshall Press, 1933.

BRIEGER, P., MEISS, M., and SINGLETON, C. S., *Illuminated Manuscripts of the 'Divine Comedy'*, Princeton UP, 1969, vol. ii.

BUCHANAN, M. A., 'At the Gate of Purgatory', *Italica*, xxv (1948), pp. 6–7.

BULFERETTI, D., *La porta del Purgatorio dantesco*, Brescia, Luzzago, 1903.

BUTI, *Commento di Francesco da Buti sopra la Divina Commedia di Dante Allighieri*, ed. C. Giannini, Pisa, Nistri, 1860.

BUTLER, A. J., *The 'Purgatory' of Dante Alighieri*, London, Macmillan, 1880.

CAETANI, G., *Domus Caetana*, Sancasciano Val di Pesa, Stianti, 1927.

CAMILLI, A., 'La Bolla giubilare di Bonifacio VIII, le indulgenze per i defunti e il ritardo di Casella', *Studi danteschi*, xxx (1951), pp. 207–9.

CAPETTI, V., 'I sette P', in id., *Illustrazioni al poema di Dante*, Città di Castello, Lapi, 1913, pp. 199–206.

——, 'Di una relazione simbolica tra i due monti Ida nel poema dantesco', ibid., pp. 47–52.

CAPITANI, O., 'Una questione non ancora chiusa: Il paragrafo 10 (ed. Toynbee) della lettera ai cardinali italiani di Dante', *Annali della Scuola Normale Superiore di Pisa*, iii (1973), pp. 471–85.

CARBONI, C., *Il Giubileo di Bonifazio VIII e la 'Commedia' di Dante*, Rome, Loescher, 1901.

CARLETTI, S., 'I luoghi santi di Roma', in *Storia e topografia dell'Anno Santo* (see Bo, V.), pp. 97-140.

CARLYLE, J. A., OKEY, T., and WICKSTEED, P. H., (eds.), *La Divina Commedia*, London, Dent, 1933.

CARROLL, J. S., *Prisoners of Hope: An Exposition of Dante's 'Purgatorio'*, London, Hodder and Stoughton, 1906.

(CATHOLIC ENCYCLOPEDIA) *The Catholic Encyclopedia*, New York, Encyclopedia Press, 1913–22.

CHARITY, A. C., *Events and their Afterlife: The Dialectics of Christian Typology in the Bible and Dante*, Cambridge UP, 1966.

CHAUCER, G., *The Canterbury Tales*, text of W. W. Skeat, Oxford UP, repr. 1958.

(CHIOSE) *Chiose Cagliaritane*, ed. E. Carrara, Città di Castello, Lapi, 1902.

—— , *Chiose sopra Dante*, Florence, Piatti, 1846.

CHYDENIUS, J., 'The Typological Problem in Dante', *Commentationes Humanarum Litterarum* (Societas Scientiarum Fennica), vol. xxv, no.1, 1958 (1960), pp. 1–159.

COMPAGNI, D., *Cronica*, ed. G. Luzzatto, Turin, Einaudi, 1968.

CONTE, P., 'Il canto ix del *Purgatorio*' (Lectura Dantis Romana), Turin, SEI, 1965.

CORNOLDI, G. M., *La 'Divina Commedia' di Dante Alighieri col comento di G. M. Cornoldi*, Rome, Befani, 1887.

CORTI, M., *Principi di comunicazione letteraria*, Milan, Bompiani, 1976.

COSMO, U., *A Handbook to Dante Studies*, transl. D. Moore, Oxford, Blackwell, 1950.

———, *Vita di Dante*, revised by B. Maier, Florence, La Nuova Italia, 1965.

DANTE, *La vita nuova*, ed. M. Barbi, Florence, Bemporad, 1932.

———, *Il Convivio*, ed. G. Busnelli and G. Vandelli, revised by A. E. Quaglio, Florence, Le Monnier, 1964, 2 vols.

———, *Opere di Dante Alighieri*, ed. F. Chiappelli, Milan, Mursia, 3rd edn., 1967.

DAVIDSOHN, R., *Storia di Firenze*, Florence, Sansoni, 1956, vol. iv.

DEFERRARI, R. J., and EAGAN, M. C., *A Concordance of Statius*, Hildesheim, Olms, 1966.

DEL LUNGO, I., *Dino Compagni e la sua Cronica*, Florence, Le Monnier, 1879, 2 vols.

DEMARAY, J., 'The Pilgrim Texts and Dante's Three Beasts: *Inf.* i', *Italica*, xlvi (1969), pp. 233–41.

———, 'Pilgrim Text Models for Dante's *Purgatorio*', *Studies in Philology*, lxvi (1969), pp. 1–24.

———, 'Patterns of Earthly Pilgrimage in Dante's *Commedia*: Palmers, Romers, and the Great Circle Journey', *Romance Philology*, xxiv (1970–1), pp. 239–58.

———, *The Invention of Dante's 'Commedia'*, Yale UP, 1974.

DE ROBERTIS, D., *Il libro della 'Vita Nuova'*, Florence, Sansoni, 2nd edn., 1970.

DI PINO, G., 'Il canto ix del *Purgatorio*', in *Nuove letture dantesche*, vol. iv, Florence, Le Monnier, 1970, pp. 35–56.

D'OVIDIO, F., *Nuovi studii danteschi: Il Purgatorio e il suo preludio*, Milan, Hoepli, 1906.

DRAGONETTI, R., *Dante pèlerin de la Sainte Face* (Romanica Gandensia, vol.xi), Ghent, 1968.

DUPRÈ THESEIDER, E., *Roma dal Comune di Popolo alla Signoria Pontificia (1252–1377)* (Istituto di Studi Romani: Storia di Roma, vol. xi), Bologna, Cappelli, 1952.

(ENCICLOPEDIA) *Enciclopedia dantesca*, Rome, Istituto della Enciclopedia Italiana, 1970–1. Entries cited:
 'Benvenuto' (F. Mazzoni)
 'Casella' (L. Peirone)
 'Monarchia' (P. G. Ricci)
 'Porta' (D. Consoli)
 'Purgatorio' (M. Aurigemma)
FALLANI, G., *Dante poeta teologo*, Milan, Marzorati, 1965.
——, 'Il canto ix del *Purgatorio*', in *Lectura Dantis Scaligera*: *Purgatorio*, Florence, Le Monnier, 1967, pp. 293–312.
——, (ed.), *La Divina Commedia*, Messina–Florence, D'Anna, 1969.
——, *Dante autobiografico*, Naples, Società Editrice Napoletana, 1975.
FERGUSSON, F., *Dante's Drama of the Mind: A Modern Reading of the 'Purgatorio'*, Princeton UP, repr. 1968.
FILOMUSI GUELFI, L., 'La struttura morale del *Purgatorio* dantesco', *Il giornale dantesco*, v (1898), pp. 362–74.
FORTI, F., 'Il dramma sacro della *mala striscia*', in id., *Magnanimitade: Studi su un tema dantesco*, Bologna, Pàtron, 1977, pp. 83–101 (originally in *Giornale storico della letteratura italiana*, cxlvi, 1969, pp. 481–96).
FOSCOLO, U., *Opere: Le Poesie*, ed. E. N. Girardi, Milan, Le Stelle, 1968.
FOSTER, K., and BOYDE, P., *Dante's Lyric Poetry*, Oxford, Clarendon Press, 1967, 2 vols.
FRANZ, A., 'Dante zitiert II', *Deutsches Dante-Jahrbuch*, xxix-xxx (1951), pp. 41–105.
FRATICELLI, P., *Storia della vita di Dante Alighieri*, Florence, Barbèra, 1861.
FRECCERO, J., 'The River of Death: *Inf*. ii. 108', in S. B. Chandler and J. A. Molinaro (eds.), *The World of Dante*, Toronto UP, 1966, pp. 25–42.
FRUGONI, A., 'Riprendendo il *De centesimo seu Iubileo anno liber* del cardinale Stefaneschi', *Bullettino dell'Istituto Storico Italiano per il Medio Evo*, lxi (1949), pp. 163–72.
——, 'Il Giubileo di Bonifacio VIII', ibid., lxii (1950), pp. 1–121.
——, 'Il carme giubilare del "Magister Bonaiutus de Casentino"', ibid., lxviii (1956), pp. 247–58.
——, 'La figura e l'opera del cardinale Jacopo Stefaneschi (*c.* 1270–1343)', *Rendiconti dell'Accademia Nazionale dei Lincei*: Classe di scienze morali, storiche e filologiche, Ser. VIII, v (1950), pp. 397–424.

——, 'Dante, *Epist.* xi. 24–5', in *Studi in onore di Alfredo Schiaffini (Rivista di cultura classica e medioevale,* vii), 1965, pp. 477–86.

GHIGNONI, P., 'Alla soglia del Purgatorio (Canto ix)', *Il giornale dantesco,* xxiv (1921), pp. 213–16.

GIAMBUZZI, L., *Cronache degli Anni Santi,* Rome, Officium Libri Catholici, 1975.

GMELIN, H., *Dante Alighieri: Die Göttliche Komödie,* transl. H. Gmelin, *Kommentar,* vol. ii: 'Der Läuterungsberg', Stuttgart, Klett, 1955.

GRANDGENT, C. H. (ed.), *La Divina Commedia,* revised by C. S. Singleton, Harvard UP, 1972.

GRECO, A., 'Roma negli scrittori dell'età di Dante', in *Dante e Roma,* Florence, Le Monnier, 1965, pp. 243–54.

GREGOROVIUS, F., *History of the City of Rome in the Middle Ages,* London, George Bell and Sons, 1900.

HARDIE, C., 'The Mountain in *Inf.* i and ii, the Mount Ida in Crete, and the Mountain of Purgatory', *Deutsches Dante-Jahrbuch,* xlvi (1970), pp. 81–100.

HEILBRONN, D., 'Dante's Gate of Dis and the Heavenly Jerusalem', *Studies in Philology,* lxxii (1975), pp. 167–92.

HOLMES, G., 'Dante and the Popes', in C. Grayson (ed.), *The World of Dante,* Oxford UP, 1980, pp. 18–43.

HÖSL, I., *Kardinal Iacobus Gaietani Stefaneschi* (Historische Studien, lxi), Berlin, Ebering, 1908.

JACOPONE DA TODI, *Le Satire di Jacopone da Todi,* ed. B. Brugnoli, Florence, Olschki, 1914.

—— , *Le Laude secondo la stampa fiorentina del 1490,* ed. G. Ferri, 2nd edn. revised by S. Caramella, Bari, Laterza, 1930.

—— , *Laudi, Trattato e Detti,* ed. F. Ageno, Florence, Le Monnier, 1953.

—— , *Le Laude,* ed. F. Mancini, Bari, Laterza, 1974.

—— , 'O papa Bonifazio', in *Poeti del Duecento* (La letteratura italiana: Storia e testi, vol. ii), ed. G. Contini, Milan–Naples, Ricciardi, vol. ii, pp. 139–43.

KEATS, J., 'Lamia', in *The Poems of John Keats,* London, Methuen, 7th edn., 1951.

LANA, *Comedia di Dante degli Allagherii col commento di Jacopo della Lana bolognese,* ed. L. Scarabelli, Bologna, Regia, 1866.

LANDINO, *Comento di Christophoro Landino Fiorentino sopra la Comedia di Danthe Alighieri poeta fiorentino,* Florence, Nicholo di Lorenzo della Magna, 1481.

LEOPARDI, G., *I canti,* ed. L. Russo, Florence, Sansoni, repr. 1974.

LESCA, G., *Il canto ix del 'Purgatorio'* (Lectura Dantis), Florence, Sansoni, 1919.

LEVI, G., *Bonifazio VIII e le sue relazioni col comune di Firenze*, Rome, Forzani, 1882.

(LIBER) *Liber Usualis*, Tournai, Desclée, 1934.

(LIBRO) *Il libro della natura degli animali*, in *La prosa del Duecento* (La letteratura italiana: Storia e testi, vol. iii), ed. C. Segre and M. Marti, Milan–Naples, Ricciardi, pp. 297–310.

LUCAN, *De bello civili—The Civil War (Pharsalia)*, Cambridge, Mass., Harvard UP—London, Heinemann, 1969.

MACCARRONE, M., *'Vicarius Christi'*, *Lateranum*, Rome, Anno xviii (1952).

——, 'Il terzo libro della *Monarchia*', *Studi danteschi*, xxxiii (1955), pp. 5–142.

——, 'Papato e impero nella *Monarchia*', in *Nuove letture dantesche*, vol. viii, Florence, Le Monnier, 1976, pp. 259–332.

MANSELLI, R., 'Dante e l'*Ecclesia spiritualis*', in *Dante e Roma*, Florence, Le Monnier, 1965, pp. 115–35.

(MANUSCRIPT) Biblioteca Laurenziana, MS Laur. Tempi, 1.

MARCHETTI LONGHI, G., *Gli Stefaneschi*, Rome, Istituto di Studi Romani, 1954.

MARIN, L., 'Essai d'analyse structurale du chant ix du *Purgatoire*, v. 1–73', in *Psicoanalisi e strutturalismo di fronte a Dante: Dalla lettura profetica medievale agli odierni strumenti critici*, Florence, Olschki, 1972, vol. ii, pp. 183–216.

MARTI, M., *Poeti del dolce stil nuovo*, Florence, Le Monnier, 1969.

MARTIN, G., *Roma Sancta*, ed. G. Bruner Parks, Rome, Edizioni di Storia e Letteratura, 1969.

MATTALIA, D. (ed.), *La Divina Commedia*, Milan, Rizzoli, 1960.

MEDIN, A., 'Le stimate di Dante (*Purg.* ix. 112)', *Atti del R. Istituto Veneto di scienze, lettere ed arti*, lxxxviii (1928–9), pp. 761–9.

MILTON, J., 'Lycidas', in *The Poetical Works of John Milton*, ed. D. Masson, London, Macmillan, 1954.

MINEO, N., *Profetismo e apocalittica in Dante*, Univ. di Catania, 1968.

(MISSALE) *Missale Romanum*, New York, Benziger, 1942.

MITCHELL, C., 'The Lateran Fresco of Boniface VIII', *Journal of the Warburg and Courtauld Institutes*, xiv (1951), pp. 1–6.

MOMIGLIANO, A. (ed.), *La Divina Commedia*, Florence, Sansoni.

MOORE, E., 'The Date Assumed by Dante for the Vision of the *Divina Commedia*', in id., *Studies in Dante: Third Series*, Oxford, Clarendon Press, 1903, pp. 144–77.

———, 'Santa Lucia in the *Divina Commedia*', in id., *Studies in Dante: Fourth Series*, Oxford, Clarendon Press, 1917, pp. 235–55.

MORGHEN, R., 'Il giubileo del 1300', in id., *Medioevo cristiano*, Bari, Laterza, 1951, pp. 304–26.

——— , *Bonifacio VIII e il Giubileo del 1300 nella storiografia moderna* (Quaderni della Fondazione Camillo Caetani, i), Rome, Elefante, 1975.

(MOSTRA) *Mostra di Bonifacio VIII e del primo Giubileo*, Rome, Ente Provinciale per il Turismo, 1950.

NORTON, G. P., 'Retrospection and Prefiguration in the Dreams of *Purgatorio*', *Italica*, xlvii (1970), pp. 351–65.

ORENGO, R., *Note polemiche sui riferimenti astronomici della 'Divina Commedia'*, publ. by author, Riva Ligure, 1974.

ORR, M. A. (Mrs J. Evershed), *Dante and the Early Astronomers*, London, Allan Wingate, revised edn., 1956.

OTTIMO COMMENTO, *L'Ottimo Commento della Divina Commedia*, Pisa, Capurro, 1828.

(OXFORD) *The Oxford Book of Medieval Latin Verse*, Oxford, Clarendon Press, 1959.

OZANAM, A. F., *Le Purgatoire de Dante*, in id., *Œuvres complètes*, Paris, Lecoffre, 2nd edn., 1862, vol. ix.

PADOAN, G., 'Il Limbo dantesco', in id., *Il pio Enea, l'empio Ulisse*, Ravenna, Longo, 1977, pp. 103–24.

PALGEN, R., 'Il quadruplo Purgatorio', *Convivium*, xxxii (1964), pp. 3–23.

PARRI, W. and T., *Anno del viaggio e giorno iniziale della 'Commedia'*, Florence, Olschki, 1956.

PASQUAZI, S., *'Dove l'acqua del Tevero s'insala'*, in id., *All'eterno dal tempo*, Florence, Le Monnier, 1972, pp. 275–81.

PATROLOGIA GRAECA (P.G.), *Patrologiae Cursus Completus: Series Graeca*, ed. J.-P. Migne. Volumes cited:

| iii | Dionysius the Areopagite and Pachymera, *De coelesti hierarchia*; *De divinis nominibus*. |
| lx | St. John Chrysostom, *Commentarius in Epistolam ad Romanos*: Homilia xxxii. |

PATROLOGIA LATINA (P.L.), *Patrologiae Cursus Completus: Series Latina*, ed. J.-P. Migne. Volumes cited:

iii	St. Cyprian, *Epistola ad Iubaianum de haereticis baptizandis*.
vi	Lactantius, *Divinarum Institutionum liber VII: De vita beata*, with notes by G. Iseo.
xxii	St. Jerome, *Epistola XV*: 'Ad Damasum Papam'.
xxv	St. Jerome, *Commentariorum in Ezechielem prophetam libri XIV*.

xxvi	St. Jerome, *Commentariorum in Evangelium Matthaei libri IV*.
xxxv	St. Augustine, *In Joannis Evangelium Tractatus CXXIV*.
lxi	St. Paulinus of Nola, *Epistola*, 13; *Poema*, 27.
lxiii	Boethius, *De consolatione philosophiae*.
lxxvii	St. Gregory, *Epistolae*, iv, no.43; xii, no.25.
cxxii	John Scotus Erigena, translations of Dionysius the Areopagite, *De coel. hier.* and *De div. nom.*
cxxvii	Anon., *Descriptio regionum urbis*; Anastasius Bibliotecarius, *Historia de vitis Romanorum Pontificum*, with prolegomenon by C. Sommier, *Tractatus analyticus de praeeminentia et auctoritate Sanctae Sedis*.
clxv	St. Bruno, *Commentaria in Matthaeum*.
clxxii	Honorius Augustodunensis, *Summa gloria de apostolico et augusto*.
clxxxii	St. Bernard, *De consideratione libri V*.
cxc	Stephen Langton, *Tractatus de translatione Beati Thomae*.
ccxx	'Index de Purgatorio'.

PEREZ, P., *I sette cerni del Purgatorio di Dante*, Turin, 1865.

PETERS, E. M., 'I principi negligenti di Dante e le concezioni medioevali del *rex inutilis*', *Rivista storica italiana*, lxxx (1968), pp. 741–58.

PETRARCH, 'Epistola metrica: Ad Iohannem Barilem', in *Opere di Francesco Petrarca*, ed. E. Bigi and G. Ponte, Milan, Mursia, 3rd edn., 1966, pp. 440–5.

PETROCCHI, G. (ed.), *La Commedia secondo l'antica vulgata*, Milan, Mondadori, 1966–7, 4 vols.

PETRONIO, G., *Bonifacio VIII: Un episodio della vita e dell'arte di Dante*, Lucca, Lucentia, 1950.

PÉZARD, A., 'Le chant premier du *Purgatoire*', in V. Vettori (ed.), *Letture del 'Purgatorio'*, Milan, Marzorati, 1965, pp. 7–35.

——, 'Le chant deuxième du *Purgatoire*', ibid., pp. 36–71.

——, 'La porte de la foi? (*Inf.* iv. 36)', in id., *Dans le sillage de Dante*, Paris, Soc. d'Études Italiennes, 1975, pp. 502–16.

PHILALETHES (King John of Saxony) (transl. and ed.), *Dante Alighieri's Göttliche Comödie: II. Das Fegefeuer*, Leipzig, Teubner, 1868.

PIETRO DI DANTE, *Petri Allegherii super Dantis ipsius genitoris Comoediam Commentarium*, Florence, Piatti, 1845.

PIETROPAOLI, C., *Il Giubileo nella 'Divina Commedia'*, Lanciano, Carabba, 1900 (reviewed in the *Bullettino della Società Dantesca Italiana*, ix, 1902, pp. 247–8).

PORENA, M. (ed.), *La Divina Commedia*, Bologna, Zanichelli, 1955.

POTTHAST, A., *Regesta Pontificum Romanorum*, Graz, 1957.

QUATTROCCHI, D. (see Stefaneschi, J.).

RAIMONDI, E., 'Analisi strutturale e semantica del canto ix del *Purgatorio*', *Studi danteschi*, xlv (1968), pp. 121–46 (also as 'Semantica del canto ix del *Purgatorio*', in id., *Metafora e storia*, Turin, Einaudi, 1970, pp. 95–122; see also 'Rito e storia nel I canto del *Purgatorio*', ibid., pp. 65–94).

RANSOM, D. J., '*Panis angelorum*: A Palinode in the *Paradiso*', *Dante Studies*, xcv (1977), pp. 81–94.

RHEINFELDER, H., 'Il mito di Roma in Dante', in *Nuove letture dantesche*, vol. vi, Florence, Le Monnier, 1973, pp. 277–98.

RICCARDI DEL VERNACCIA, F., *Lezione sopra i sette P. ricordati da Dante nel canto ix del 'Purgatorio'*, Florence, Pezzati, 1837.

RICCI BATTAGLIA, L., 'Polisemanticità e struttura della *Commedia*', *Giornale storico della letteratura italiana*, clii (1975), pp. 161–98.

ROPES LOOMIS, L., *The Book of the Popes*, New York, Columbia UP, 1916.

ROSSETTI, G., *Comento analitico al 'Purgatorio' di Dante Alighieri*, ed. P. Giannantonio, Florence, Olschki, 1967.

ROSSETTI, M. F., *A Shadow of Dante*, London, Longmans, Green and Co., 1894.

RUSKIN, J., *Modern Painters*, London, George Allen, 1903–5.

——, *Sesame and the Lilies*, London, George Allen, 1905.

SAPEGNO, N. (ed.), *La Divina Commedia*, Florence, La Nuova Italia, 1958 (also revised edn., 1968).

SAROLLI, G. R., 'Noterella biblica sui sette P', *Studi danteschi*, xxxiv (1957), pp. 217–22.

SAYERS, D. L. (transl. and ed.), *The Divine Comedy: Purgatory*, Penguin Books, 1955.

SCARPINI, M., 'I gradini della porta del Purgatorio', *La Rassegna*, xlvii (1939), pp. 197–9.

SCARTAZZINI, G. A. (ed.), *La Divina Commedia*, Leipzig, Brockhaus, 1875.

——, and VANDELLI, G., *La Divina Commedia . . . col commento scartazziniano rifatto da Giuseppe Vandelli*, Milan, Hoepli, 21st edn., repr. 1974.

SCOTT, J. A., 'The Rock of Peter and *Inf.* xix', *Romance Philology*, xxiii (1969–70), pp. 462–79.

SINCLAIR, J. D. (transl. and ed.), *The Divine Comedy: Purgatorio*, Oxford UP, repr. 1971.

SINGLETON, C. S., '*In Exitu Israel de Aegypto*', in J. Freccero (ed.), *Dante: A Collection of Critical Essays*, Englewood Cliffs, Prentice-Hall, 1965, pp. 102–21.

——, 'Campi semantici dei canti xii dell'*Inferno* e xiii del *Purgatorio*', in *Miscellanea di studi danteschi*, Genoa, Bozzi, 1966, pp. 11–22.

——, (transl. and ed.), *The Divine Comedy: Purgatorio*, Princeton UP, 1973, 2 vols.

SPERONI, C., 'Dante's Prophetic Morning-Dreams', in R. J. Clements (ed.), *American Critical Essays on the 'Divine Comedy'*, New York UP – London UP, 1967, pp. 182–92.

STAMBLER, B., *Dante's Other World: The 'Purgatorio' as Guide to the 'Divine Comedy'*, New York UP, 1957.

STATIUS, *Achilleid*, ed. O. A. W. Dilke, Cambridge UP, 1954.

STEFANESCHI, J., *Iacobi Sancti Georgii ad Velum Aureum Diaconi Cardinalis de Centesimo seu Iubileo Anno Liber*, ed. D. Quàttrocchi, *Bessarione*, vii (1900), pp. 299–317.

STICKLER, A., *Il Giubileo di Bonifacio VIII: Aspetti giuridico-pastorali* (Quaderni della Fondazione Camillo Caetani, ii), Rome, Elefante, 1977.

SUMPTION, J., *Pilgrimage*, London, Faber and Faber, 1975.

TAFUR, P., *Andanças é Viajes*, ed. M. Jiménez de la Espada (Colección de Libros Españoles Raros o Curiosos, vol. viii), Madrid, Ginesta, 1874.

(TEMPLE CLASSICS) *The 'Purgatorio' of Dante Alighieri*, London, Dent and Sons, 1933.

THOMAS AQUINAS, St., *Summa theologica*, ed. Nicolai, Sylvius, Billuart, and C.-J. Drioux, Paris, Bloud and Barral, 17th edn.

——, *S. Thomae Aquinatis in Evangelia S. Matthaei et S. Joannis Commentaria*, Turin, Marietti, 1925.

TRÒCCOLI, G., *Il Purgatorio dantesco: Studio critico*, Florence, La Giuntina, 1951.

VALENTINI, R., and ZUCCHETTI, G., *Codice topografico della città di Roma*, Rome, Istituto Storico Italiano per il Medio Evo (Fonti per la Storia d'Italia). Volumes cited:

iii (1946) John the Deacon, *Liber de Sanctis Sanctorum*; Pietro di Mallio, *Opusculum Historiae Sacrae*.

iv (1953) *Memoriale de memorabilibus et indulgentiis quae in urbe romana exsistunt*; Giovanni Rucellai, *Della bellezza e anticaglia di Roma*.

VALLONE, A., 'Il Dante perduto', *L'Alighieri*, xi (1970), no.2, pp. 3–8.

——, *Dante* (Storia letteraria d'Italia), Milan, Vallardi, 1971.

VAYER, L., 'L'affresco del Giubileo e la tradizione della pittura monumentale romana', in *Giotto e il suo tempo*, Rome, De Luca, 1971, pp. 45–59.

VELLUTELLO, A., *La Commedia di Dante Aligieri con la nova espositione di Alessandro Vellutello*, Venice, Francesco Marcolini, 1544.

VENTURA, G., *Memoriale Guilielmi Venturae civis Astensis*, in L. A. Muratori (ed.), *Rerum italicarum scriptores*, Milan, 1727, vol. xi.

VERNON, W. W., *Readings on the 'Purgatorio' of Dante*, London, Macmillan, 1889.

VILLANI, G., *Cronica*, Florence, Magheri, 1823, 4 vols.

VILLANI, M., *Cronica*, Florence, Magheri, 1825, 3 vols.

VILLARI, P., *The Two First Centuries of Florentine History*, transl. L. Villari, London, Fisher Unwin, 1895, vol. ii.

VIRGIL, *Aeneidos*, in *P. Vergili Maronis Opera*, ed. F. A. Hirtzel, Oxford, Clarendon Press, repr. 1959.

——, *P. Vergili Maronis Opera*, ed. J. Conington, London, Whittaker, 1871, vol. iii.

VOSSLER, K., *Medieval Culture: An Introduction to Dante and his Times*, transl. W. C. Lawton, London, Constable, 1929.

WATT, J. A., 'Dante, Boniface VIII and the Pharisees', in J. R. Strayer and D. E. Queller (eds.), *Post Scripta: Essays on Medieval Law and the Emergence of the European State in Honor of Gaines Post* (Studia Gratiana, xv), Rome, 1972, pp. 201–15.

WOOD, C. T. (ed.), *Philip the Fair and Boniface VIII*, New York, Holt, Rinehart and Winston, 2nd edn., 1971.

Index